THE GAME THAT SAVED THE NHL

THE GAME THAT SAVED THE NHL

The Broad Street Bullies, the Soviet Red Machine, and Super Series '76

ED GRUVER

FOREWORD BY JOE WATSON, PHILADELPHIA

FLYERS ALL-STAR DEFENSEMAN

Essex, Connecticut

An imprint of Globe Pequot, the trade division of
The Rowman & Littlefield Publishing Group, Inc.
4501 Forbes Blvd., Ste. 200
Lanham, MD 20706
www.rowman.com

Distributed by NATIONAL BOOK NETWORK

British Library Cataloguing in Publication Information available

Library of Congress Cataloging-in-Publication Data
Names: Gruver, Ed, 1960- author.
Title: The game that saved the NHL : the Broad Street Bullies, the Soviet Red Machine, and
    Super Series '76 / Ed Gruver ; foreword by Joe Watson.
Description: Essex, Connecticut : Lyons Press, [2023] | Includes bibliographical references and
    index.
Identifiers: LCCN 2023014468 (print) | LCCN 2023014469 (ebook) | ISBN 9781493074976
    (cloth) | ISBN 9781493079445 (epub)
Subjects: LCSH: Super Series '76 (Hockey) | Philadelphia Flyers (Hockey team)--History. |
    TSSKA (Hockey team : Moscow, Russia)--History. | National Hockey League--History.
Classification: LCC GV847.7 .G78 2023 (print) | LCC GV847.7 (ebook) |
    DDC 796.962/640974811–dc23/eng/20230411
LC record available at https://lccn.loc.gov/2023014468
LC ebook record available at https://lccn.loc.gov/2023014469

∞™ The paper used in this publication meets the minimum requirements of American National
Standard for Information Sciences—Permanence of Paper for Printed Library Materials, ANSI/
NISO Z39.48-1992.

For Michelle, whose January 11 birthday is the same date as this famous game and who saw the Broad Street Bullies play in the Spectrum

CONTENTS

Foreword

Forty-seven years have passed since the famous game at the Spectrum in Philadelphia between the two-time defending Stanley Cup champions and the Red Army (CSKA) team on January 11, 1976. It was the final in a series of games pitting the world-renowned Red Army team and the lesser but still formidable Soviet Wings (*Krylya Sovetov*) against National Hockey League (NHL) clubs.

The Red Army team was unbeaten heading into their game against the Flyers. They'd been tied by the Montreal Canadiens at the Montreal Forum, but no one had defeated them—that is, until they met the Flyers. We beat 'em, 4–1 on the scoreboard, and finished with 49 shots on goal to their 13.

Over the years, reporters and hockey fans alike have asked me the same questions: How did the Flyers do it? Did the big win surprise you? Did you realize the significance of the win at the time? How on earth did you—a defensive defenseman hardly known for scoring goals—manage to score a shorthanded goal against legendary goalie Vladislav Tretiak?

There was no "secret" to our win. We had, in my opinion, the best coach in the world at the time in Fred Shero. We executed Freddy's game plan, no more and no less.

There probably was not one person outside of Russia who knew and understood Russian hockey as well as Freddy did. He had even traveled behind the Iron Curtain during the NHL off-season for international coaches' clinics and had befriended the father of Russian hockey, Anatoly Tarasov.

As such, Freddy knew the Red Army system inside and out. He studied it and he knew how to beat it. The way to beat it was to let them circle and weave all they wanted. Don't chase the puck. Keep them to the perimeter. The key for us was to control the net-front areas and the four corners of the rink. I remember that Freddy told us before the game, "We'll show them a real Iron Curtain"—and that's what we did.

The Red Army never adjusted their strategy. That was the fault of their coach, Konstantin Loktev. They were still doing the same thing in the third period—weaving around the perimeter, back passing—that they did in the first period. They kept playing right into our hands.

The convincing win may have surprised outsiders, but no, it did not surprise our players or the fans at the Spectrum. By our second Cup-winning year of 1974–1975, there were a lot of nights when we held teams to about 15 to 20 shots. Especially at the Spectrum, we expected to win every night, no matter what team we were playing. Boston, Montreal, Buffalo, the freakin' Red Army: it didn't matter.

We played the same kind of game and had the same identity. We knew who we were, and we knew we had great coaching, too. Above all, we didn't get outworked by anyone.

I don't think our guys dwelled too much on the political aspects of the game against the Red Army. At least I didn't. It was always about hockey, from my point of view: our team versus their team, not the United States versus the Soviet Union or a battle to show the superiority of Canadian hockey or Russian hockey. It was the Flyers versus the Red Army, and it was in our building. We all wanted to show our team was better than theirs.

To feel that way, even if you don't like the other team, you've got to respect them. We didn't fear the Red Army. We respected them, and they respected us, too. Beating them the way we did was one of the best experiences in my career.

As far as my goal goes, I wish there was a better story about how it happened. There was nothing fancy to it. Don Saleski shot the puck, and I had nothing but open ice in front of me to get to the net. The rebound came right to me, and I backhanded the puck into the net. That was a pretty neat moment, but it wasn't a dramatic play.

The funny part came afterward, when Fred Shero said Soviet hockey had been set back twenty years because I'd scored against them. That has always made me chuckle.

In 2017, I took a trip to Russia with the Flyers Alumni team—a three-city tour of Kazan, St. Petersburg, and Moscow—to play against Russian hockey alumni teams. While we were there, reporters inevitably asked me about that long-ago game from 1976 and the goal I scored. Most of the reporters were too young to have even been born yet at the time of the game against the Red Army.

I think that was when I finally started to have a complete understanding of just how big that Red Army game was in the history of our NHL game. All I can say is that I was honored to be a small part of it.

I'm happy to write the foreword for Ed's book *The Game that Saved the NHL*, the first book ever written on the Flyers' historic showdown with the Red Army and groundbreaking Super Series '76. I hope you enjoy reading about this great slice of hockey history.

Joe Watson

Philadelphia Flyers defenseman

PROLOGUE

The Russians Are Coming (Russkiye Idut)

ON SUNDAY, JANUARY 11, 1976, A FEVER SEIZED PHILADELPHIA.

Veteran Flyers defenseman Joe Watson felt the fervent intensity that gripped the city as he headed to the Spectrum, the home of the Philadelphia Flyers, located at 3601 South Broad Street. "The atmosphere in Philadelphia that day," he recalls, "was electric."

Joe's younger brother, fellow Flyers defenseman Jimmy Watson, was so excited for the highly anticipated and historic Sunday afternoon showdown between hockey superpowers—the two-time reigning Stanley Cup champions versus the international champion Central Red Army—that he had barely slept the past two nights.

"We're the reigning Stanley Cup champions and the Russians come over and they're blowing out the Rangers and the Bruins," Jimmy remembers. "We knew they were a tremendous team and that we were in for a real fight. For two nights I was trying to figure out how we were going to deal with this. I hardly slept."

Jimmy's teammate Ross Lonsberry slept, but it was hardly peaceful. Dreaming that the Flyers fell behind the Soviets, 5–1, in the second period, the left winger woke up in a cold sweat. Such was impact the Flyers' impending collision with the Soviet Red Army squad was having on players, coaches, and fans. It was one of the biggest international hockey events ever, a contest that would be watched by more than a quarter of a billion people worldwide. The Flyers were set to host the Russians in the climactic game of Super Series '76, a groundbreaking series matching Soviet championship squads HC CSKA Moscow (translated to Central

Sports Club of the Army Moscow, or Central Red Army Club) and their comrades Krylya Sovetov (Wings of the Soviet, shortened by North American media to Soviet Wings), against eight of the NHL's top teams.

NHL schedule makers indulged their sense of drama by matching their champion Flyers against the Soviet champion Red Army in the series finale. "The Russians were the envy of hockey in Europe, and we were the envy of hockey in North America, and it all came down to a one-game series," Joe Watson says. "We had to uphold the prestige of hockey in the NHL."

Sportswriter Barry Wilner said at the time that not since the 1972 Team Canada versus USSR series had there been "so much fan interest in one game." It would be an extraordinary meeting of two of the more iconic teams in sports history—the Flyers' "Broad Street Bullies" and the Soviet Red Army. Drawn by the enormity of the event, large crowds gathered on the steps of the Spectrum on game day. Bundled in brightly colored clothing against 15 mph winds and temperatures expected to climb no higher than 35 degrees Fahrenheit, many picketed the presence of the Soviets. Jewish activist groups protested the USSR's harassment and imprisonment of Russian Jews. Their gloved hands thrust picket signs into the icy air demanding "Free Soviet Jews." Before the day was done, fights would break out and blood would be spilled on the Spectrum steps. "It was crazy," remembers Bullies defenseman André "Moose" Dupont. "Politics became involved in that game."

A sellout crowd of 17,077 arrived to fill the arena—then just over eight years old—and cheer their beloved Bullies. They clutched coveted game tickets depicting the red, white, and blue stars and stripes of the United States and the yellow-on-red hammer and sickle of the Union of Soviet Socialist Republics. The flags were crossed, and each ticket carried the hopeful words, "May We Live in Peace." A play on those words was carried out by fans protesting Russia's treatment of Soviet Jews, who unfurled a banner inside the Spectrum reading "May We Live in Peace, Let Soviet Jews Live in Peace." The Red Army objected to the banner, and it was removed.

Sunday games at the Spectrum sometimes transformed into what Flyers fan Dana T. Graf called "doomsday in the Roman Colosseum" in his 1976 book *Hockey Mad*. Graf wrote that fans could go from "rabid to bloodthirsty," mimicking the ancient Romans with chants of "Get that guy! Kill him!" As he approached the Spectrum, Flyers goalie Wayne Stephenson experienced a nervous excitement. Subbing for the injured Bernie Parent, the league's top goalie the previous two seasons, Stephenson was in his sixth NHL campaign and backstopping the Bullies to the greatest regular season record in franchise history. Stephenson felt uptight heading into this first matchup of the champions of hockey's two worlds. He agreed with fellow goalie Glenn Hall that net minding in the NHL was "sixty minutes of hell." This game might be more evidence of that, Stephenson thought, since the Flyers had everything to lose in their battle with the Soviets.

The Stanley Cup champs also had much to gain. A victory over hockey's international champions would give the Bullies bragging rights to being the best team not only in the NHL but in the world. The pressure began building on the Bullies four nights earlier. After dealing a 7–3 loss to Toronto at Maple Leaf Gardens, the Flyers left the ice to a frenzied call to beat the Soviets. "The NHL hated us because they were envious of us and because we won, but the fans in Toronto were screaming at us to beat the Russians," Joe Watson recalls. "They followed us to our bus and were screaming, 'Beat the Russians!' I thought, 'This really means a lot to everybody.'"

Jimmy Watson came to the same realization. "We were hated throughout the NHL for what they called our roughhouse tactics," he said. "But the other [NHL] teams that played the Russians hadn't won, so here we were, suddenly the league's last hope."

Flyers coach Fred Shero found irony in the situation. For years critics had been calling his Broad Street Bullies bad for the NHL because of their rough play. Now they were supposed to save the league from the Soviets. Shero chortled at the thought. For the first time, his Broad Street Bullies were the good guys. On a personal note, Shero, the maverick coach of perhaps the most maverick team in sports history, thought the throwdown with the Russians represented the high point of his professional life. Even after claiming consecutive Stanley Cup titles in 1974 and 1975, Shero told reporters he would never consider his team world champions unless they beat the Red Army, whose dominance eventually led to their "Red Machine" moniker. Defeating the Soviets, Shero knew, would help dispel the belief held by hockey traditionalists that his Broad Street Bullies were little more than a goon squad.

"I've been waiting a long time for this game," Shero said before facing the Red Army. "The fact that nobody in the NHL has beaten them and left it up to us means something. The players want to do something about it."

Shero's son, Ray, was thirteen years old in 1976 and remembers the enormous energy surrounding this game. "There was a huge buildup," he says, and the intense interest was something the Flyers had never experienced, not even in their two Stanley Cup Finals. No team in the history of the NHL has ever experienced the enormous pressure felt by the Flyers on the day they faced the Red Army. The pressure was suffocating, and Fred Shero felt it was "choking us to death," adding that losing to the Soviets would be "worse than dying." A Renaissance man who read books on history, philosophy, law, and literature, Shero's attitude toward his Bullies' impending battle with the Soviets was Shakespearean: "Sound trumpets! Let our bloody colours wave! And wither victory, or else a grave."

Central Red Army (in Russian, *Tsentral'naya Krasnaya Armiya*), so named because of its affiliation with the Red Army military, is one of the legendary teams in the history of sport. No hockey team, not even Original Six royalty like the Montreal Canadiens, is as decorated as Central Red Army. Beginning in 1948, two years after the club was founded and up through its meeting with the Flyers, the Red Army rampaged to nineteen Soviet championships, was runner-up on eight other occasions, and skated to nine USSR Cups and six European Cups. Playing NHL stars for the first time in the 1972 Summit Series, the Soviets were in charge until a controversial slashing penalty by the Flyers' Bobby Clarke and a late goal in the deciding game in Moscow gave Team Canada the narrowest of victories. The Russians' revenge came two years later when they routed a squad of World Hockey Association stars, including Bobby Hull and an aging Gordie Howe, in the 1974 Summit Series, winning the eight-game series, 4–1–3.

By 1976, the Soviets stood astride the hockey world like a goliath. Sending a chill down the collective spine of North American hockey players, coaches, owners, and fans was the ominous Russian phrase *"Russkiye idut"*—"The Russians are coming." By extension they represented the Communist political system, and to many outside the Soviet Union, acrobatic goalie Vladislav Tretiak; electrifying winger Valeri Kharlamov, idolized by future star Evgeni Malkin; flashy forward Aleksandr Maltsev, the hero of Alex Ovechkin; and punishing defenseman Valeri Vasiliev, tough as a Soviet T-34 tank, were nothing less than a Red Menace. Enlisted in the Soviet military, the players had one job: to train, practice, and play hockey. The Russians were reputed to be the world's preeminent players, and on May 30, 1975, the Soviet government announced it was sending its two top teams—Central Red Army and Soviet Wings—to North America for a post-Christmas tour of eight NHL cities. The official Soviet party line, espoused by Wings coach Boris Kulagin—a taskmaster considered to be the Russian version of Vince Lombardi—was that the games would be "friendlies."

Despite claiming these games were exhibitions, the Soviets added ringers to their Red Army team, raiding Moscow Dynamo for Vasiliev and Maltsev and SKA Leningrad for forward Slava Solodukhin. The Wings were likewise fortified, receiving a forward line from Spartak Moscow that included Aleksandr Yakushev (who was Hull's choice as the best left winger in the world), Vladimir Shadrin, and Viktor Shalimov, along with defenseman Sergei Glukhov. It was clear that unlike the title of the 1963 James Bond film, these Soviets were not arriving "From Russia with Love."

Celebrating its Bicentennial, the United States braced for the Soviet invasion. So did the NHL, and no team more than the Flyers of Philadelphia, the birthplace of American democracy. Flyers assistant coach and former all-star defenseman Barry Ashbee stated that a game against the Soviets would not be just another exhibition. The Russians were preparing for the Olympics, he noted, and playing the pros would get them primed. Ashbee said the series meant a lot to the NHL as well. "The 1972 Series was a great eight games, and these eight games will be even better," he told reporters. "The matchups of an NHL club, not an all-star or national team, against their individual clubs will be very interesting. I know all the coaches in the league are looking forward to the chance to beat them—everybody wants to beat the best."

After seven games in Super Series '76, the best is what the Soviets appeared to be. Relying on precision passing and buzz saw skating, the Russians lit up NHL clubs like Katyusha rockets. The Red Army proved particularly impressive, frustrating Phil Esposito and the New York Rangers, 7–3, at Madison Square Garden and beating the Bobby Orr-less Bruins, 5–2, at Boston Garden. Its lone non-win was a thrilling 3–3 final against Scotty Bowman's Canadiens in the Montreal Forum. The game ranks as one of the greatest ever, and with much of the NHL landscape now scorched earth, the Red Army rolled into Philadelphia for the finale of Super Series '76. Awaiting them were the Broad Street Bullies, reviled by the rest of the NHL as an outlaw band of brawlers, but suddenly called upon to defend the league's honor. It was an unfamiliar position for an outfit derided by hockey's old guard as heathens who had stormed the citadel and seized the game's Holy Grail—Lord Stanley's cherished chalice—the past two years.

"The Soviet Union game was a classic," Flyers Hall of Fame winger Bill Barber says. "North America was on the shoulders of the Flyers for that game."

Bossed by Clarke and emboldened by enforcers Dupont, Dave "The Hammer" Schultz, Bob "Hound" Kelly and Don "Big Bird" Saleski, the ferocious Flyers had first gained notoriety three years earlier. Their nickname was coined by *Philadelphia Bulletin* scribe Jack Chevalier and headline writer Pete Cafone on January 3, 1973, following a bloody beat down of the Flames in Atlanta.

"The image of the fightin' Flyers is spreading gradually around the NHL, and people are dreaming up wild nicknames," Chevalier wrote. "They're the Mean Machine, the Blue Line Banditos, and Freddy's Philistines." On the flight back to Philadelphia, Chevalier had a moment of inspiration. Calling the *Bulletin* newsroom, he asked that his "Blue Line Banditos" reference be changed to the "Bullies of Broad Street." Cafone seized on the phrase and wrote the accompanying headline for the next day's edition: "Broad Street Bullies Muscle Atlanta."

As the gritty Bullies battled to consecutive Cup titles, Shero's system of organized mayhem enraged the league. His club went after opponents in waves and pounded them into submission. The Flyers elevated fighting to a tactic, embracing Conn Smythe's maxim: "If you can't beat 'em in the alley, you can't beat 'em on the ice." Their slam-bam style scarred—and scared—opponents. Former Maple Leaf muscleman Borje Salming once said that if a modern NHL team played like the Bullies, their players would be suspended for life. A former boxer who won lightweight and middleweight titles, Shero didn't apologize for his team: "If we can, we'll intimidate our rivals. We try to soften them up, then pounce on them. There are a lot of ways to play this game. Our way works."

Schultz, the Flyers' top bully boy and Public Enemy No. 1 in the eyes of opposing players and fans, glamorized his goon role. Fans in opposing cities held up placards reading "Flyers: Animals on Skates." Life-sized dummies dressed in Flyers jerseys were hung in effigy in NHL arenas. When the Bullies arrived in enemy cities, newspaper columnists warned readers to hide their women and children—the barbarians were at the gates. Yet confronted now with a Soviet steamroller, North America suddenly rallied behind the Broad Street Bullies. "It was their all-star team against our regular franchises, and they were winning," Flyers founder and chairman Ed Snider said. "They came in here and we were the defending Stanley Cup champions. We were the team everybody was hoping would finally beat these sons of bitches."

Sports and politics became so intertwined it was impossible to separate the two. The Cold War was white hot, and the Bullies saw deep meaning in their battle with the Russians. This faceoff with the Soviets, Clarke said at the time, was all about defeating the Communist lifestyle. A goodwill banquet before the game was fraught with tension. Jimmy Watson recalled "daggers" being stared by both squads. This game, he thought, represented nothing less than the free world versus the Communist Bloc. Inside the Spectrum on game day, technicians and broadcasters of the Canadian Broadcasting Company prepared for a massive viewing audience. Ralph Mellanby, executive producer of *Hockey Night in Canada*, picked the Flyers–Red Army game as the highlight of Super Series '76 and had four additional cameras installed inside the Spectrum.

CBC sportscasters Bob Cole and Dick Irvin Jr., the voices of the vener-ated broadcast, would be joined in the booth by New York Islanders star defenseman Denis Potvin. Potvin had played against the Soviet Wings the night before in the Nassau Coliseum, the Russians winning, 2–1, over an Islanders squad boasting Bryan Trottier, Clark Gillies, Bobby Nystrom, and other members of a budding dynasty.

Irvin arrived in Philadelphia on the eve of the game and was struck by the excitement in the city. "The Philadelphia fans were wild," he says. "Their attitude was anti-Russian." The following day, as the clock ticked toward the 1:05 p.m. EST face-off, an estimated 250 million people were tuning in, including 150 million in the Soviet Union, where the time was fast approaching 9 p.m. Flyers announcer Gene Hart, who would be doing the national broadcast with Rangers announcer Marv Albert, thought there had never been a hockey game, other than a Stanley Cup Game 7 or Olympic final, that created as much interest as this one. Fred Cusick, for forty years the voice of the Bruins, summarized the collision of conflicting styles that captured the imagination of so many: "The Rus-sians came over, nobody had ever seen that kind of hockey. The Broad Street Bullies, nobody had ever seen anything like that before."

The Red Army and the Flyers represented two distinctly different and unique ways of interpreting the same sport. European hockey was less linear than the North American approach. The Soviet style was based on blurring speed and intricate passing. Hockey as played by the Flyers was an immense physical struggle, an ancient siege. They loved to hit and fight for the puck along the boards, in the corners, and in front of the nets. What everyone was waiting to see was how the Red Army and the Broad Street Bullies would cope with each other's tactics. "In the Rus-sians and Flyers," *New York Times* hockey writer Gerald Eskenazi noted, "the fan has the two classic examples of the different ways the game can be played." Writer Larry Bortstein believed the encounter would provide a stark contrast in strategy: "The Flyers play a hitting game that seems to crowd out the opposition by sheer force. The Russians play a skating and passing game that works best in the larger European rinks."

East and West believed this game to be war by proxy. Back in the USSR, politburo members tuned into renowned Russian announcer

Nikolai Ozerov's broadcast from the Spectrum. A young KGB agent named Vladimir Putin was intensely interested in the outcome. At his home in Moscow, thirteen-year-old Arthur Chidlovski stared transfixed at the televised sight of the Soviet champions on the same ice as the NHL champions. He had persuaded his mother to allow him to stay up to watch a sports spectacle that had no precedent. The extraordinary event would lead him to become a historian of Russian hockey. "Everybody in Russia watched that game," Chidlovski recalls. "It was huge."

From his seat in the press box high above the Spectrum ice, *Philadelphia Inquirer* columnist Bill Lyon noted the nearly overwhelming intensity and noise inside the building. "It was howling, yowling chaos," Lyon remembered. "It was the height of the Cold War, and the mighty Red Machine was invincible. It had dominated the hockey world for decades." And the Flyers? "The rest of hockey detested them," stated Lyon. But the NHL now had to rely on the Bullies to rescue the league. The Flyers' intensity ratcheted up when NHL president Clarence Campbell made a surprise trip to their locker room before the opening period.

"Boys," Campbell told the Bullies, "you have *got* to win this game."

The Bullies sneered. "He didn't even want to be on the ice with us after we won the Stanley Cup the previous two years," Joe Watson says. "But he came into our dressing room before we played the Russians and told us we had to win this game—*at all costs*." The Flyers responded to the NHL president in a manner true to the Bullies' belligerent ways. "We told him to get the hell out!" Joe Watson says. "We knew what we had to do."

What the Stanley Cup champions had to do was play the game of their lives. But they wouldn't do it for Campbell. "Campbell hated us," defenseman Larry Goodenough says. "I was startled when he came in and made his speech. We didn't need it. We hated to lose anyway, and we wanted to win this game so much. We were charged up."

Jimmy Watson looked around at the faces of teammates who had won Stanley Cups but never faced a challenge like the Red Army. He looked at Clarke, who in Jimmy's opinion was one of the best leaders not only in the NHL but in all sports. Jimmy knew that Clarkie, as teammates called their captain, didn't always do the talking; sometimes Jimmy would exhort his teammates: "Let's go, boys! We can do it!" Clarke talked to teammates when he needed to. More often he led by example. "What a great example he set," says Goodenough. "He was the best leader I've ever seen in hockey."

Jimmy Watson would see Clarke half-dressed in his white, orange, and black uniform as much as *two hours* before a game. A diabetic, Clarke had gone through his pregame ritual—dissolving three spoonsful of sugar into a Coca-Cola—and sat in front of his locker getting himself focused to play. The captain had a fear—not a physical fear, but a fear of losing. The Russians, Clarke knew, were hard men, "real tough sons of bitches." Jimmy looked at his brother Joe, at Barber, at Rick "Hawk" MacLeish, at Terry Crisp, at fellow defenseman Ed Van Impe, with whom he would be paired to slow the Soviets' top line of the Mercury-quick Kharlamov, feisty Boris Mikhailov, and Maltsev, a forward Clarke remembered from the 1972 Summit Series and considered the best he ever faced. Jimmy went right on down the row of Flyer faces—Schultz, who Jimmy credited with giving the Bullies courage; Saleski; Goodenough; Orest Kindrachuk. Jimmy knew they all wanted to prove that the Soviets weren't hockey supermen.

The Flyers didn't like the Russians and believed the Red Army didn't respect them. Hadn't Soviet players stated that the Flyers were "much inferior" to Montreal? Goodenough had seen the Soviets watch them practice and laugh. The Bullies seethed. This game, Kelly thought, is "going to be a war." It would be the final war waged in Super Series '76, and in Philadelphia it felt like Armageddon. The Broad Street Bullies, perceived by purists as malcontents, miscreants, misfits, and delinquents from Devil's Island, were ready for the Russians. "The boys were a little quiet in the locker room before that game," Goodenough remembers. "I wanted to get on the ice and get that first hit in. Then I could just play hockey."

Writing in *Pravda*, the official newspaper of the Soviet Union's Communist Party, Russian correspondent Alexander Pumpyansky stated that the final game between the Red Army and the Flyers, "with the help of tendentious propaganda, was built up as not only the culmination of the tournament but as a game that would stand for the whole tournament."

As referee Lloyd Gilmour skated to center ice to drop the first puck between Clarke and Maltsev, both sides knew this was something special. The throbbing intensity inside the Spectrum was proof of that. This was a collision not just of great hockey teams, but of ideologies and politics; the Red Army was told, presumably by Soviet officials, that it would be "very bad" for them not to win. "There was so much involved that it became more than a hockey game," Dupont recalls. "We couldn't let them go back to Russia saying they were better than us. We had to beat them."

Jimmy Watson thought there was no way the Flyers were going to lose this game. Dupont believed the Broad Street Bullies were ready to die on the ice to defeat the Red Army. Preparing for the faceoff at center ice, Maltsev stared at Clarke and saw a gap-toothed grin: a half-smile, half-sneer that may have reflected NHL referee-in-chief Scotty Morrison's message to the Flyers before the game. Knowing the fearsome reputation of Russia's Red Machine (*Krasnaya Mashina)*, the NHL brass, desperate for victory, made a startling decision.

"Boys," Morrison told the Bullies, "we're going to let you play *your* game."

CHAPTER 1

Broad Street Bullies

THEY HAILED FROM VARIOUS POINTS OF THE FROZEN NORTH—FLIN Flon, Manitoba; Trois-Rivières, Quebec; Smithers, British Columbia; Waldheim, Saskatchewan; Callandar, Ontario.

Long before they skated indoors in historic arenas, they spent their youths on frozen ponds. Snowbanks predated the wooden boards of the indoor rinks; snow shovels cleared the ice rather than Zamboni machines. The air they breathed was brittle. Subzero cold stung their lungs and great clouds of steamy vapor accompanied their movements on icy sheets that sparkled like diamonds when lit by the winter sun.

The games they played in these enchanted settings were more than sport; they were something of a spiritual experience. They would happily spend an hour shoveling snow freshly fallen in the overnight to reveal the clear, crystalline ice of their local lake. They would grab their skates, hockey sticks, and woolen winter hats and play until the sun set behind the great green pines that cast dramatic shadows across white, wintry landscapes.

Such is the soul of the sport beloved by Canadians. Their ponds predate the great indoor ice rinks of the National Hockey League. Glamour games were played inside the Montreal Forum and Maple Leaf Gardens, Madison Square Garden and Boston Garden, Detroit's Olympia Stadium and Chicago Stadium, but the roots of hockey remained firmly planted in the great outdoors.

"When you're six, seven years old and you're skating on a frozen lake, it's the longest breakaway you've ever seen, and it's always Game 7 of the Stanley Cup Finals," Broad Street Bullies defenseman Larry Goodenough says. "That's where the dream begins."

The dream ran thick in the blood of North American boys whose goal was to don the sweater of an NHL club. So, too, did the frequent and sometimes violent body contact of a fast, physical sport. Nowhere was the game played with as much violence as in Philadelphia in the 1970s, and at the height of the Broad Street Bullies' reign, Flyers captain Bobby Clarke delivered a chilling message to the rest of the NHL: If you're going to beat us, you're going to pay a price.

Many NHL players weren't willing to pay the price that beating the Bullies demanded. Lancaster, Pennsylvania, sportswriter Jeff Young once called the City of Brotherly Love the "City of Brotherly Shove," and in 1976 it seemed to mirror the place Frank Sinatra sang of in "This Town"—"a love-you town, shove-you town, and push you 'round-town." Opponents arriving at the Spectrum sometimes developed the infamous "Philadelphia Flu." It was an illness that afflicted even the most red-blooded rink rats. Arriving at the Spectrum, opponents felt as if they were arriving at the gates of hell. "It's unique what the Spectrum was like in those years," former *Philadelphia Inquirer* sports columnist Bill Lyon recalled. "A lot of players dreaded it and developed mysterious maladies."

Burly Bullies defenseman Andre "Moose" Dupont chuckles at the memory of opposing players coming down with the dreaded Philly Flu. "They got a little shy," the Moose says. From his seat in Section 82, Flyers fan and author Dana T. Graf noted in 1975 that the Spectrum had become a "House of Horrors" for opponents. "Teams trekking into town," he wrote, "do so very warily." They were concerned, said Graf, "not with winning but with surviving."

Dave "The Hammer" Schultz remarked, in Ross Bernstein's book *The Code: The Unwritten Rules of Fighting and Retaliation in the NHL*, that the Flyers were proud that opponents were struck with the Philly Flu, since it indicated they were intimidated. The Hammer heard stories that opponents would laugh and joke on their team bus from the Philadelphia airport, but as the bus approached the Walt Whitman Bridge, the entire team would fall silent as the grave. The Flyers joked that as opponents arrived at the arena and the driver turned off the engine, the bus kept shaking. The Philly Flu was no joke to the rest of the league, even to physical players from the NHL's rough-and-tumble past, like Glen Sonmor, a battler for the New York Rangers in the early 1950s. Sonmor said the Philly Flu was real and that opponents didn't want to play the Bullies. The Flyers, he stated, "won with fear and opposing players were truly scared of them."

Outfitted in burnt orange and black uniforms and brandishing bristling mustaches and long locks, the Flyers were imposing, visually and physically. NHL referee Ray "Scampy" Scapinello heard about the Philadelphia Flu, and while he wasn't sure if anyone ever claimed illness or injury to avoid playing in Philadelphia, he was certain they at least thought about it. Scapinello thought the Spectrum's visiting locker room was the quietest in sports, due to nerves. The Bullies' harsh treatment extended to referees. "Just drop the puck!" Clarke would growl at Scapinello in a faceoff circle. "Nobody came here to watch you!" Says defenseman Jimmy Watson, "We were a tough, hard-nosed team. Nothing wrong with that."

Center Bill Clement remembers that the Bullies didn't care what anyone thought. "We were like masked marauders," he says. "We rode into town, beat the hell out of their team, drank their beer, and rode out of town. The Broad Street Bullies intimidated with fists and sticks. Teams that do the intimidating are hated, and that hatred is never forgiven." Intimidation through aggression was a big gun in the Bullies' arsenal, but it wasn't their only weapon. The two-time Stanley Cup champions also boasted top talent: Clarke, left winger Bill Barber, goalie Bernie Parent, and head coach Fred Shero are enshrined in the Hockey Hall of Fame.

Tutored by the great Jacques Plante, Parent was the league's best goalie in 1973–1974 and 1974–1975, winning the Vezina Trophy as the NHL's top goaltender and the Conn Smythe Trophy as the Stanley Cup playoffs' Most Valuable Player both seasons. "When Bernie got to Toronto, Plante taught him so much," recalls Clement. "Bernie was the missing piece for us."

Many NHL historians consider Parent's performances from 1973 to 1975 as the best back-to-back campaigns ever produced by an NHL goalie. Legendary NHL broadcaster Dick Irvin Jr. says he's never seen a goalie put together better back-to-back seasons. Parent punctuated both years with Stanley Cup–clinching shutouts of Hall of Famers Bobby Orr, Phil Esposito, and the "Big, Bad Bruins" in 1974 and Buffalo's famed "French Connection" line of Hall of Famer Gil Perreault and All-Stars René Robert and Rick Martin in 1975. As backstop for the Bullies, Parent was an invaluable member of the Flyers. The greatest goalie in team annals and one of the best in NHL history, Bernie's bravura performances allowed the Bullies to play their style, since Clarke, Schultz, and company knew Parent would provide the equalizer in shorthanded situations created by the Bullies' battles.

Flyers fans knew it as well, and it became common in Philadelphia and surrounding communities to state that "only the Lord saves more than Bernie Parent." The phrase became so favored in Philadelphia during the Bullies' glory years that it was fashioned into a popular bumper sticker. Thunderous chants of "Ber-nie!" filled the Spectrum as Parent's play proved pivotal to the Flyers becoming the first expansion team to claim Lord Stanley's Cup and barging their way to a second consecutive Cup in 1975.

Parent was part of a nucleus that included talent both homegrown and imported. Winger Reggie Leach was of the latter variety. Nicknamed the "Riverton Rifle" for his rapid release and unerring accuracy, Leach led the Stanley Cup champs in goals in 1975, with 45, and was considered by opponents in a poll to have one of the NHL's best slapshots, estimated at 100 miles per hour. His backhanders could be just as difficult to defend against, and he intimidated defenses as he brought the puck past the blue line.

Born in Riverton, Manitoba, to teenage parents, Leach grew up in an atmosphere of alcoholism and poverty. Several members of Reggie's household died young due to alcohol-related issues. Before Reggie was born, his father left to work in the mines; his mother, a Cree Indian, soon left as well, leaving Reggie to be raised by his grandparents. Like Parent, Leach found playing hockey to be his passion. Leach proved so proficient he was tabbed at age thirteen to play alongside adults on a semipro club. Not long after, he became a member of the best junior hockey club in Manitoba, the Flin Flon Bombers. He became wingman to Bombers' center Bobby Clarke, and after Leach spent time with the Bruins and Oakland Seals, it was Clarke who is said to have urged the Flyers to trade for his former linemate one week after Philadelphia claimed its first Stanley Cup.

Joining Clarke and Barber on the Flyers' first line, Leach struggled in the early stages of the 1974–1975 season. Shero was critical of Leach's lack of intensity and his play in the Bullies' defensive zone. Compounding the difficulties was the Rifle's surprisingly popgun attack, netting five goals in the season's first six weeks. Admonished by Shero and Clarke, Leach knew his NHL career hung in the balance. Taking dead aim on defenses, the Rifle shot bullseyes. Scoring 40 goals in the next 60 games, Leach helped propel the Bullies back into the playoffs. Reggie was a key factor in the Flyers' run to a second Stanley Cup, lighting the lamp eight more times in the postseason. The Rifle would be even more deadly in 1975–1976. As the Soviet Red Army team prepared to storm North America, Leach was enjoying a campaign that would see him lead the NHL in goals with a career-high 61 while posting another career best with 91 points.

The LCB Line—Leach, Clarke, and Barber—left opponents woozy. Leach's flame-belching blasts and bewildering backhanders blended beautifully with Clarke's competitiveness and tireless intensity and Barber's all-around skills. The LCB Line ranked as one of the most electric in the sport, along with the Sabres' French Connection line of Perreault, Martin, and Robert; the Montreal Canadiens' Dynasty Line of Steve Shutt, Guy Lafleur, and Jacques Lemaire; the World Hockey Association's Winnipeg Jets' Hot Line of Anders Hedberg, Bobby Hull, and Ulf Nilsson; and the Red Army's Valeri Kharlamov, Vladimir Petrov, and Boris Mikhailov.

Leach's penchant for producing goals in flurries prompted *Philadelphia Bulletin* sportswriter Jack Chevalier to give him the "Riverton Rifle" nickname. While Leach's linemate Barber was never bestowed as catchy a moniker, the words used to describe his play are just as meaningful. He was called a "model of consistency" and "all-around player" whose skills proved a perfect complement to Leach and Clarke. Clarke would dig the puck out of the corners, Barber would set up the play, and Leach would redirect the rubber past the goalie.

Like Clarke, Barber played his entire career with the Flyers. One of six Flyers to have his jersey number retired, Barber's 420 goals remained a franchise record until Claude Giroux eclipsed it on December 30, 2021. An eight-time NHL All-Star, Barber earned league honors every season from 1974–1975 through 1981–1982. Growing up in Callander, Ontario, Barber benefited from his family's love for the game. Bill and his four brothers played on a backyard rink built by their father. Lights were strung so the Barber boys could play night games.

Barber idolized Detroit Red Wings great Gordie Howe and attended Howe's hockey camps during the summer. The experience helped Barber become a star centering the top scoring line for the Kitchener Rangers in the Ontario Hockey Association. Selected seventh (his eventual uniform number) by the Flyers in the first round of the 1972 NHL Entry Draft, Barber was assigned to Philadelphia's American Hockey League (AHL) team, the Richmond Robins. Scoring 9 goals in his first 11 games with the Robins earned Barber a call-up to the Flyers. Switched from center to left wing by Shero, Barber initially teamed with Rick "Hawk" MacLeish and Gary Dornhoefer on the second scoring line before he was bumped to the top scoring line with Clarke and "Cowboy" Bill Flett.

Flyers assistant coach Mike Nykoluk said at the time that Barber owned the attributes the club was seeking: "poise, a hard shot, a smart sense with the puck, strength, and good skating ability." At 6-foot-1 and 195 pounds, Barber was big enough to battle for the puck while still being quick enough to outskate opponents. He produced 64 points (30 goals, 34 assists) his rookie season and finished second to Steve Vickers of the New York Rangers in the Calder Trophy voting for Rookie of the Year. Barber contributed to the Flyers reaching the Stanley Cup semifinals, and his 69 points (34 goals, 35 assists) the following season helped boost the Bullies to their first championship. In 1974–1975 Barber upped his points total to 71, and as the Flyers prepared to square off with the Soviets, he was on his way to enjoying his greatest NHL season, with a career-best 112 points, in which he recorded 50 goals and 62 assists.

The Flyers had snipers up and down their lineup ready to greet Red Army goalie Vladislav Tretiak. Second-line center MacLeish ranked second to the Rifle on the Flyers' list of goal scorers in 1974–1975, with 38, and was said to own the best wrist shot on the team. Centers Orest Kindrachuk and Mel Bridgman and wingers Dornhoefer and Ross Lonsberry added scoring depth to a lineup whose eventual 348 goals dwarfed the league average of 273. Even enforcers like Schultz and Don Saleski were capable of scoring 20 goals in a season, as the Hammer did in 1973–1974 and "Big Bird" did in 1975–1976. As the Flyers prepared for the Soviets, their celebrated LCB Line was in the process of setting an NHL record for goals in a season with 141. Clarke was on his way to claiming his second straight—and third overall—Hart Trophy as the league's MVP. It was enough to propel the Flyers to the best record (51–13–16) in franchise history.

The Bullies were an enigmatic team fronted by an enigmatic coach—Freddy "The Fog" Shero. It was a nickname Shero detested, but it was attributed to him due to his detached personality and quirky quotes—"People generally get what's coming to them, unless it has been mailed"—and because his famous "system" was beyond the grasp of many of his fellow coaches. "People know the fighting of the Flyers, but St. Louis and Boston were fighting, too," says Fred's son Ray, an NHL executive. "The Flyers had an image, but they had good players. I'm sure he was proud to say that he was a true 'player's coach.' His players wanted to play for him. They played hard for him, and they won."

The Flyers won because Shero developed a systemized approach that saw his squad working in cohesive five-man units, a strategy he borrowed from the father of Soviet hockey, Anatoly Tarasov. "I figured if the Russians could use complete five-man units with defensemen who were used to a certain forward line, we could," Shero told *Hockey Pictorial* magazine in 1977. "Then it dawned on me to make everyone on the team be able to drop into any of those positions. Everyone became interchangeable, based on the center or the defense combination."

Once he grasped Tarasov's methods, Shero built a system based not on ad-lib shooting but on finely honed units employing a disciplined approach to defensive hockey. NHL writer Frank Orr detailed the Shero system in a 1976 edition of *Hockey Illustrated* magazine: "The defensemen stand up at the blue line, the back-checking wingers turn opposition attacks towards the middle of the ice and the team never is outnumbered in its own zone. The Flyers have set patterns to working the puck out of their own zone and forechecking it in the attacking zone."

In addition, the Flyers became the first NHL team to employ a full-time assistant coach (Nykoluk) and the first to undergo in-season conditioning, study game films, and have a regular morning skate—revolutionary ideas at the time, now long since adopted by every NHL club. From a technical standpoint, the Shero system was less mysterious than the man whose name it bore. It involved three main parts: forechecking in the opponent's end, a five-man system of interchangeable players, and physical play. The basic tenets were a calculated use of physicality and disciplined positional play.

As there are four corners in a rink and two pits, one in front of each net, Shero knew that to win, a club has to control those areas. The Bullies would both give and take punishment in the corners and pits, leading to the Flyers having more fights than most teams.

Shero knew whereof he spoke. A former fighter, he has been credited with being one of just two players who ever fought Gordie Howe to a draw on the ice. The physical play his Flyers engaged in would have worn them down had Shero not practiced another revolutionary idea: short, one-minute shifts for players. He wanted his players to skate like hell, and get off the ice.

After the Flyers' first Stanley Cup victory in the spring of 1974, Shero made a pilgrimage to the Soviet Union to study the intricacies of Russian hockey. While the rest of the NHL was practicing the North American system of taking the puck behind their own net, Shero had his Flyers adopt the Soviet system of quick counterattacks, rapidly moving the puck to the open man.

The Shero system was disparaged by some. Howie Meeker, an analyst for *Hockey Night in Canada* in the 1970s, scoffed that Shero learned from the Soviets. Former Detroit Red Wings star Ted Lindsay told *Hockey Illustrated* in 1976 that while Shero talked about the Russian influence, "in watching his team play, I'd say he's been influenced a hell of a lot more by Hap Day."

Clarence "Hap" Day guided the Toronto Maple Leafs to five Stanley Cups from 1942 to 1949, including three straight from 1947 to 1949. The Leafs employed a clutch-and-grab style, emphasizing positioning. Four, sometimes five, Leafs players lined up along the blue line awaiting the opponent's attack. Day augmented his disciplined defense with intimidation tactics, carried out by enforcers like "Wild" Bill Ezinicki.

A student of his sport, Shero acknowledged that he borrowed as freely from Day as from Tarasov. He believed his Flyers didn't do anything the Toronto Maple Leafs of the late 1940s didn't do. There were a few refinements to accommodate the modern game, but Shero's Flyers were basically playing the same style as Day's Maple Leafs. The Bullies would send one man in to forecheck—usually the center—and their wings would peel back and pick up enemy wings along the boards. For the opposition to force its way free, it would have to make perfect passes, or the Flyers would steal them.

Shero's strategies succeeded in wearing out Bruins superstar Bobby Orr in the 1974 Stanley Cup Finals and shackling Buffalo's French Connection line in the 1975 Cup Finals—and opposing coaches took note. "The Montreal Canadiens play more interesting hockey, but the Flyers will keep on winning because their system is one which takes advantage of the other team's mistakes and uses those mistakes to beat you," Sabres coach Floyd Smith told *Hockey Pictorial* in 1977. "The Flyers don't really try to score themselves; they just wait for a mistake in the other guy's end and then capitalize on it."

By 1976, even Bowman's freewheeling Montreal Canadiens were using a version of the Shero system. So, too, were Don Cherry's Bruins and Al Arbour's New York Islanders. The Canadiens and Islanders would combine to win eight consecutive Stanley Cups from 1976 to 1983. "There is no doubt we copied much of the system from Shero and the Flyers," Bowman acknowledged at the time in *Hockey Pictorial*. "We had to copy from Freddy to beat him." Cherry admitted the same. "When you look at the Bruins, the Bruins are the Flyers," he said in a 1977 article in *Hockey Pictorial*. "If I've had any success as a coach, it's because I've imitated Freddy Shero."

Canadiens Hall of Famer Ken Dryden had a goalie's-eye view of the Flyers and told the *Montreal Gazette* that the more he saw of the Shero system, the more impressed he became: "They seem to have specialists for everything. They have their scorers—MacLeish, Lonsberry, Barber, Clarke, and Leach. They have those defensemen who are impossible to dislodge in front of the net. They have a designated workhorse in Dornhoefer, who's as good at his job as anybody. They have designated fighters like Schultz and Saleski."

Lonsberry and Saleski represented the yin and yang of the Bullies' lineup. One was the "Rabbit"; the other, "Big Bird." One was a scorer; the other, a checker. One arrived via trade; the other, via the NHL Draft. One was a left wing; the other, a right wing. Yet they pooled their talents to form a productive line critical to the Flyers' success. Lonsberry locked down the left wing slot on the line with MacLeish and Dornhoefer. Called "Rabbit" or "Roscoe" by his teammates, Lonsberry had come to the Flyers in a 1972 deal with the Los Angeles Kings. Alongside his shaggy-haired mates, Lonsberry stood out in part because he was one of the few Flyers in this era to wear a helmet. The Bullies joked that Ross wore his helmet not to protect his head but to protect his toupee.

Lonsberry was a two-way forward who hustled on both ends of the ice. He was tough enough to battle for the puck and skilled enough to score 32 goals in the regular season and add 13 points in 17 Stanley Cup games, as he did in 1973–1974. He was also durable enough to take the ice in more than one thousand regular-season and postseason games combined. A native of Humboldt, Saskatchewan, Lonsberry proved a perfect fit for Shero's system. So, too, did Saleski. The mop-topped 6-foot-3, 205-pound Saleski was nicknamed "Big Bird" for the Sesame Street character, and like the Rabbit, was a native of Saskatchewan, hailing from Moose Jaw. Saleski manned the right wing after being taken by the Flyers with the 64th pick in the 1969 NHL Draft.

Like Lonsberry, Saleski was a solid two-way forward unafraid to fight for the puck. Where Lonsberry was a prolific point producer, Saleski was a checker who excelled as a penalty killer and on-ice policeman.

His 205 penalty minutes in 1972–1973 marked a career high and cemented his status as one of the baddest of the bad-boy Bullies. Still, there was more to Big Bird than penalty killing and punch-outs. Beginning with the 1975–1976 season, Saleski started finding the back of the net with regularity. With the Russians on the horizon, Big Bird posted the first of three straight 20-goal seasons and reached a career best in points, with 47.

In his autobiography *The Game*, Dryden wrote that the Flyers were a "good but limited team" that needed the Shero system to be successful. "To be effective they needed to play just one way," Dryden wrote, "and to play it so well they could overcome any team." Still, it was the Flyers' free-swinging ways that garnered the most attention. Battling their way to a second straight Stanley Cup title in 1975, the Bullies led the league in penalty minutes, with 1,969, a startling average of nearly 25 minutes per game. Leading the way were Schultz (with 472 penalty minutes, an NHL record that still stands) and Moose Dupont (with 276). A 200-pound defenseman, Dupont had no illusions about why the Flyers had brought him to the big club after he posted a ridiculously high number of penalty minutes in the Central League. Moose told inquiring minds that he was brought in to hit.

Schultz's penalty minutes in 1975 shattered the previous record (348) he had set the season before. The Hammer became the poster boy for the Broad Street Bullies. In his book *The Hammer: Confessions of a Hockey Enforcer*, Schultz lamented the amount of brawling he had done on the ice. Still, he realized that fighting was an integral part of the NHL in the 1970s. "Hockey is a contact sport for men," Schultz wrote. "It's not the Ice Follies."

Shero said Schultz was aware he didn't have an abundance of speed or skill; he was there to be a physical force. The national media took note. Playing on the name of the popular TV series *Mod Squad*, *Newsweek* magazine dubbed the fighting Flyers the "Mad Squad." *Sports Illustrated* called the Bullies the "notorious Mean Machine." *Time* magazine put the Flyers on its cover and titled the story, "War on Ice: Courage and Fear in a Vortex of Violence." In his book *A Thinking Man's Guide to Pro Hockey*, Gerald Ezkenazi of the *New York Times* noted that the trouble with the

Flyers was that "they were so good when they began their streak of Stanley Cup victories that their violent nature received more publicity than if they had been an also-ran team."

There had been other tough teams in NHL history—including the Big, Bad Bruins of 1969–1974 and the 1969–1972 Blues—and ironically, it was the Bruins and Blues who proved instrumental in the Flyers adopting their Wild West style. Fronted by defenseman "Terrible" Ted Green, the Bruins of the early 1970s were labeled "The Animals." When they took the ice at New York's Madison Square Garden, organist Eddie Layton taunted Boston's bad boys by playing a bouncy version of the song *Talk to the Animals*. Before there was the Philly Flu, there was the Boston Flu. Even Schultz was not immune. Orr and Esposito sought to intimidate the Hammer by skating up to him and delivering a snarling message: "Hey, the boys are going to get you tonight."

In the 1969 playoffs, the Blues' Noel Picard and the Plager brothers—Bob and Barclay—battered the fledgling Flyers. "The Plager brothers and Noel Picard bludgeoned opponents with their sticks," recalls Clement. "The Blues brutalized the Flyers in the playoffs." Determined that his team would never again be physically intimidated, Flyers owner Ed Snider instructed his front office brass to draft bigger, stronger players. In time, the Flyers brought in a bevy of beefy enforcers, and the Broad Street Bullies were born. Urged by Shero to "take the shortest route to the puck carrier and arrive in ill humor," the Hammer, Moose, Big Bird, and Bob "Hound" Kelly posted penalty minutes at alarming rates. In the process, they cleared a path for skilled players Clarke, Leach, Barber, and MacLeish.

Kelly, also known as "Mad Dog," was a grinder and a battler. Dropping his gloves, he threw punches in bunches and earned another moniker—"Machine Gun" Kelly—for his rapid-fire deliveries. Whatever nickname he went by, Kelly produced one of the signature plays from the 1975 Stanley Cup Finals. In its design, in the determination and physicality in which it was carried out, and in its successful execution, this singular play symbolized an era in the NHL. Kelly's Cup-winning score 11 seconds into the third period of Game 6 in Buffalo Memorial Auditorium paved the way for the Bullies to hoist the Cup for the second straight spring. A video review shows Kelly fighting off a hard check from behind the net by tough defenseman Jerry Korab, getting a screen from Clarke, breaking the puck free, faking goalie Roger Crozier and then beating him with the backhander. Philadelphia fans heard this radio call from Flyers play-by-play man Don Earle and color analyst Gene Hart:

Earle: "Kelly bumped behind the net by Korab, Kelly scores!"

Hart: "The Hound does it again! Arf, arf!"

"It was super sweet," remembers Kelly. "The first [Cup in 1974], we worked hard to get there. The second [title] showed we weren't a fluke." Joe Watson believes the goal exemplified the pregame planning of Shero and the grit of guys like Kelly and Clarke, the latter freeing the Hound to make the play by checking the monstrous Korab. "Bob Kelly played three shifts that whole game; Freddy puts him in and he scores the winning goal," Watson says. "That shows what Coach was like. He had foresight— Hound scores the winning goal on a play we practiced all year."

Kelly was a member of a ferocious foursome that gave the Flyers their fearsome reputation. But the Bullies paid a price for their meat-grinding ways. "Their style of play didn't come easy," said Bill Lyon, a frequent visitor to their postgame locker room. "They counted their stitches after games."

"We threw a lot of body checks, and it was tough for us," Dupont recalls. "But it was tougher for [opponents]." The Bullies took as much as they gave. In the 1973–1974 campaign Clarke was jumped by Barry Cummins of the California Golden Seals and took twenty stitches in his scalp. The Flyers found balm for their bruises at a blue-collar bar/restaurant called Rexy's. Situated in South Jersey, Rexy's featured superlative sausage pizza and pulsating music and was a favored haunt of the Flyers and their fans and groupies. Graf called it the place players and fans went to replay the game, "drowning the sorrows of a grueling loss or toasting the heroes of a hard-fought victory." It was the Bullies' second home, and at least half the Flyers' squad showed up after games at the Spectrum.

"Rexy's was part of our routine," says Dupont. "We'd meet after games and talk for an hour or so."

The Flyers played hard and lived hard, and Shero built a brotherhood among his battling Bullies. They bonded behind a bunker mentality, and their ability to overcome all obstacles led to much chagrin throughout the NHL. Chicago Black Hawks star Bobby Hull bolted to the rebel World Hockey Association perhaps in part to escape the enforcer era in the NHL and what the Golden Jet called "harem-scarem" tactics. New York Rangers coach Emile Francis declared the Bullies bad for hockey, and Dryden admitted having a "tortured ambivalence" toward the Flyers. Dryden considered Clarke the fiercest competitor of the era and he admired Parent and Shero, but he despised the Bullies' brawling and intimidation.

"The rest of hockey detested it and made no bones about it," recalls Lyon. "To this day you can't read about those Flyer teams without a reference to the Broad Street Bullies. It's as indelible as a tattoo." Ray Shero recalls the Bullies having an image, but also having good players, and Joe Watson agrees, saying the Bullies never received just due for their talent. "We had guys who worked hard and had skill and were never given credit," says Watson.

Clement believes the reason the Flyers were never given credit for their skill was because they were rough. "We played within the rules and paid the price when we strayed. But we were far more skilled than we were given credit for," he says. Dupont remembers Phil Esposito calling the Bullies tough but talented. "Everybody talks about the Broad Street Bullies, but we didn't win Stanley Cups with only strong players," he says. "We had Fred Shero's system, and everybody played their roles. We played tough, but we could score goals."

Borrowing from the Bruins, Blues, Leafs, and Russians, the Flyers won with a brand of hockey never seen before nor since. "We started physically going after teams," Clarke said in the documentary *Names on the Cup*. "We were tired of getting beat up. And when we started beating them up, there was a lot of whining going on. They liked it better when we were small and getting the crap beat out of us."

The rise of the Bullies in 1972–1973 resembled the rise of the Bruins in 1967–1968. The Bruins had been pushed around but got bigger and stronger by trading for Black Hawks forwards Phil Esposito, Ken Hodge, and Fred Stanfield, and bringing up Derek "The Turk" Sanderson. In Philadelphia, Snider and Flyers general manager Keith Allen followed suit. Fed up with being brutalized by opponents, the Flyers' front office built a club of talented, tough players. The former coach and first-time GM Allen earned renown as "Keith the Thief" for his skillful trades and drafts, becoming, in the words of Philadelphia sportswriter Jay Greenberg, "the second most important person in the history of the franchise."

Greenberg notes that it was Allen who, as assistant GM in 1969, listened to rookie scout Gerry Melnyk and convinced GM Bud Poile to draft the diabetic Clarke. And it was the Thief who brought in skilled players—Parent, Barber, Ashbee, MacLeish, Leach—as well as Fred Shero. Snider and Allen complemented one another, the owner being young and brash and his GM seasoned and calculating. Greenberg thought Snider and Allen set the bar together—Snider with his drive and ambition and Allen with his eye for talent and emphasis on courage.

Clement says the Flyers were built from a plan and with a purpose. "The DNA of our team was created intentionally," he notes. "And we won our way." The club Snider and Allen built embodied the blue-collar lifestyle of their city, and the Flyers' fame spread far beyond South Philly. By 1976, the Bullies transcended their sport. "Fans knew they were going to get their money's worth when they went to see the Broad Street Bullies play," says Joe Watson. He recalls a *Los Angeles Times* headline publicizing their upcoming game with the Kings, warning fans: "The Animals Are Loose. Lock Your Doors." An embattled Clarke asked in 1974 that if the Bullies are so bad, why hadn't they been locked up?

Perhaps the reason lay in the fact that brawling had been a part of the NHL since long before the Bullies were built. Years before the Flyers took to fighting, Stan Fischler quoted Canadian novelist Hugh MacLennan in a 1968 *Sport* magazine article: "Hockey breeds the insane emotions of the Roman circus." Before there was Schultz there was Eddie Shore and Eddie Shack, and forty years before there was Shero defending his Bullies there was Toronto Maple Leafs coach Dick Irvin telling reporters that fans like rough, tough hockey and that teams had to play that way to please them.

Despite the furor over their style, the Bullies became big box office for the NHL. They appeared regularly on national TV, sharing the screen with NBC announcers Tim Ryan and Ted Lindsay, and the rink side duo of Brian McFarlane and Peter Puck. They sold out arenas in NHL cities and were featured on the covers of national magazines. Songs about the Bullies hit the airwaves. Decades later, they were immortalized on *The Simpsons*, their lineup joining notorious figures from history on a "Jury of the Damned."

Hockey traditionalists thought the high-gloss treatment given to the Flyers was a black eye for their sport. Some NHL veterans, however, saw nothing wrong with the Bullies. Hockey Hall of Famers Lindsay, Henri Richard, and Dick Irvin Jr. praised the Flyers. Richard believed the Flyers worked harder than any other club. Lindsay thought the Bullies played hockey the way it should be played. Irvin broadcast numerous Bullies' games and recalls being impressed: "I thought they had a terrific team."

January 1976 brought a new challenge for the Flyers. As their cold war on ice with the Russians approached, the question on the minds of many was: How would the Broad Street Bullies match up with the Soviet Red Army?

CHAPTER 2.

The Red Machine (*Krasnaya Mashina*)

LITERATURE'S FIRST OUTDOOR ICE-SKATING SCENE WAS PENNED BY Russian author Leo Tolstoy in his 1877 classic *Anna Karenina*—fitting from the viewpoint of Russians, whose love for hockey rivals that of the Canadians. Like their youthful counterparts in Montreal, Edmonton, and Toronto, boys in Moscow, St. Petersburg, and Gorky take to frozen ponds and played from sunrise to sunset for the love of the game.

Young hockey players in the USSR were taught early they must compete fiercely to join the high-level team in the area. This reality made for ferocious struggles for ice time, and the players who emerged as elite were hardened competitors. The internal strife paid off in external competition, with the Soviets dominating international hockey from the 1950s through the 1980s. Bobby Clarke knew better than anyone in Philadelphia the immense challenge the Flyers faced in Central Red Army, a club that would become known internationally as the Red Machine (in Russian, *Krasnaya Mashina*).

Clarke was a fourth-line center for Team Canada in the historic 1972 Summit Series, a series the Canadians entered overconfident and underconditioned. "No doubt, the Soviet players were much better prepared physically than us," Clarke told writer Slava Malamud in 2006. "Another thing that played against us was probably the arrogance [of Team Canada]. There was not a player on our team who doubted we'd win easily." The Canadians were quickly proven wrong. Worse, they had the hell scared out of them. Following the first period of Game 1, the Canadians realized they could not keep up with the Russians.

After five games, the Soviets led the series, 3–1–1. Vladislav Tretiak impressed with stunning saves in goal, but it was left winger Valeri Kharlamov, the idol of thousands of Russian youths—including future great Pavel Bure, also known as the "Russian Rocket"—who dazzled the NHL professionals. Team Canada defenseman Don Awrey thought Kharlamov so fast he was difficult to defend. The original Russian rocket kept Team Canada on its toes.

Russian hockey historian Arthur Chidlovski recalls Kharlamov's flash-and-dash performance in the 1972 Summit Series as otherworldly. "Kharlamov intimidated the Canadians," he says. "He made them look like they were seventy-year-old men."

Team Canada coach Harry Sinden, who helped build the Big, Bad Bruins, had seen his share of great players in the NHL and was not easily impressed. Yet even Sinden was awed by Kharlamov's blurring speed and slick stickwork. Seldom had Sinden seen anyone come down on NHL defensemen and beat them to the outside, go around them and then in on the net. It wasn't done, except Kharlamov did it. By Game 6, played in the Palace of Sports in the Central Lenin Stadium, Team Canada assistant coach John Ferguson had seen enough. The former Montreal Canadiens enforcer looked at Kharlamov and said, "Someone needs to do something about this guy." His players understood. Team Canada saw the Summit Series as "Us versus Them." Kharlamov was killing the Canadians, so somebody had to do something.

That somebody was the Flyers' captain. Ferguson knew no one but Clarke would do it. That's how Bobby played the game. He played to win. Kharlamov likewise played with a fierce intensity, and matched against Kharlamov's line, Clarke was familiar with the Soviet winger's feisty style; he felt Kharlamov's hockey stick in his stomach more than once. Rare film shows Clarke closing in on an unsuspecting Kharlamov, then cutting him down with a two-handed slash. "I kind of hunted him down," Clarke recalled once, "and gave him a whack across the ankle. He speared me, and I slashed him. . . . It was something done during the heat of battle."

Kharlamov, his left ankle fractured, had to be helped by teammates to the bench. The Soviets seemed shocked by the attack. "I am convinced that Bobby Clarke was given the job of taking me out of the game," Kharlamov said later. "I looked into his angry eyes, saw his stick which he wielded like a sword, and didn't understand what he was doing. It had nothing to do with hockey."

As far as Clarke and the Canadians were concerned, it had everything to do with hockey. "Bobby would do what he had to do to win," says Bill Clement, Clarke's teammate on the Broad Street Bullies. Kharlamov missed Game 7 and was ineffectual in Game 8 as the Canadiens rallied to a narrow victory. "One of the villains of the Summit Series was Bobby Clarke, because of what he did to Kharlamov," remembers Chidlovski. "But if you ask me now who I want on my team if I am a GM, I will say Bobby Clarke because he gave everything to win. He gave 100 percent."

The advancing armies of Napoleon and Hitler had been stopped at the gates of Moscow, but with Kharlamov neutralized, Team Canada became the first foreign army to conquer Russia on its home ground. Asked by venerable hockey journalist Dick Beddoes about the slash, Clarke, a native of the hardscrabble mining town of Flin Flon, shrugged. "If I hadn't learned to lay on a two-hander once in a while, I'd never have left Flin Flon."

The youngest team captain in NHL history, Clarke left Moscow with an enhanced reputation among his fellow Canadians and newfound confidence that he belonged among the NHL's elite. He also left with a greater understanding of hockey behind the Iron Curtain. At the time, the Canadians played a vertical game—"north to south," from one goal to the other. Canadian hockey was direct and aggressive. In Europe, because of the larger rinks, the emphasis was on a horizontal game—"east to west," between the boards. Russian players held the puck longer, passed it more, and moved it between the blue lines. The Soviet style was in direct contrast to the Canadians, who would storm the blue line and launch laser-like shots in the style made famous by Bernie "Boom Boom" Geoffrion. Where the Soviets would back skate and reform their attack, NHL players had a dump-and-chase mentality.

The difference between the Russian game and Canadian game was not in the complexity of each side's strategy, but in its direction and speed. The direction of the game as played in the USSR was first choreographed by Anatoly Tarasov, the father of Russian ice hockey. To some, he was a dictator who ruled the sport in the same iron-fisted manner that Soviet strongman Josef Stalin ruled the Eastern Bloc. Tarasov had, in fact, been directed by Stalin to build a hockey superpower, and he treated his players as human chess pieces in a grand strategy. He received from them total dedication to *his* team and *his* strategies. "He viewed hockey as art, with the coach as choreographer, the players as performers," Roy MacGregor wrote in the *Ottawa Citizen*. "The principles of dance and piano—endless practice, repeated movements, perfected technique—would create a base from which true artistry could grow."

Tarasov developed the weave-and-pass style of play that became a signature of the Soviets. He laid the foundation for what became known as the "Soviet hockey school." Prior to his being tasked to build a national program in 1946, ice hockey had been virtually unknown in the Soviet Union. The popular Russian ice sport since the mid-1800s had been bandy, a sort of field hockey on skates played outdoors, eleven players to a side, on an ice surface the size of a soccer field. In time, it became a popular spectator sport, and bandy leagues spread throughout Russia.

In the bloody aftermath of World War II, which had seen a staggering 20–27 million Soviet citizens die, the Russians, wary of the outside world, turned their collective focus inward. The arts—the Bolshoi Ballet, Moscow Symphony Orchestra, and Moscow Circus—flourished and became internationally renowned. So, too, did the sciences and technology, funded as they were by the Kremlin. While the strength of the Soviet Union was displayed for the world to see via weapons and armed forces, the USSR also sought to display the alleged superiority of communism over capitalism in the athletic arena. Due in large part to the Red Army's drafting of top young players into the military, Tarasov built a program that within a decade was producing Olympic and world championship teams.

Working at first with just a few hockey rule books, Tarasov converted bandy players to ice hockey and within eight years was dominating the international scene with an elegant—and seemingly unbeatable—pass-oriented style of play. "Everything they did was adapted from bandy and soccer," former Columbus Blue Jackets and Canadian national team coach Dave King told the *Montreal Gazette* in 1999. "The buildup of the play, the drop passes, the way they see the ice—it all started with bandy."

It was at the conclusion of a bandy match in February 1946 that ice hockey was introduced to a curious Russian audience at Dynamo Stadium. Spectators watched as two teams of university students from the Moscow Institute of Physical Education took to the ice to play a game that was earning international renown due to its popularity in the Olympics. In 1945, Nikolai Romanov, chairman of the All-Union Committee for Physical Culture, told soccer and hockey department head Sergei Savin to report on Canadian ice hockey. When Savin declared the sport to be at the "center of attention" of the Olympic Games, Romanov insisted that Canadian hockey become a priority for the Russians.

Grainy black-and-white photos from this early era of games show Russian players bundled in long pants, heavy sweaters, and thick gloves and breathing frosty vapor as they battle for the puck on sunny but scarred ice surrounded by snowbanks. Moscow Dynamo became the first USSR ice hockey champion, winning the title in 1947. Just seven years later, the Soviet national team took to the ice in Stockholm for its inaugural appearance in the world championship competition. On March 7, 1954, the Russians rocked the sports world, defeating Canada, 7–2.

Tarasov built Soviet hockey into a formidable machine feared around the globe. His teachings influenced generations of Russian players and teams, and his influence spread beyond the Soviet Union to North America following the 1972 Summit Series. Tretiak is of the opinion that the European and North American styles of hockey began merging in 1972. It was then, Tretiak believes, that the NHL received a boost in creativity, tactics, and discipline, the fundamentals of Tarasov's system.

Until the 1975–1976 Super Series, the Summit Series marked the high point for Russian and North American ice hockey. John Kreiser noted in a 2012 article on NHL.com that the 1972 Summit Series shaped the modern NHL, the hockey world being "fundamentally changed by the start of an eight-game series between national teams from Canada, loaded with NHL players in their prime, and the Soviet Union—considered the two best hockey-playing nations in the world at the time—that played out across the month of September." The series, he wrote, "was a must-follow for hockey fans across the globe and after its dramatic conclusion—a 4–3–1 series win for the Canadians—there was no question that the NHL would never be the same again."

The much-anticipated series began on September 2, 1972. Team Canada boasted the best players in the NHL, minus Bobby Orr, Bobby Hull, and Gordie Howe. Orr was sidelined by injury, Howe retired, and Hull ineligible due to his involvement in the WHA because Team Canada officials opted for NHL players only. The absence of Hull in particular meant Team Canada should have been named Team NHL, as not all Canadian players were allowed on the team. In contrast to Team Canada's professionals, the Soviets competed under "amateur" status. Technically, many were members of the Red Army military—Central Red Army being linked to the Soviet Army, the Wings a part of the Soviet Air Force, and Dynamo Moscow sponsored by the Soviet Ministry of Interior and the KGB—but it was evident that their military jobs were to train year-round and compete in amateur competitions such as the Olympics and world championships. "The Russians played eleven months out of twelve," Chidlovski recalls. "That was Soviet hockey at that time."

The Red Army won Olympic gold in 1964, 1968, and 1972, but the quality of their victories was called into question as they were veterans competing against amateurs. Kreiser noted that when the Soviets arrived on North American shores in 1972, they were still a mystery. "Scouting back then was nowhere near as developed as it is now," he wrote, "and none of the Canadian players had seen much of the Soviets."

New York Rangers forward Rod Gilbert, a member of the famous GAG (Goal a Game) Line, said once that pro players didn't know anything about the Soviets and had no idea how good the Russians were. Before the series, a *Hockey News* poll of Canadian journalists revealed expectations of a sweep of all eight games by the NHL stars. Team Canada forward Paul Henderson said the pros didn't take the Soviets seriously. They knew the Russians were good players, but with the lineup Team Canada had, how, Henderson wondered, could they lose?

But lose Team Canada did, and in humiliating fashion in Game 1, when the Soviets stormed back from a quick 2–0 deficit and overwhelmed the NHL stars, 7–3. Team Canada rallied to take Game 2, but the Russians rebounded, winning three of the first five games and tying a fourth. Canada was in an uproar over the prospect of being defeated in its national game by the Soviets. There was enormous pressure on Team Canada, their players laboring under the realization that they couldn't lose the series.

The format for the Summit Series was for the two teams to play eight games, four in each country, and Team Canada turned the Series around in the Soviet Union, winning the final three games in Moscow. Henderson's heroic game-winning goal in the final minute of Game 8 on September 28 prompted New Year's Eve–style celebrations throughout Canada, North America's national game having been saved from being co-opted by communist Russia. "The series, and especially Henderson's third winner in as many games, became a landmark cultural event in Canadian history and a huge source of national pride," wrote Kreiser. "But it also showed that the Soviets' 'amateurs' were just as good as the NHL's professionals."

Boris Mikhailov saw the series as a meeting between two schools of hockey. Tretiak told the *Sporting News* in 2012 the Soviets and Team Canada were both winners in 1972. "It was a great series for all of hockey," Tretiak said. "The best that Russia had and the best of the NHL. The winner was the game of hockey."

Two years later, Howe, Hull, and WHA stars were similarly stunned by the Soviets in the 1974 Summit Series. When the Russians arrived for their first practice in Quebec City, the host of Game 1 of the series, Howe and Hull were watching. "Let's show them what we can do," Mikhailov, the Soviets' star center, told teammates. What followed, wrote Lawrence Martin in his book *The Red Machine: The Soviet Quest to Dominate Canada's Game*, was a practice "as fast, as intense, and as technically perfect as the Soviets could possibly make it." When practice ended, Howe turned to Hull: "Hey, Bobby, put your eyeballs back in your head!"

"Did you see those guys handle the puck?" Howe asked Hull. "I saw one guy blow a pass in the entire practice and one of the coaches called him aside and gave him hell."

By the time the Red Army headed to North America in December 1975, it was considered by many the premier hockey team in the world. The Soviets had won every Olympic and world championship tournament from 1963 to 1972—they would strike Olympic gold again in 1976—and their Summit Series with the NHL and WHA proved they could compete with North America's top professionals. "I had seen them play in 1972 and they were so skilled," Joe Watson remembers. "They had a lot of talent. They should have been professionals because they were part of the Red Army. But their big thing was winning the Olympics and world championships."

Clarke, having played against the Russians in the Summit Series, knew the high skill level of the Soviets. "Kharlamov was an incredible player, and he could play physically, too," Clarke told Malamud. "What he was doing with the puck was unbelievably beautiful." When Clarke played against Aleksandr Maltsev in 1972, he thought Maltsev was the best forward he ever faced. Clarke considered Maltsev great in every aspect of play, be it controlling the puck, face-offs, or physical play.

Clarke called Alexandr Yakushev "the best player" of the series, reminiscent of the great Jean Beliveau. Clarke said Yakushev had "that special grace" that Beliveau had. Yakushev's style, said Clarke, was "clean, beautiful, precise, strong, and with this one-of-a-kind grace."

Clean, beautiful play were not attributes associated with the team that would serve as the Soviets' final opponent in Super Series '76—the Broad Street Bullies. The Soviet teams traveling to North America in 1975–1976 were different than their predecessors in 1972 and 1974 in that they were wiser to the ways of North American hockey. They had learned from their Canadian counterparts the benefits of forceful forechecking and tight defense. Heading the Soviet contingent was coach Konstantin Loktev. A former player for CSKA Moscow in the Soviet Hockey League, the forty-two-year-old Loktev had been inducted into the Soviet and Russian Hockey Hall of Fame as a player in 1964. In 1976, he would be inducted into the USSR Hall of Fame under the category of Builder.

Lining up at right wing, the 5-foot-7, 165-pound Moscow native was a little big man. Loktev helped Moscow (CSKA Moskva in Russian) win the Soviet Championship in 1955, the first of nine USSR titles he would contribute to as a player. Loktev's skill on the ice earned him numerous awards, both USSR and international. He teamed with Aleksandr Almetov and Veniamin Aleksandrov to form one of the top lines in Russian history. The trio was largely responsible for the success of Soviet hockey in the 1960s, producing more than 250 goals in some 100 games.

Loktev began his coaching career in 1968 with the Soviet Defense Ministry team and succeeded Tarasov as head coach of CSKA Moscow. Loktev briefly coached Partizan Belgrade in 1974 before winning the first of two Soviet Championships in 1975 with CSKA Moscow. In 1976, Loktev began working with the Soviet national team, winning Olympic gold that same year.

The Red Army club Loktev brought to North America in the winter of 1975–1976 was brimming with talent. Tretiak had been named by the IIHF Best Goaltender in 1974 and in 1976 would claim his third consecutive USSR Most Valuable Player award and his sixth straight selection to the USSR All-Star squad. He would be named to every Soviet All-Star team from 1971 until 1984 and enshrined in the Hockey Hall of Fame in 1989. Kharlamov was a winger small in stature (5-foot-8, 168 pounds) but nonetheless dynamic, a playmaker who used his unique combination of skill and speed to dominate opponents. Kharlamov combined with fellow winger Mikhailov and center Vladimir Petrov on a fearsome line that listed three future members of the IIHF Hall of Fame.

"The 1976 Red Army team was a great team," says Chidlovski. "We were between two coaching czars—Tarasov and [Viktor] Tikhonov. Loktev was a legendary player from the Aleksandrov Line. He was one of the greatest, classiest players in Soviet hockey. Loktev was brought up in the system."

Mikhailov, a 5-foot-9, 165-pound Muscovite, was one of the primary leaders of the Red Army club. His willingness to do the unglamorous work in front of the net and on rebounds allowed him to lead his line in scoring. While Petrov and particularly Kharlamov grabbed headlines with slick skating, flashy scores, and spectacular skills in the open ice, it was Mikhailov who produced a record 427 career goals to become the all-time leader among Soviet goal scorers. That Mikhailov was a remarkable player was evident in his being named captain of CSKA and Team USSR following the 1972 Summit Series with Team Canada. "Kharlamov was not our best player on the ice," Chidlovski says. "He was the flashiest, but he was not the backbone of the team. Mikhailov was the backbone."

It was fitting that Mikhailov was a member of not only the mighty CSKA but also Lokomotiv Moscow, for he was a high-impact performer and personality. As the Red Army prepared for the Broad Street Bullies, Mikhailov had already won USSR gold six times (1968, 1970–1973, 1975), world championship gold six times (1969–71, 1973–1975), and Olympic gold twice (1972, 1976), leading the USSR in goals in 1975 and 1976, and was a four-time USSR All-Star (1969, 1973–1975). On the international front, Mikhailov was named World Championship (WC) Best Forward in 1973, was an IIHF All-Star in 1973, and WC scoring leader in 1974. In the 1974 Summit Series, Mikhailov again distinguished himself by producing 4 goals and 2 assists in seven games.

Serving as lynchpin on the legendary line was Petrov, the 6-foot, 187-pound product of Krasnogorsk, a playmaker who was a force on both ends of the ice. Petrov's value could be found on both the power play and penalty-killing units. One of the superlative centers in Soviet hockey history, Petrov enjoyed tremendous chemistry with wingers Kharlamov and Mikhailov. When CSKA was on defense, Petrov played a physical game in the tradition of top Soviet blue liners. As the Red Army attacked, Petrov's stickhandling, open ice skills, and strong slapshot proved too much for even the best defenders.

Petrov plied his trade for CSKA and the Soviet Wings. He won USSR gold in 1969, 1970–1973 and 1975, world championship gold in 1969–1971 and 1973–1975, and Olympic gold in 1972 and 1976. That he figured prominently in Flyers boss Fred Shero's game plan was a given, as Petrov paced the USSR in goals scored 1970 and 1973 leading up the battle with Bullies and was the Russian national scoring leader in points in 1973 and 1975. Petrov earned fame on the international front, being named an IIHF All-Star in 1973 and leading the world championship in scoring that same year.

Vladimir Popov, a third-line right wing, was primed for what many would consider his finest performance on the international stage. A veteran of the Summit Series, Popov joined the Red Army team in 1971, his path to the Elite Russian League having begun in 1966 when he joined the CSKA youth program. As an eighteen-year-old, Popov had been thrilled to be a member of the magnificent Red Army team headed by Tarasov. Playing in the Elite League from 1971–1983, Popov produced 109 goals in 350 games. Popov proved so solid a winger that he was included on Red Army teams that earned USSR gold in 1971–1973 and 1975 before gearing up for the 1976 Super Series. For the NHL tour, Popov would team with Viktor Kutyergin and Aleksandr Lobanov.

Also gearing up was fellow right winger Vladimir Vikulov. A member of CSKA's second line, Vikulov was thought by teammates and opponents alike to be one of the top playmakers of the era. At 5-foot-9 and 176 pounds, Vikulov was slick with the stick and a consistent point producer. He excelled in one-on-one situations, his skill and creativity leading to rapid, unerring shots on goal and well-crafted assists to linemates like Boris Alexandrov. NHL teams knew Vikulov was a scoring threat to be dealt with; playing for Team USSR in international competition, Vikulov would net 109 goals in 191 games from 1965 to 1977.

Aleksandr Gusev likewise was ready for the trip to North America. One of the best scoring defensemen in Russian history, the 6-foot, 189-pound Moscow native blended strength with skill to become one of the Red Army's most respected players in both national and international competition. Gusev was a physical player whose hard hits reverberated in arenas around the world. Opponents considered him one of the best blueliners in the game, a sturdy presence whose athleticism and technical proficiency made it difficult for enemy skaters to get past him with the puck. Gusev joined the Red Army youth ice hockey program in 1957 and first pulled on the cherished CSKA sweater in 1967. His Red Army teams won national gold in 1968, 1971–1973, and 1975, and world championship gold in 1973 and 1974. He earned IIHF All-Star status in 1973 and played in the 1972 and 1974 Summit Series, scoring the winning goal in Game 5 of the latter.

Gusev would team with Valeri Vasiliev, one of the greatest players in Russian history, on the Red Army's top defense line. Gennadi Tsygankov joined Gusev and Vasiliev as one of the premier defensemen in Soviet hockey in the 1970s. At 5-foot-11 and 187 pounds, Tsygankov was one of the top team players in Soviet history, a player who had no fear when it came to battling for the puck in corners or blocking enemy shots with his body. He would go on to be the first defense partner of Slava Fetisov. A native of Vanino, Tsygankov used his speed to outrace opponents to the puck and was an outstanding penalty killer. His willingness to put team goals ahead of personal achievements allowed him to be a valued member of Elite League clubs CSKA, SKA Khabarovsk, and SKA Leningrad. On the eve of Super Series '76, Tsygankov had already been a key contributor to USSR gold teams in 1970–1973 and 1975, world championship winning teams in 1971, 1973, and 1975, and the Olympic gold winner in 1972.

Centering Popov's third line was Alexei Volchenkov. Physically strong, Volchenkov was a product of the CSKA youth program and had been a member of the Red Army team since 1970. His fourteen-year career with the Red Army and SKA Leningrad would see him score 155 goals in 446 games. A steady, consistent forward, Volchenkov played several positions for USSR gold-winning teams. The NHL agreed to allow Vasiliev and Aleksandr Maltsev of Dynamo Moscow and Slava Solodukhin of SKA Leningrad to join the Red Army club as reinforcements.

Maltsev was a force in Russian hockey for three decades. Playing in the Soviet League from 1967 to 1983, he scored 329 goals in 529 games. As a member of Team USSR from 1968 to 1982, Maltsev was even more productive, delivering 212 goals in 301 games. The 5-foot-9, 174-pound native of Kirovo-Chepetsk had the same flashy speed as Montreal Canadiens star Yvan Cournoyer and was as stylish and creative in one-on-one situations as the Habs' Guy Lafleur.

Maltsev was a masterful puck handler and as quick in making the right decisions as he was in avoiding the hard hits of frustrated opponents. The latter was said to be a reason Maltsev's performance in the 1972 Summit Series was considered lacking by some observers, who thought the right winger was intimidated by the hard body checks of the

Canadiens. Still, Maltsev's smooth strides and puck movement impressed NHL players, and his team-first attitude and willingness to play any forward position to help the Soviet national squad's cause was highly valued by his comrades, his *tovarishchi*.

Maltsev's impact on both the USSR team and Dynamo Moscow was evident in the number of championships and personal awards he earned. Heading into Super Series '76, Maltsev's collection of trophy hardware included Olympic gold in 1972 and world championship gold in 1969–1971 and 1973–1975. He was MVP of the USSR League in 1972, a Soviet All-Star in 1970–1972 and 1974, an IIHF All-Star in 1970–1972, and world championship scoring leader in 1970 and 1972, earning World Championship Best Forward awards both years. Like Maltsev, Vasiliev, a native of Gorky, played his entire career with Dynamo Moscow, and he stands as one of the best players in the long history of Russian ice hockey. Recognized as rough and physical, he was criticized by some media members for using "dirty tricks," but respected Soviet sports journalist Yuri Vanyat was quoted by Chidlovki as stating that NHL players in the 1972 Summit Series made the Russian star look "like one of the cleanest players in the world."

Vasiliev's skill and strength as a member of junior teams impressed recruiters enough that he advanced to Dynamo Moscow in 1967. Vasiliev combined flash with force, and he relished hard hits and body checks at the blue line. "Maybe it is not being very humble," he said then, "but I think the Canadians know now that Russians can hit the same way they can."

Vasiliev was only 5-foot-11 and 187 pounds, but his bodychecks bruised and sometimes bloodied opponents, veterans of NHL wars included. Physical play and defense were key components of Vasiliev's game; so, too, were skating, scoring, and passing. Playing for Team USSR from 1970 to 1982, Vasiliev beat opposing goalies 44 times in 279 games. His list of achievements, team and individual, as he prepared to meet the Bullies was impressive. He won WC gold in 1970 and 1973–1975 and Olympic gold in 1972. Vasiliev was a Soviet All-Star from 1973 to 1975, won WC Best Defenseman in 1973, and was an IIHF All-Star in 1974 and 1975.

Born in Leningrad, Solodukhin began playing ice hockey at Lenmyasokombinat Club and moved on to the SKA youth program in 1964. The 5-foot-11, 185-pound center played most of his career for SKA Leningrad in the Elite League, and he soon earned renown as an attacker on offense and a steady performer on defense. Playing for Team USSR in 1972 international competition, Solodukhin scored 12 goals in 15 games. Having gained international experience playing for the Soviet national team and winning a silver medal in the 1972 World Championship, Solodukhin was invited by Soviet national coach Vsevolod Bobrov to participate in the 1972 Summit Series.

In the 1950s, Russian hockey was pioneered by players who formerly played bandy and soccer. The 1960s saw the Soviets dominate the international scene, winning world championships and the Olympics. Chidlovski notes that due to the undeniable talent of the Soviet stars of the early 1970s, Soviet hockey reached its highest levels: "Although the first Super Series against the best NHL players was won by Team Canada, the Soviet hockey style received its recognition among the inventors of the game. By many accounts, it proved to be equal to the well-established Canadian style and, in some areas, even more superior."

On the eve of the 1970s, North Americans questioned just how good Russian hockey players were. In the October 1969 issue of *Sports Canada*, Jean Beliveau told writer Pat Hickey he didn't think the Soviet squad would impress NHL players. "I'd like to play against the Russians," Beliveau said. Foreshadowing Super Series '76, he added that "it would be better if we played as NHL teams . . . on our terms," noting that the Soviets should agree to play more than one game. "I think that we could fit it into our schedule if we had a Russian team tour Canada and play six or seven games against different teams."

Did Beliveau think the Soviets could give the NHL's pros a good game? Not at that time, he said. He believed the Russians knew they couldn't compete with NHL players. "I think they want to play [NHL pros]," Beliveau told Hickey, "because they realize they're not getting any better. I think the next step for them is to play a pro team."

The Soviets' games with Team Canada packed arenas in North America and in the Soviet Union. NHL owners took note, and details of a series between the Soviets and NHL clubs began emerging during the Summit Series. No deal was made, and the opportunity passed. Club owners wanted the Soviets back, not only for financial reasons but because they believed the Summit Series had not shown their players at their best. The NHL wanted the world to see its top teams play the Soviets in midwinter games when North American players would be in peak physical condition. They also believed NHL players would benefit from playing alongside their regular teammates rather than with fellow stars on a makeshift squad.

In June 1975, NHL governors and Russian negotiators met in Montreal to discuss a super series. Hammering out an agreement, they announced plans for Super Series '76. The two best teams from the USSR—the Central Red Army and the Soviet Wings—would fly to North America in December 1975 to face eight NHL clubs. The series would start in New York City just after Christmas and end in Philadelphia two weeks after New Year's Day.

Sportswriter Larry Bortstein wrote in the 1975 issue of *Hockey* magazine that sports fans on both continents wondered, "How would match-ups between Russian league teams and professional teams from North America come out?" Bortstein noted the "geographical imbalance" existing in the Soviets' tour: Games were concentrated in the east, with Chicago being the westernmost city the Russians would visit. NHL executive director Brian O'Neill explained the reason for the scheduling. "Before we scheduled the games," O'Neill said, "we asked our teams which of them wanted to participate in the series. About 12 teams said yes."

The geography factor dictated that the Los Angeles Kings, who had boasted one of the better records in the NHL the season before, would not host the Soviets. The NHL was paying the Russians' travel expenses, O'Neill said, and it wasn't feasible from a financial standpoint to send the Soviets to LA for a single game. Bortstein believed the Super Series would be of greater benefit to the Soviets than to NHL teams. The Winter Olympics loomed, and the Russians would be heading to Innsbruck, Austria, less than a month after the series. The Soviets would gain experience playing the pros, all but ensuring they would be favored to claim Olympic gold.

"Sure, the Russians will benefit from playing our teams before the Olympics," O'Neill told Bortstein. "But to be honest, the Olympics is their secondary concern. Obviously, their games against our teams are more important to them than the Olympics are."

Rangers general manager and former bench boss Emile "The Cat" Francis fairly purred at the prospect of NHL clubs playing the Soviets. Francis believed players on both sides would benefit from the series, and since the teams would be in top condition because the NHL season was underway, it would be a better test of hockey than the Summit Series.

The Soviets versus NHL schedule of games captured the attention of millions:

December 28—Red Army at New York Rangers

December 29—Soviet Wings at Pittsburgh Penguins

December 31—Red Army at Montreal Canadiens

January 4—Soviet Wings at Buffalo Sabres

January 7—Soviet Wings at Chicago Black Hawks

January 8—Red Army at Boston Bruins

January 10—Soviet Wings at New York Islanders

January 11—Red Army at Philadelphia Flyers

The game at Boston Garden was of particular interest since Orr had never played against Tretiak, Kharlamov, and the rest of the Red Army. Shortly after leading the Bruins to their second Stanley Cup title in three seasons with a victory over the Rangers, Orr was sidelined for the 1972 Summit Series by a knee operation. When the Super Series was announced, the Red Army's game in Boston promised a not-to-be-missed meeting between Orr, the NHL's best defenseman, and the offense-oriented Kharlamov.

The New Year's Eve meeting in Montreal likewise looked to be a classic. "No city in the NHL is more conscious of Canada's proud national hockey tradition than Montreal," wrote Bortstein, "and that pride will be on the line the evening of Dec. 31."

The series finale was fitting in that Soviet champion Red Army would face the two-time Stanley Cup champion Flyers. The 1975–1976 Red Army club ranks with the 1972 national team as one of Russia's great international squads. Its lineup—listing defensemen pairings of Vasiliev–Gusev, Vladimir Lutchenko–Tsygankov, and Viktor Kuzkin–Alexei Volchenkov and forward lines of Mikhailov–Petrov–Kharlamov, Vikulov–Victor Shluktov–Alexandrov, and Popov–Solodukhin–Maltsev, with Volchkov, Sergei Glazov, and Viktor Kutyergin providing depth—may have been better than its 1972 predecessor, as it was more experienced in international play.

In Philadelphia, Shero eagerly awaited the arrival of the Soviets. "Freddy watched films of the Russians," Joe Watson remembers. "He told us, 'They have an Iron Curtain over there. We're going to show them an iron curtain in North America.'"

CHAPTER 3

Freddy the Fog

HE WAS A FORWARD THINKER, A MAN AHEAD OF HIS TIME. YET AS MUCH as Fred Shero was revered, his team was reviled. And while he was nicknamed "Freddy the Fog," for decades it was the Hockey Hall of Fame selection committee that appeared to be in a daze as it continually snubbed one of the game's great coaches.

"The legacy of my father should be as an innovator," Ray Shero says. "I believe he was ahead of his time in many facets of the game on and off the ice."

Dick Irvin Jr. recalls Shero, a 2013 Hockey Hall of Fame inductee, as one who "changed things a bit in his approach to the game. I didn't get to know him that well, but who did?"

Flyers fan Dana T. Graf called Shero an innovator and improvisor, a coach with "an uncanny knack for line juggling, for coming up with the right combination of five players to best handle a particular situation." Shero, wrote Graf, was "not afraid to flip-flop his wings, to change his defensive pairings, or to break up a successful forward line."

Former *Philadelphia Inquirer* sports columnist Bill Lyon remembered Philadelphia's sports scene in the early 1970s as a "toxic wasteland." That changed when Shero arrived wearing photo gray glasses and checkered blazers to build what Lyon recalled as a team of "toothless, fearless Canadians with a penchant for nicknames and fisticuffs."

A son of Russian immigrants, Shero borrowed from the Soviet style and popularized "system" hockey in the NHL. The success of Shero's system prompted Scotty Bowman, Al Arbour, and Glen Sather to borrow freely from the Fog as they built dynasties with the Canadiens, Islanders, and Oilers, respectively.

"He came to us out of nowhere," Bob Kelly recalls. "He had been in the Rangers' system, but he really typified what it meant to be a Flyer."

What it meant to be a Flyer in the mid-1970s was to be a lifelong member of the Bullies brotherhood. It was a point vividly illustrated in a chalkboard message Shero scrawled prior to winning the 1974 Stanley Cup against the Bruins: "Win today, and we walk together forever." The Flyers won, and as Shero promised, they walk together still. This is testimony to the brotherhood Shero helped his team build.

Born October 23, 1925, in Winnipeg, Manitoba, Shero was seventeen years old when he was signed by the New York Rangers to his first professional contract. The 5-foot-10, 185-pound defenseman divided his first season in the Eastern Amateur Hockey League playing for the New York Rovers and Brooklyn Crescents. The advent of World War II saw Shero join the Royal Canadian Navy and serve on the HMCS *Chippawa*, where he continued to play hockey. Following the war, Shero returned to the Rangers and played two more years in the minors before being called up to the big club.

Shero's NHL debut came on October 16, 1947, in the regular season opener against the Montreal Canadiens. He played 19 games in the NHL his first season and spent time with the St. Paul Saints in the United States Hockey League. Shero's moniker, "The Fog," was first bestowed upon him in a 1948 game in St. Paul, Minnesota. Indoor ice surfaces are susceptible to fog due to high humidity, and in this game the arena grew so dense with fog that Shero said he was the only player able to see the puck. His statement led to his being called "Freddy the Fog"—though it was also believed to have applied to Shero often being lost in thought.

After seeing limited action for the Rangers in the 1947–1948 campaign, Shero broke through the following year and became a regular in the Blueshirts' rotation. In 1949–1950, the Rangers qualified as the fourth seed in what was then still a six-team league. New York shocked top seed Montreal in the first round and pushed star-studded Detroit to seven games before falling in double overtime. Shero was dealt in 1951 to the Cleveland Barons of the American Hockey League.

The Barons were an AHL powerhouse, capturing consecutive Calder Cup titles in Shero's first two seasons with the team. Shero's contributions to the club earned him AHL All-Star status in 1954, and he continued his winning ways when he went to the Winnipeg Warriors of the Western Hockey League (WHL) for the 1955–1956 season. In his first season with Winnipeg, Shero served as captain of a club that claimed the WHL title. He spent one more season with the Warriors before joining the Shawinigan Cataractes of the Quebec Hockey League. It was while he was with the Cataractes in the 1957–1958 season that Shero began coaching. He was a player and assistant coach when he captured his fourth minor-league championship in six seasons. Shero retired as a player in 1958 and spent thirteen highly successful years coaching in the minors, where he earned six first place finishes and was runner-up five times.

Shero coached the St. Paul Saints to the 1960 and 1961 International Hockey League titles and three years later took the St. Paul Rangers to the finals of the Central Professional Hockey League. In 1965, Shero returned to the AHL and five years later bossed the Buffalo Bisons to the Calder Cup crown. He was named AHL Coach of the Year and received the Louis A. R. Pieri Memorial Award. Shero headed back to the Central Hockey League (CHL) for the 1970–1971 season and led the Omaha Knights to the title.

Despite his stunning success at coaching minor-league hockey, Shero was not seriously considered by New York Rangers brass to be a prospective heir to Blueshirts boss Emile Francis. Like Shero, "the Cat," as Francis was known, was a former Rangers player and had served as the club's head coach and general manager since the 1965–1966 season. Francis later took New York to the Stanley Cup Final in 1971–1972 and had a memorable encounter with Shero in the 1974 Stanley Cup semifinals.

While Shero was unable to move up in the Rangers organization, the Flyers were searching for a new head coach to replace Vic Stasiuk, who was fired following the 1970–1971 season. Stasiuk played left wing on Detroit's Stanley Cup winning teams in 1952, 1954, and 1955 and made NHL history in 1957 1958 when, as a member of the Bruins, he teamed with fellow Ukranians Johnny Bucyk and Bronco Horvath on the Uke Line, the first NHL line to produce three 20-goal scorers in the same season.

Following the end of his playing career in 1966, Stasiuk coached the AHL's Pittsburgh Hornets and Quebec Aces and the Eastern Hockey League's Jersey Devils before taking over as headman of the fledgling Flyers in 1969. A single point separated Philadelphia from the NHL playoffs in Stasiuk's first season behind the bench, but he took them to the promised land the following season, where they were eliminated in the first round. Criticism of Stasiuk from Flyers players led to his dismissal as head coach on May 27, 1971. Though he was offered an opportunity by Flyers owner Ed Snider to stay with the organization as a scout, Stasiuk opted instead to accept the head coaching position with the California Golden Seals, who had been recently purchased by Charles O. Finley, maverick owner of Major League Baseball's Oakland A's.

Needing to fill the head coaching position with the Flyers, Keith Allen, who had been the Flyers head coach their first two seasons in 1967–1968 and 1968–1969 and replaced Bud Poile as general manager following the 1970 season, recommended Snider hire the Rangers' minor-league coach. Allen didn't know Shero personally, but he knew of his successes. "He had won everywhere," Allen said in the Flyers book *Full Spectrum*. "[H]is record was so good, and I'd never heard anyone say a bad word about him."

Shero's success in the Rangers organization impressed Allen and Snider, and on June 2, 1971, the Flyers made him the third head coach in the franchise's young history. Buoyed by his previous coaching success, Shero predicted the Flyers would not finish lower than second place in the West Division, which was formed in 1967 when the NHL followed the lead of the other major sports and expanded. For the NHL, that meant adding six new clubs—Los Angeles, Minnesota, Philadelphia, Pittsburgh, St. Louis, and San Francisco/Oakland—to the Original Six: Boston, Chicago, Detroit, Montreal, New York Rangers, and Toronto.

Flyers announcer Gene Hart's initial impression of Shero was that he was a much different man than his predecessors. Where the dignified

Allen had served as the club's first bench boss and the rambunctious Sta-siuk the second, Hart thought Shero "a small, bespectacled, withdrawn older gentleman, introverted, and even eccentric."

The Flyers floundered in Shero's first season, finishing fifth in the West with a 26–38–14 record and seven fewer points in the standings than they had managed the previous season. Still, they remained in play-off contention heading into the season's final day. Playing Buffalo in the Memorial Auditorium, the Flyers forged a 2–0 lead. The Sabres tied the score, but a win or tie would vault the Flyers into the playoffs, and Hart counted down the remaining time on Flyers radio: "*Five minutes . . . Four . . . Three . . . Two . . . One . . .*"

With seconds remaining, former Flyer Gerry Meehan shot from sixty feet out. The puck flew over the left shoulder of Philly goalie Doug Favell. Listeners heard Hart's agonizing call: "*Shot, score! And that does it for the Flyers. Three-two Buffalo with four seconds left. The Flyers are elimi-nated from the playoffs . . .*" A disheartened Hart then muttered, "Son of a bitch!"

Shero struggled during his initial season because he leaned heavily on the talents of his players rather than on the system he had used in the minors. Before his second season, Shero instituted the strategies he would become famous for. He named Mike Nykoluk, a former center with the Maple Leafs in 1956–1957 and the Rochester Americans and Hershey Bears of the AHL from 1956–1957 to 1971–1972, the NHL's first full-time assistant coach. Critics questioned why Shero would need an aide-de-camp when no other NHL coach did, but the Fog proved he was a clear thinker as the Flyers fashioned a season of franchise firsts: the first winning season (37–30–11) in team history, first recognition as the Broad Street Bullies, and first playoff series victory.

The Flyers' reputation was enhanced on November 9, 1972, when tough guy Keith Magnuson and the Chicago Black Hawks arrived at the Spectrum. Schultz rained right hands down on Magnuson, who gave nearly as good as he got. Magnuson's mouth was bloodied and his jaw reportedly broken by Schultz's hammering. The brawl established the Flyers as a team to be feared. Hart later remarked that from that point forward, the Flyers "marauded through the NHL, earning the scorn of many but pride and reverence from their growing legion of fans."

Flyers fans celebrated the talents of Bobby Clarke, Bill Barber, Ross Lonsberry, Orest Kindrachuk, and crew while also embracing with equal fervor enforcers Schultz, Kelly, and Don Saleski. In 1972–1973, the Hammer, Hound, and Big Bird took to heart Shero's credo to play with swaggering aggression and founded the Flyers' "200 Club"—each acquiring more than 200 penalty minutes during the season. Schultz headed the trio with 259 PIMs, followed by Kelly (238) and Saleski (205). The addition of defenseman Andre Dupont during that season added more muscle to the Bullies' lineup, and Moose would join the "200 Club" when he posted 216 PIMs the following season and a career-high 276 in 1974–1975.

Shero considered it tough hockey and swore he never told a player to attack another player. He told his players if they ever heard him say to attack another player, they could break a stick over his head. Shero asked only that his Flyers play aggressively.

Flyers owner Ed Snider told author Adam Kimelman in his book *The Good, the Bad, and the Ugly: Heart-Pounding, Jaw-Dropping, and Gut-Wrenching Moments from Philadelphia Flyers History* that intimidation was not the Flyers' goal. "We became intimidators because we were so strong and tough," Snider said.

Flyers defenseman Wayne Hillman believed the Bullies could see enemy players casting a wary eye upon entering the Spectrum. Opponents heard that the Flyers were a bunch of animals and didn't want any part of them. Says Jimmy Watson, "Intimidation was a big part of the game back then."

It was the birth of the Philly Flu, and Flyers' winger Gary Dornhoefer thought the combination of the Bullies' physical play and the deafening crowd noise made the Spectrum an intimidating place to play. The Flyers were just as intimidating on the road. Kindrachuk knew that going into an opponent's arena and taking two points from them following a win was what the Bullies cared about. Everybody loved to hate the Flyers, and they loved to be hated. It inspired the Bullies even more.

Inspiration and intimidation fueled the Flyers' surge in 1972–1973. Shero's approach opened avenues of ice for Philly's snipers, and the offense flourished, fashioning five scorers with at least 30 goals. Clarke claimed the Hart Trophy after producing a team-best 104 points on 37 goals and 67 assists. The captain's relentless style impressed his peers, who voted him the Lester B. Pearson Award as the league's top player. Rick MacLeish etched his name in the record book by becoming the eighth player in NHL history to score 50 goals in a season and the first Flyer to do so. Bill Flett added a career-high 43 goals, and Barber (who led all rookies in scoring) and Dornhoefer scored 30 each.

Shero's system included a breakout play that benefited the Bullies immensely. It involved all five Flyers on the ice and utilized short, sharp passes to prevent defenses from forechecking. Long passes on the breakout were not attempted unless the center or wing was wide open. Another play in the Shero system focused on the forecheck, with the center in deep to pressure the puck and both wings positioned high along the boards with a defenseman, while the other defenseman stayed back. "Freddy was ahead of his time, and he was one of a kind," Jimmy Watson remembers. "He was a pioneer, and he changed the NHL."

The Flyers finished in second place in the West, returned to the playoffs for the first time in two years, and defeated the aging Minnesota North Stars in six games. The key contest for Shero's squad was Game 5 on April 10, 1973. With the series tied at two games apiece, MacLeish stepped up, the Hawk swooping in early in the second period to post his second power-play goal of the game. MacLeish's score gave the Flyers a 2–1 lead, but Bill Goldsworthy tied it at the thirteen-minute mark of the third, and the teams headed to overtime. At the eight-minute mark of OT, Dornhoefer took the puck at center ice and, upended by defenseman Tom Reid, went airborne to beat goalie Cesare Maniago for the game winner.

Dornhoefer's memorable moment from Game 5 is immortalized by a bronze statue outside the Spectrum of him scoring while parallel to the ice. The Flyers closed out the North Stars in Game 6, then faced the Canadiens in the semifinals. The series was close, with Philadelphia taking Game 1 in overtime, but the Canadiens won four straight to end the Flyers' season. Losing to Montreal convinced Flyers management it needed to improve the team's goalie situation. To upgrade the position, the Flyers let the past serve as prologue, reacquiring their former goalie Bernie Parent. His skills polished by two years in Toronto with his idol, Jacques Plante, Parent returned to the Flyers on May 15, 1973, not the raw talent he had once been but a finished product. With Bernie back-stopping a strong defense, the Flyers began the 1973–1974 campaign certain they could win it all.

The Flyers started fast, topping Toronto, 2–0, on October 11 as Parent made 28 saves, and Terry Crisp and Barber beat former teammate Favell for goals. The season-opening game, the lone NHL contest that night, was noteworthy for another reason—Kate Smith's appearance at the Spectrum to sing "God Bless America" live for the first time at a Flyers game. The famous singer's history with the team dated to December 11, 1969, when her recorded version of "God Bless America" was played in place of "The Star-Spangled Banner." The decision to play Smith's song had been made by Flyers vice president Lou Scheinfeld, who had tested tapes and records of patriotic songs on the Spectrum's PA system before deciding on "God Bless America."

Scheinfeld's decision to replace the traditional "Star Spangled Banner" surprised the 10,059 fans in attendance and infuriated Snider. The Flyers' 6–3 victory over Toronto after the playing of Smith's song tempered the dismay of fans and Snider, and when Scheinfeld played it again on December 21 and Philly pounded Pittsburgh, 4–0, reporters pointed out that the Flyers were 2–0 when Smith's recording was aired.

Smith was familiar with Philadelphia, having sung on the Steel Pier in the 1930s. But she had resisted efforts by the Flyers to bring her to the Spectrum to sing live; time after time the response from the singer's Long Island home was a firm "no." The Flyers were confused until it was learned that Smith kept declining out of concern about how a hockey crowd would greet an aging singer whose career had peaked decades earlier. It wasn't until Fred Ditmars, an uncle to Smith, sent her newspaper articles detailing the Flyers' success following the playing of her song that she agreed to appear live for the 1973 season opener. Her appearance was kept secret from fans; no announcements were made prior to the game, and Snider sent a chauffeured limousine to Long Island to pick up the singer and bring her to Philadelphia. Following player introductions, a red carpet was rolled onto the ice, and a floor microphone and small organ were brought out. Flyers public address announcer Lou Nolan leaned into his microphone: "At the beginning of this new season, would you all please rise and join us in the singing of 'God Bless America' with Kate Smith!"

The sight of Smith walking onto the carpet gave rise to a roar from the crowd that drowned out the remainder of Nolan's address. Hart recalled that the Spectrum "literally exploded with an ovation that rose in a crescendo until it was absolutely deafening." Smith said the fans' cheers went right through her. The singer had played before larger crowds but had never received such an ovation. Moved by the crowd's reaction, Smith rose to the occasion. "She sang beautifully," Hart remembered—so beautifully that her final notes were eclipsed by another ovation, and she departed with a smile and wave, blowing kisses to the crowd. Favell heard the roar and tossed his goalie gloves in the air in resignation. "I knew right then we didn't have a chance."

Buoyed by their good-luck charm, the Bullies earned a triumph that improved their record at the time to 29–3–1 when Smith's "God Bless America" rang through the rafters at the Spectrum. Parent returned to his former team in style, recording a 2–0 shutout. He earned a second straight shutout two days later by blanking the Islanders in the Nassau Coliseum. Bernie would hold scoreless five of the Flyers' first twelve opponents. Shero, who'd had his doubts about dealing for Parent, was convinced. In time, he would consider Parent the best goalie he'd ever seen.

Parent, in turn, credited Shero's system for his success. "It's a great system we play, from Fred Shero and Mike Nykoluk," Parent told Flyers announcer Don Earle. "If you don't make any mistakes in your own end, they don't score any goals."

The broadcasting tandem of Hart and Earle provided a soundtrack of the season for Flyers fans. Approaching his forty-fifth birthday, Hart had been with the Flyers since their inception. The former high school history teacher and part-time sports announcer had submitted tapes of his broadcasts to the team for consideration. Because the fledgling Flyers could not at the time afford a premier Canadian announcer, they hired the New York City native on a part-time basis. "I wish I could say they had 288 tapes and mine was the best," the self-effacing Hart said. "But it was really a matter of expediency. I was the right guy at the right time in the right place."

Originally serving as the team's public address announcer and color analyst for Stu Nahan (later featured as a ring announcer in Sly Stallone's films featuring fictional Philadelphia fighter Rocky Balboa), the boy-hood New York Rangers fan became the voice of the rival Flyers for the next twenty-nine years. Hart's style was heavily influenced by legendary NHL broadcaster Foster Hewitt. Hart's high-pitched voice and frenetic delivery suited both radio and TV, and he became as closely identified with the Flyers as the team's players and coaches. In their early years, the Flyers had to pay for airtime, and only the third period of each game was broadcast.

Like Hart, Earle traced his beginnings in broadcasting to high school games. Two years older than Hart, Earle had broken into the big time at the same time as Gene. From 1967 to 1971, Earle broadcast Boston Bruins games for WSBK-TV, capturing the excitement of the Bruins' 1970 Stanley Cup season. He then joined Hart broadcasting Flyers action on WTAF-TV Channel 29 in Philadelphia. Hart and Earle alternated in the roles of announcer and analyst, their voices synonymous with Flyers hockey broadcast simultaneously on TV and radio. They developed a signature call, awarding a case of Tastykake desserts to every Flyer who scored a goal. Tastykake was a sponsor of the Flyers, and the cases of desserts were usually donated by the players to charity. Hart's signature call—"Score!"—often preceded the call for "a case of Tastykake!" Earle opened every Flyers broadcast by stating, "Let's go, Flyers. Let's go, Gene Hart." Hart would end each broadcast with, "Good night and good hockey."

Flyers fans found Hart and Earle to be pure poetry, the pair painting word pictures describing the colorful action on the ice below:

Hart: "Barber along the near side. Shot . . . score! Billy Barber from the point for a case of Tastykakes!"

Earle: "Dornhoefer back to MacLeish. Drop pass. Dornhoefer scores for a case of Tastykakes!"

On March 30, the Flyers faced the Bruins in a game Hart called the most important of the regular season. Philadelphia fronted the West Division, Boston the East. The Flyers had not beaten the Bruins in their previous twenty-seven encounters, going 0–24–3. With a sellout crowd of 17,007 packing the Spectrum, the Bullies won, 5–3. The Flyers celebrated clinching their first division title by swigging from champagne bottles and dragging the 280-pound Hart—the "Mound of Sound"—into the locker room shower.

By regular season's end, the Flyers had earned their first 50-win season and won the West with 112 points, one point lower than Boston's league-leading total. Parent set an NHL record that would stand for seventeen seasons by playing 73 of the Flyers' 78 games. Parent set additional NHL marks for wins in a season (47) and led NHL goalies with a 1.89 goals-against average and a league-leading 12 shutouts. Schultz led the league with 348 penalty minutes. The Hammer also scored 20 goals. Lonsberry and MacLeish netted 32 goals apiece, Barber 34, and Clarke a team-high 35 goals and 52 assists. The captain's 87 points ranked fifth best in the league. Postseason awards poured in. Parent shared the Vezina Trophy with Chicago's Tony Esposito, becoming the first Flyers goalie to be so honored. Parent also finished second to Boston's Phil Esposito for the Hart Trophy. "Skill and toughness, combined with goaltending, is tough to beat," says Bill Clement.

After guiding the Flyers to their best season in the team's short history, Shero received the NHL's Jack Adams Award as Coach of the Year. "Freddy was way ahead of his time in people's skills, even thought he was an introvert," says Clement. "We were kids trapped in men's bodies, and he wanted us to have fun. We loved Freddy, we all did. He was a gentle man, the first coach who respected his players. He broke the mold in a lot of ways. But there was a method to his madness."

Dupont believes the same. "Freddy was an innovator," he says. "He had a system, and he knew how to motivate a team, that was his strong suit."

Shero's motivation included a set of rules that were a blueprint for victory:

1. Never go offside on a three-on-two or two-on-one.

2. Never go backward in your own end except on a power play.

3. Never throw a puck out blindly from behind your opponent's net.

4. Never pass diagonally across ice in your own end unless 100 percent certain.

5. Wings on wings in the neutral zone—unless intercepting a pass.

6. Second man goes all the way in for a rebound.

7. Defense with puck at opponents' blue line—look at each teammate before shooting.

8. Wing in front of opponents' net must face the puck and lean on the stick.

9. Puck carrier over center with no room and no one to pass to must shoot the puck in.

10. No forward must ever turn his back on the puck.

11. No player must be more than two zones away from the puck.

12. Never be outnumbered in the defensive zone.

13. On delayed penalty, puck carrier must look for the extra man.

14. Be alert to time left on the opponent's penalty.

The Flyers followed Shero's rules and swept the Flames in four games in the first round of the playoffs. Schultz scored an overtime game winner and bloodied Bryan Hextall with a barrage of blows. Game 3 at the Omni in Atlanta saw a bench-clearing brawl break out. The Bullies were leading, 2–1, when Clarke clipped Curt Bennett. The big Flames center dropped his gloves and then dropped Clarke. Flett rushed to Clarke's defense, but the Cowboy fared as poorly as his captain. The entire Bullies team jumped the boards, Schultz leading the way. The Hammer squared off with Butch Deadmarsh, while Ed Van Impe sized up southpaw John Stewart. Players were soon fighting even in the penalty box. It took 25 minutes to sort out the melee, and referee Dave Newell dealt out 90 minutes in penalties. After the game, Shero took his customary walk and returned with cuts and scratches on his face. "I was either mugged, or I walked into a telephone pole," he said. Clement says the Flyers believed it was the former. "He was drinking one night in Atlanta and got beat up. Mike Nykoluk found him in a pool of blood." Taking over as head coach for Game 4, Nykoluk told the Bullies, "Win the game for the guy who should be behind the bench."

Blood would be a byword for the next round, the conference final against the Rangers that still stands as arguably the roughest in NHL history. The series was built up by the media as the fighters from Philadelphia versus the nice guys of New York. The Flyers-Rangers Metroliner semifinal had multiple layers. Shero and Francis shared similar background ties, both having played and coached for the Blueshirts. The two were teammates on the 1948–1949 and 1949–1950 Rangers clubs, the latter losing to Detroit in a seven-game Stanley Cup Final. Shero's Broad Street Bullies would bring their style to bear against Francis's GAG Line of right wing Rod Gilbert, center Jean Ratelle, and left wing Vic Hadfield, and goalies Bernie Parent and Ed Giacomin would match their skills in net.

Francis had stepped down as Rangers coach to concentrate on his general manager duties following the 1972–1973 season but returned to the bench following an unimpressive start by his successor, Larry Popein. The high-salaried Rangers were dubbed by frustrated fans "The Cat's Fat Cats," and with the Blueshirts in danger of missing the postseason, Francis fired Popein and reclaimed the coaching reins. Righting the Rangers' ship, the Cat bossed the Blueshirts on a playoff drive. Although the Flyers had won 50 games to the Rangers' 40, NHL experts predicted Philly would fall in six games.

What ensued was a series so violent that *Sports Illustrated* ran a cover photo of Clarke colliding with Rangers center Pete Stemkowski, Bobby eliciting a grin as his stick finds a place between Stemkowski's legs. The headline on the magazine's cover told the story of this series:

MAYHEM ON THE ICE

Philadelphia Wars with New York

Mark Mulvoy's cover story, titled "It's Sockey, the Way They Play It Here," detailed the numerous altercations between the players and, to a lesser extent, the strategies employed by the Fog and the Cat.

The Bullies opened the semifinals in typical bruising fashion, delivering a 4–0 beatdown of the Blueshirts on Spectrum ice in Game 1. MacLeish opened the scoring by sending the puck past a horizontal Giacomin. The Hawk also closed the scoring, sandwiching his scores around goals by Lonsberry and Barber. The tone for the series was set when Rangers tough guy center Walt Tkaczuk, six weeks removed from a broken jaw, was dropped to his knees and left dazed by Clarke and Dupont. "Moose pushed me," Clarke innocently claimed in *Sports Illustrated*, "and my shoulder accidently hit Walter in the head."

Tkaczuk took the ice for Game 2 outfitted in a protective helmet equipped with two football-style bars covering his jaw. Lined up against Clarke, Tkaczuk called the Flyers captain a backstabber. The Bullies boss responded by cussing out Tkaczuk. The war of words quickly escalated into something far more physical, with Hound Kelly taking on Bugsy Butler. Kelly was starting at left wing because Shero believed Francis would start one of the Blueshirts' big boys, Ron Harris. Shero knew Harris had been hurt in Game 1 and thought a good hit from Kelly would get him out of Game 2 early. Francis's decision to start Butler, however, didn't change Kelly's plans. "Kelly jumped the other guy instead," Shero told reporters.

Using his twenty-pound weight advantage, Kelly claimed what Mulvoy called "a unanimous decision" over the Rangers rookie. Noting the Hound's ability to deliver punches in bunches, Clarke spoke admiringly of his teammate's ability to land "three or four punches before the other guy even realizes he's in a fight."

Said Kelly, "They sure don't pay me to score goals." Clarke tormented the Blueshirts with what Mulvoy described as "a quick stick, a pair of quicker elbows, and the fastest mouth in the game." When Stemkowski was bloodied on the forehead following a first-period fight with Jim Watson, Clarke told the Rangers center, "I didn't think Ukranians bled when they got hit." An angry Stemkowski retaliated with a rapid response. "If there were still only six teams in the league," he snapped at Clarke, "you wouldn't be around."

Clarke and Tkaczuk continued their private struggle. Mulvoy reported that Clarke slashed Tkaczuk and took an elbow in return. On another occasion the two centers waved their sticks menacingly in each other's faces, and their animosity was heightened when Tkaczuk slashed Clarke and Bobby speared Walt. Mulvoy wrote that the Bullies bludgeoned the Blueshirts in the corners and that the Flyers' "body-bending" forechecking forced the Rangers to make blunders. Dornhoefer and Flyer forwards harassed Giacomin enough to provide openings for two goals by Lonsberry and one each by MacLeish, Clarke, and Van Impe, and Game 2 went to the Bullies, 5–2.

Schultz had been relatively quiet in the first two games in the Spectrum, surprising for a man who had set an NHL record for PIMs in 1973–1974. The Fog expected his enforcer to be more active in the Big Apple. "Schultz," he told Mulvoy, "does most of his fighting on the road." Rangers fans greeted the Hammer in Game 3 in Madison Square Garden with chants of "We want Schultz!" They got their wish two minutes into the game when the Hammer barreled onto the ice and into defenseman Brad Park. Schultz rammed into Park again, dropped him to the ice, and pummeled him with punches. As the linesman separated the two, Schultz continued to pound away, delivering four blows to Park's midsection. Joe Watson drove Bruce MacGregor into a goalpost and held him in place while Saleski swooped in and gave MacGregor a facewash with his gloves. The Hawk and Moose beat Giacomin with early goals, but rather than be routed, the Rangers ripped the game from the Flyers' grip. Defenseman Jim Neilson hit Kelly with such force in a corner that he knocked the gloves off the Hound's hands.

Dornhoefer's power play goal midway through the second period made it 3–1 Philadelphia, but the Flyers, having hit the Rangers for three straight games, now hit a wall. "We just died," Clarke remarked to Mulvoy. "Hitting someone all the time can be very tiring." Park knew the Bullies were wearing down. "You can't be a hitting team 60 minutes a game," he told Mulvoy. "It's exhausting." The Rangers rallied, netting four straight goals in a 5–3 victory. Just as importantly, the Blueshirts brought the battle to the Bullies. Harris crashed Kelly into the boards, his hip check sending the Hound to the locker room with damaged ligaments in his knee. Steve Vickers pummeled Dornhoefer and Park one-punched MacLeish. As the Flyers filed to their team bus, which was not parked inside the Garden due to equipment being stored for another event, Rangers fans were waiting. They cursed the Bullies and threatened Schultz.

Police were stationed behind the Bullies' bench during the games at the Garden to prevent fans from throwing objects at Flyers players and coaches. So volatile was the situation that arena security increased its personnel to more than 125 to curtail potential violence. This Garden was no Eden for the Bullies, their series lead evaporating entirely in Game 4 as Gilbert took a feed from Vickers and put the puck past Parent in overtime. The 2–1 win evened the series at two games apiece and proved particularly satisfying for Gilbert, who had been forced to fend off the Hammer throughout the game. Gilbert didn't completely escape punishment; following his OT goal he was, in Mulvoy's words, "pitchforked" to the ice by Joe Watson.

The win was controversial, as New York appeared to have had too many men on the ice at the time of Gilbert's goal, and another disputed goal, this one by Blueshirts right winger Bobby Rousseau in the second period, denied Parent a second series shutout and effectively ended the career of Flyers All-Star defenseman Barry Ashbee. Rousseau's shot struck Parent's stick and landed outside the goal line. The goal judge ruled that the puck was inside the net when it glanced off Bernie's stick, equalizing the first period goal scored by Joe Watson. The controversial score forced OT, during which Ashbee was struck in the eye by a shot from Dale Rolfe. Ashbee was carried from the ice on a stretcher and after weeks of examinations by doctors was told his playing career was finished.

Returning to the Spectrum for the pivotal Game 5, the Flyers got two more goals by the ubiquitous MacLeish, as well as scores by Tom Bladon, who was playing for Ashbee, and Simon Nolet. Parent yielded just one counter in the 4–1 final, but back at MSG two nights later, the Rangers evened the series with their own 4–1 win.

Game 7 was played before a packed house at the Spectrum and a national television audience. The Flyers brought the raucous crowd to its feet by playing Kate Smith's recording of "God Bless America." The Rangers quieted the house with an early goal by Bill Fairbairn, but MacLeish tied it with his 11th goal of the postseason. The Flyers forged a 3–1 lead on a pair of second period scores by Kindrachuk and Dornhoefer. Vickers tightened the scoring nearly nine minutes into the third, but Schultz turned the tide in the Flyers' favor. With the puck in the corner, Schultz, Rolfe, and Park all sought control. Believing he had been challenged physically by Rolfe, Schultz hammered his over-matched opponent. Rolfe fell to the ice, and Hart noticed that during what he called a "terribly one-sided confrontation," not one Ranger ran to Rolfe's aid.

Park thought the way to stop Schultz was simple. He thought about taking a swing with his stick at Schultz's head but decided that if he had to maim someone to win the Stanley Cup, he didn't want to win it. Park told reporters he was fed up with the nonsense the Flyers were pulling and wanted to give it right back.

Schultz's battering of Rolfe inspired the Bullies. Less than a minute later, Dornhoefer beat Giacomin to the stick side. MacLeish had much to do with Dornhoefer's eventual game winner, jarring the puck loose from Park by bashing him into the end board. Lonsberry corralled the loose puck and fired it to Dornhoefer. Dornhoefer's goal came at the 9:01 mark, and though New York got a score from Stemkowski five minutes later, the Flyers secured a 4–3 win and earned their first berth in the Stanley Cup Finals. As the final seconds melted from the clock, the Spectrum scoreboard saluted the team's amulet with the message "God Bless Kate Smith."

The Flyers were the first expansion team to defeat an Original Six squad in a playoff series. The Bullies not only ended New York's quest for its first Cup since 1940, they expedited the end of the most famous line in Rangers history; the GAG line was broken up in 1974 when Hadfield was traded to Pittsburgh. Ratelle was then traded to Boston in '75. "The Rangers had a tremendous team, but they didn't have togetherness," Dupont remembers. "That was the difference between them and us."

The marauding Bullies were shipping up to Boston, and oddsmakers installed the upstart Flyers as underdogs, predicting a victory in five games for Bobby Orr and the Big, Bad Bruins. For the first time in this postseason, the Flyers wouldn't have home ice advantage, and they had dropped three games to the Rangers in New York. Philadelphia would also be missing Ashbee against a Bruins squad that boasted the NHL's best offense and the league's top four scorers, three of whom recorded more than 100 points. The Bullies would have to battle history as well. The Flyers had beaten Boston just four times in seven years and had won only once on Boston Garden ice, that victory coming in the first meeting between the teams in 1967. Clarke promised the Flyers would show up. The Bullies had come too far to quit now, he told reporters.

Orr recalled in his autobiography his awareness that the Flyers had arrived: "Philadelphia may have been an expansion team, but they were not to be taken lightly." Orr thought Parent a goalie who could steal games, Clarke a captain who would do anything to win, and the Bullies a team that "didn't take a backseat to the Big, Bad Bruins when it came to toughness."

The series opened on Tuesday night, May 7, in Boston Garden. A confrontation between the NHL's two toughest teams since 1969—the Big, Bad Bruins and Broad Street Bullies—and arguably the league's hardest workers in the two Bobbys—Orr and Clarke—promised a memorable Stanley Cup Final. Orr was of special interest to Shero, who agreed with those who believed he took dives to influence penalty calls. Black Hawks head coach Billy Reay said it was "brutal" what Orr got away with, and Shero concurred. It looked to the Fog like officials were afraid to call a decision against Orr in the Boston rink. The trouble, said Shero, is that the referees thought Orr was God.

Just as Orr had thought of Howe as his most impressive opponent in the late 1960s, Clarke considered Orr one notch above everyone else in the NHL in the mid-1970s. The Flyers' captain believed Orr to be the only guy in the NHL with the potential to take the puck behind his own net, skate through the defense, and score a goal at the opposite end of the ice. The Flyers knew they would not beat Boston if, as Shero said, they "treated Orr like the Pope." Every NHL club attempted to forecheck Orr with a single player standing in front of the Bruins net, waiting for him to make his move and then trying to skate with him. Shero saw that as futile, and Clarke agreed, considering it an almost hopeless job since there weren't many players who could skate with Orr.

Shero's scheme to combat Orr was to send three forwards in a crossing pattern in front of the Boston net. By flooding the area with moving roadblocks, the forwards would force Orr to reconsider his lanes to open ice. "The idea," said Shero, "was to make Orr work harder than he normally does." The Fog's plans also included having his forwards chase Orr behind the net when he had the puck and pin him to the boards, thus forcing faceoffs in the Bruins' end. Should Orr escape his pursuers and carry the puck past center ice, Shero told his defenders to greet Bobby with body checks. Traps were also laid for Esposito, the linchpin of the Nitro Line he centered with wingers Wayne Cashman and Ken Hodge. Espo was touted as the "World's Greatest Center," and bumper stickers in Boston read, "Jesus Saves, But Espo Scores on the Rebound!" Shero instructed the tenacious Clarke and MacLeish to take turns opposing Espo on faceoffs. Nor did Shero forget Bruins goalie Gilles Gilbert. The Bullies had provided plenty of traffic in front of Giacomin and planned to do the same to Gilbert.

Dornhoefer knew he wouldn't be the only guy getting in front of Gilbert. The Flyers would look to get in front of the Bruins' goalie in an effort to bother him. They reasoned that if Gilbert couldn't see the puck, he would be in trouble. The Flyers thought it important that somebody be stationed in front of Gilbert to trouble him.

Fans saw the finals as a heavyweight championship, and it was the Big, Bad Bruins who got the jump in Game 1 in steamy Boston Garden, putting two early goals past Parent. Kindrachuk and Clarke tied it, but

Orr would be the difference. Earlier in the game, his blue line bullet was redirected for a goal by Cashman, who was stationed in front of Parent. With 22 seconds left in the third period, Orr escaped Shero's traps, sped down the ice, and scored the game winner. "I'd like to say I took aim and fired a perfect shot, but I didn't." Orr saw Ken Hodge with the puck, and when the pass came out, Bobby let it rip.

Dupont and the Bullies were defiant in defeat. The Moose believed the Bullies should be more encouraged than the Bruins, even though the Flyers lost. Dupont thought Boston had to get a lucky goal to win. Dupont made a more declarative statement in Game 2, which looked to be a repeat of the opener when the Flyers fell behind, 2–0. Philadelphia halved its deficit, and with 50 seconds left, Dupont tied the game and celebrated with his Moose shuffle. A hip check from Lonsberry in over- time left Orr crumpled on the ice. "Seeing Bobby down on the ice like that," Lonsberry said, "had to depress the other Bruins."

Parent's stoning of veteran Johnny Bucyk at the 10-minute mark kept the Flyers alive, and at 12:01, Clarke took a shot from close range, battled for the rebound, and lifted the winning shot over a prone Gilbert. Clarke exulted, thrusting both arms high into the air and jumping with joy. "I don't see how anybody can have doubts about us now," Clarke said at the time. "We know we can beat them."

Joe Watson, who had roomed with Orr when both were Bruins during Bobby's rookie season, recalls that Game 2 was when the Flyers "really had an idea we could beat this team." The Bullies proved as much in Game 3 in the Spectrum, winning 4–1 behind goals by Bladon, Crisp, Kindrachuk, and Lonsberry alongside great goaltending by Parent. The Flyers followed by taking a 2–0 lead in Game 4. The Bruins tied it, but Shero's strategy of tiring out Orr appeared to have an effect in the third period when Lonsberry beat the Bruins superstar to the puck in the Boston zone and fed Barber, who rocketed a 40-foot blast past Gilbert. Dupont's insurance goal closed the scoring at 4–2 and gave the Flyers a 3–1 series lead.

Returning home to Boston Garden, Orr scored twice in Game 5 to fuel a 5–1 victory. "What can you say about Orr?" Parent asked. "He's really something." The night before Game 6, Jimmy Watson thought, "My gosh, if we win tomorrow, we win the Stanley Cup!" In the Spectrum, the Fog went to the green chalkboard and wrote his soon-to-be-famous message about winning now and walking together forever.

Snider promised Philadelphia Mayor Frank Rizzo that the Flyers would win it all on Sunday, May 19. Outside the Spectrum it was 78 degrees, and a scent of spring sweetened the air. Inside the sold-out arena, 17,007 fans thundered their approval at the sight of Kate Smith stepping to the microphone down on the ice. Standing on the ice amid the bedlam, Parent was comforted by his philosophy that it was the Flyers and 17,000 fans against the Bruins.

Listening to Smith's voice, Parent thought the Spectrum roof was going to come down. "God bless her," he thought. Hoping to break Smith's spell on the Flyers—the Bullies having gone 35–3–1 when her song was played, Esposito approached and asked, "Couldn't you sing 'As the Caissons Go Rolling Along'?" Espo and Orr sought to share in the good fortune by shaking hands with Smith. What the Bruins didn't know was that the Bullies not only boasted Kate but Bennie as well. Elton John's hit single "Bennie and the Jets," released the previous February, had become another good luck charm for the Flyers, a harbinger of victories when it aired on Philadelphia radio stations.

The Bruins outshot the Flyers, 16–8, in the first period, but the Bullies left the ice with a 1–0 lead, MacLeish deflecting Dupont's shot into the net for a power play goal at 14:28. The Hawk had won a face-off with Gregg Sheppard and sent the puck skittering to Dupont, who was forty feet away from Gilbert on the left point. MacLeish flashed toward the net as Dupont delivered a wrist shot. The puck deflected off the stick of MacLeish. "The puck hit my stick, changed direction and went in," MacLeish told reporters. "Gilbert would have had it if it hadn't gone off my stick."

With the Bullies still leading in the third, 1–0, Parent kicked aside a pair of shots by Orr. "We had a good defense, and we had Bernie," Dupont recalls. "He made saves that were unbelievable." As the seconds counted down, Parent looked up at the scoreboard just as Orr sent in a long screamer toward the Flyers' goal. "I never saw it," Parent later admitted. "If it had been on net, it would have gone in."

The Flyers faithful counted down the final moments, and at precisely 5:02 p.m. Hart provided a memorable call that has been compared to Russ Hodges's classic, "The Giants win the pennant!":

Ladies and gentlemen, the Flyers are going to win the Stanley Cup! The Flyers win the Stanley Cup! The Flyers win the Stanley Cup! The Flyers have won the Stanley Cup!

Years later, Snider would still get goose bumps when he thought of Hart's call. "It will go down in sports history," he said, "as one of the greatest broadcast moments of all time." In the postmortem, the Bruins praised the Bullies. "The Flyers were hungrier than we were," Orr said. "They worked their butts off for three periods a game. We didn't. They knocked us off the puck and outworked us in the corners."

Jimmy Watson remembers the Bullies priding themselves on outworking opponents. "We worked hard and grinded it out every day," he says. "Our thoughts were, 'Let's not get outworked, boys.'"

Clement, who fought back from injury to play one of the finest games of his career in Game 6, recalls Shero's strategy for dealing with hockey's greatest player. "We contained Bobby Orr. Every time we got a chance we rubbed him, we isolated him from the play, and when you cut him off, you killed the Bruins."

Orr paid tribute to Shero and Nykoluk's strategy. Match the Flyers man-for-man with the top teams in the NHL, he said at the time, and there were probably better individual players on other clubs. Yet it was the Flyers who owned the Cup. Granted, Parent was strong in the nets, but Orr believed Shero's coaching made a strong contribution to the Flyers' success.

Philadelphia became the first expansion team to hoist Lord Stanley's hardware. Fans flowed onto the ice, and the next day's newspapers trumpeted the Bullies' triumph, the *Philadelphia Inquirer* proclaiming, "Miracle Flyers Take the Cup, and City Goes Wild With Joy," and the *Evening Bulletin* blaring, "We're Number One! City of Winners Erupts in Joy." Two million fans turned out to fete the Flyers in a sun-splashed victory parade in the city. Mayor Rizzo congratulated the champions at Independence Mall. Police Commissioner Joseph O'Neill eyed the massive celebration in awe. "I've never seen anything to compare to this."

Shero had said that if the Flyers won, he'd retire from coaching and return to law school. Instead, the would-be teacher turned student and traveled to Russia, to the land his parents emigrated from, to learn ice hockey strategies that could help his Flyers defend their Stanley Cup.

Less than two years following his visit to Russia, the Fog would find himself studying the Soviets again. His motivation now was to beat the hell out of what he called "a machine."

CHAPTER 4

Moscow's Mr. Go and Mr. No

(Moskovsky Mister Go yi Mister Nyet)

ONE WAS A SNIPER, THE OTHER A STOPPER. MOSCOW'S MR. GO AND MR. No; in their native tongue, "*Moskovsky Mister Go yi Mister Nyet.*"

The nicknames were first applied in the early 1970s by *Sports Illustrated* to the NHL's Esposito brothers, Phil and Tony, respectively. Phil was the sharpshooter forward for the Boston Bruins, Tony the Chicago Black Hawks goalie whose shutouts earned him the moniker "Tony 0"—as in zero goals surrendered.

By the eve of Super Series '76, the names Mr. Go and Mr. No aptly described Soviet superstars Valeri Kharlamov and Vladislav Tretiak. Kharlamov, the left wing on the Red Army's top line, was an idol of the Soviet Union. Russian hockey historian Arthur Chidlovski recalls Kharlamov's grace and beautiful play and likens him to a poet—"a poet of the game." So impressed were hockey fans in North America that many Canadian children chose the Russian star as their favorite player.

When *Sports Illustrated* writer Mark Mulvoy visited the Soviet Union in 1975 to preview the Russians before the historic Super Series '76, he compared Kharlamov to the Bruins' charismatic star Derek Sanderson. Mulvoy wrote that like Derek, Valeri was "a well-heeled bachelor who squires only chic young ladies to the best Moscow discos in his luxurious Volga, which is equipped with a stereo tape deck, dual rear-seat speakers, reclining bucket seats, and a large pocket on the front right-side door for parking tickets."

Andrei Vasilyev wrote on *Russia Beyond* that Kharlamov was "one of Moscow's great mods, one of the few who would wear a golden necklace as thick as a finger during the rough Soviet times." Vasilyev also noted that Valeri heeded the "calls of his Spanish blood, performing fiery flamencos and exhilarating rock and roll."

Yet, unlike the outspoken Sanderson, Kharlamov was soft-spoken to the point of being shy, at least when dealing with the media. When interviewed, Kharlamov spoke in a rapid Russian monotone, telling Mulvoy that he was twenty-seven years old, single, and would not marry until his playing career with the Central Army club team was concluded. "Some girls may have selected me," Russia's most eligible bachelor said, "but I have not yet selected a favorite girl."

At the time, Kharlamov was a student at the State Institute of Physical Culture and Sport. Like fellow Soviet standout Aleksandr Yakushev, who was loaned to Krylya Sovetov by Spartak for Super Series '76, Kharlamov looked to become a coach once his playing days were done. He was not the Soviet Union's first star hockey player, but he was the USSR's first *super*star. Anatoli Firsov preceded Kharlamov as Russia's best player, but he was thirty-four years old in 1976 and did not receive the international acclaim Valeri earned as the Soviets prepared for the Super Series.

To get his international champions ready for their NHL games, Red Army coach Konstantin Loktev ran his charges through a rigorous practice routine. Kharlamov, Boris Mikhailov, Vladimir Petrov, and the rest of the team did push-ups, sit-ups, knee lifts, deep knee bends, and toe touches prior to practice. When Kharlamov fouled up a three-on-two rush with what Mulvoy described as a "fancy but unrequired behind-the-back pass to Petrov," Loktev ordered his star to do a dozen push-ups.

By 1976, Kharlamov was acknowledged by most hockey experts as the premier left winger not only in talent-rich Russia, but in the entire sport. Tretiak called Kharlamov's hockey talents "God-given" and claimed Valeri "could do practically everything—a smart play, a tricky pass, a precise shot." Tretiak would look up ice, see Kharlamov performing magic with the puck, and think Valeri made the game look "so easy, so elegant." Tretiak thought Kharlamov's execution of hockey was "aesthetic" to the degree that Valeri amazed millions. In his article on Kharlamov, Vasilyev called him the "little genius of the big game."

Kharlamov had come a long way from his blue-collar beginnings. He was born into an international family on January 14, 1948, close to the Sokol subway stop in Moscow. Valeri's parents, Boris and Carmen Orive-Abad were laborers at Moscow's Kommunar plant. Boris was a metalworker; Carmen, a turner. Called Begona by her family, Carmen was born in Bilbao, Spain, the daughter of a Spanish communist, and had fled the Spanish Civil War and Francisco Franco regime as a child in 1937. Valeri was named after Soviet pilot Valery Chkalov. At age eight, Valeri moved with his mother from the Soviet Union to Spain, where they lived for several months before returning to Russia. Half Basque, Valeri was called "The Spaniard" during his career.

Vadim Nikonov, Kharlamov's childhood friend and later a renowned soccer player and coach, thought Kharlamov's mix of Russian and Spanish blood made him unique on the ice and in life. Kharlamov's love for hockey began at age seven, though some sources say age five. His first pair of skates were his father's blades fastened onto Valeri's shoes; Boris had played hockey as well. Small and thin and suffering poor health, Valeri endured tonsilitis and rheumatic fever and was found by doctors to have a heart defect. He was hospitalized for several months and told by doctors to discontinue playing sports. Kharlamov's desire to play soccer and hockey despite his physical shortcomings was such that Boris took him, without Begona's knowledge, to CSKA hockey school. Valeri tried out for the school, was accepted, and eventually debuted for the CSKA senior team in a game against HC Sibir on October 22, 1967.

Anatoly Tarasov wasn't impressed with young Kharlamov's skill set. Part of the reason may have been that the creative Kharlamov did not feel at ease around the strict Tarasov. "It was interesting to play for Tarasov," Kharlamov once said. "However, it was hard. You couldn't really relax with him, make a joke or something. You always felt stiff with him."

After fifteen games, Tarasov sent Kharlamov, who had scored two goals in that span, to CSKA farm club Zvezda Chebarkul. Located in the Urals, Chebarkul would gain renown in February 2013 when a meteorite hit the town; Kharlamov lit a similarly bright light decades earlier, scoring 34 goals in 32 games for the third-division team. It was enough for Boris Kulagin to talk his boss, Tarasov, into returning Kharlamov to the CSKA squad.

Kulagin's prodding paid big dividends for Kharlamov and Russian hockey. Kharlamov scored 37 goals in 42 games in his first full Soviet League season, then made a memorable debut in the world championships, producing 13 points in 10 games to claim his first international gold medal. It was the first of his eleven straight appearances in the world championships, and in March 1968 Valeri won his first USSR gold medal with Central Red Army. The following October, Kharlamov was teamed for the first time with right wing Boris Mikhailov and center Vladimir Petrov, a line that would become one of the most dominant in hockey history. In December 1968, Kharlamov played his first game for Team USSR.

The Spaniard upped his game in the 1969–1970 season, winning the Soviet scoring title after averaging a goal a game over 33 contests for Central Red Army, which won the first of four straight league championships. For the second straight season, Valeri followed the Soviet season with a strong performance in the world championships, producing 10 points in 9 games and fueling a second consecutive gold medal.

A celebrated star by the 1970–1971 Soviet season, Kharlamov registered career highs of 40 goals and 52 assists in 34 games. His 17 points in 10 games led to the Soviets' third consecutive gold medal and his first world championships All-Star selection. Kharlamov was even better in the 1971–1972 season and was named MVP of the Soviet League for the first time in his career. In the 1972 Winter Olympic Games in Sapporo, Japan, Kharlamov's point production helped lead the Soviets to another gold medal. The following spring, Kharlamov again gained All-Star honors in the world championships as the Soviets secured a silver medal.

Constant training helped Valeri overcome his physical shortcomings and build muscle mass. The 5-foot-8, 165-pound Kharlamov's speed and skill would later draw comparisons with Wayne Gretzky. Three years before his electrifying performance in the 1972 Summit Series, Kharlamov received the prestigious title Merited Master of Sport from the Russian Ministry of Sports. Over fourteen seasons with Central Army,

Kharlamov produced 507 points in 436 regular season games. His 293 goals and 214 assists helped fuel CSKA to eleven league titles, including two sets of four straight (1970–1973 and 1977–1980). Kharlamov competed in eleven straight International Ice Hockey Federation and European championships and captured eight gold medals, two silver, and one bronze. Four times he was named to tournament All-Star teams, and he competed in three Olympics from 1972 to 1980, earning two more gold medals.

Kharlamov's clutch performance in championship competition earned him renown as a big-game player, a reputation he enhanced with his prime-time performances against NHL stars. His second-period goals against Ken Dryden in Game 1 in the 1972 Summit Series keyed a shocking victory and earned him Russia's game MVP honors. Another second-period goal in Game 3, this time against Tony Esposito, forged a tie. By Game 6 in Moscow, Team Canada was so flustered by Kharlamov's on-ice wizardry that they knew *something* had to be done or the Soviets would win the series. "He was our main target," Harry Sinden said later. "I was tormented each night by thoughts on how to contain this guy." It was left to assistant coach John Ferguson to make a desperate decision. "I remember John Ferguson giving the pep talk between the first and second period," Clarke said. "He kept repeating that someone had to take care of Kharlamov. I looked around the room, and realized he was talking to me."

Clarke tracked Kharlamov down and delivered a two-handed whack to the Russian rocket's ankle. Valeri fell to the ice and Clarke was sent to the sin bin for slashing. With Kharlamov out of the game, the Canadians held on to win, 3–2, then won Game 7, 4–3, as Kharlamov remained sidelined. He returned for the eighth and final game of the series and registered an assist on Vlad Lutchenko's first-period goal against Dryden that gave the Soviets a 2–1 lead. But Kharlamov was still hurting from Clarke's slash, and with one of their stars at considerably less than 100 percent, the Russians lost the game, 6–5, and the series, 4–3–1.

Kharlamov produced 7 points on 3 goals and 4 assists for the series. His hockey intelligence, inspirational play, and tremendous natural talent made him a global household name. Two years later in a Summit Series against the WHA, Kharlamov contributed 2 goals and 6 assists as the Russians romped, winning four games, losing one, and tying three times. Kharlamov's 39 points in 31 games in 1974–1975 contributed to Red Army's recapturing the Soviet title, and his 16 points in 9 games led to another gold medal in the world championships. "I love to play beautifully," Kharlamov said at the time. "I love to score beautiful goals."

Chidlovski believes Kharlamov's goals belong more to a poetry book than a stat sheet. Kharlamov, Chidlovski says, "was a legend among Russian hockey legends. He was a true genius of the game. He became a truly inspirational personality for generations of Russian players."

Kharlamov's moves on the ice, Chidlovski recalls, couldn't be learned from a hockey manual or school. Nor were they precalculated patterns practiced by the Red Army. They were, according to Chidlovski, "the truly amazing moves of a hockey genius. In all their beauty and unpredictability, those were his moves. I doubt that they could have been repeated or reenacted by anyone."

Several of Kharlamov's greatest goals have been captured and preserved on film for hockey historians to study. Yet as Chidlovski remarks, "The secret of Kharlamov goals can't be figured out in a frame-by-frame replay on a tape. Tarasov once outlined the key components of the game, the three speeds of hockey—the speed of moving, the speed of reflexes, and the speed of thinking. Kharlamov's play was a perfect match of all three blended with the magic of his personality."

Videos show Kharlamov, his number 17 swaying on his sweater as he drives in on Dryden, Tony O, or Gerry Cheevers and maneuvers the puck past them. He changes direction at lightning speed and skates past Espo and Clarke, Dennis Hull (brother to Bobby), and Howe. Kharlamov played 40 games against North American professionals, and produced 48 points on 19 goals and 29 assists. Alexey Mosko writes on *Russia Beyond* that North American hockey enthusiasts were greatly impressed by Kharlamov: "This small but tightly built player had better skills and was a faster thinker than his stronger and taller Canadian counterparts."

Team Canada defenseman and future Hall of Famer Serge Savard watched Kharlamov blaze past defenders and control the puck at brilliant speed, calling him one of the top five hockey players ever. Sinden said

Valeri had "the skill and ability of any player in the NHL at the time." NHL owners agreed, and Mikhailov revealed that the Toronto Maple Leafs offered him, Kharlamov, and Petrov contracts to play for the team; sources say Kharlamov was offered a million dollars, a sizable sum in 1972. Fans thrilled at the prospect of Kharlamov showcasing his skills in NHL arenas on a nightly basis. Kharlamov, however, did not defect to North America. "We had been brought up with different values," Mikhailov later explained. "We had to prove that our Soviet system was the best."

Kharlamov dominated international play against amateur teams, registering 156 points (74 goals, 82 assists) in 105 games in world championships and 36 points in 22 Olympic games. "By all means he was one of the game dominators and the brightest star on the Red Army and Team USSR roster of the 1970s," Chidlovski says.

Kharlamov impacted generations of Russian players and fans. He became as much a source of Russian pride as the Bolshoi Ballet. In Soviet society, Kharlamov was regarded with almost the same awe and respect as Russian cosmonauts, whom he resembled to a degree with his red protective helmet. Chidlovski notes that Russian star and NHL veteran Ilya Kovalchuk was two years from being born when Kharlamov was killed in a car crash in 1981, but the biggest honor in Kovalchuk's professional life was to wear Kharlamov's uniform number 17 on his jersey at the 2002 Olympics.

Kovalchuk paid homage to Kharlamov, as does Pittsburgh Penguins' great Evgeni Malkin, who wears number 71—Kharlamov's number 17 in reverse. From an historical standpoint, Kharlamov's style has been compared favorably to Gretzky, their creativity and overall game being greater than their shooting or skating skills. Yet hockey writer Bill Schoeninger called Kharlamov "the most overrated player in history," acknowledging that Kharlamov was "a tremendous offensive talent" who "played a very 'beautiful' and 'pure' style of hockey" and that one of Kharlamov's greatest traits was that he played his best in big games. With interest in ice hockey peaking in the Soviet Union in the early 1970s, there were no bigger games than those against North American players. Thus, images of Kharlamov excelling against top NHL players in the Summit Series in 1972 and 1974 became indelible in the minds of those who watched.

According to Schoeninger, the recent emergence of more complete records for USSR hockey allows for more in-depth comparison involving Kharlamov and the other four most well-known Russian forwards—linemates Mikhailov and Petrov, contemporary Aleksandr Maltsev, and 1980s winger Sergei Makarov. "In terms of top 10 finishes in Soviet scoring, Kharlamov's finishes are the worst," he wrote. "They appear to be better than Maltsev's by a hair, but when you consider Kharlamov played on the best team in the league, CSKA (who was essentially the Soviet National team), and that Maltsev played for Dynamo with significantly worst teammates, it's clear that Maltsev's finishes are more impressive."

Makarov leads the comparisons in All-Star and MVP finishes and is "clearly superior in every category," wrote Schoeninger. "For a player with the legendary status of Valeri Kharlamov, you would certainly expect better results." He concluded that Kharlamov was a tremendous player, a top-ten all-time Russian hockey player, just not the best. "Until the perception of Kharlamov changes (if it ever does), he will remain the most overrated hockey player in history."

Chidlovski notes that "some of [Kharlamov's] teammates scored more in their careers. There were faster skaters. There were players with more powerful shots. And, of course, there were many players that were much better than Kharlamov in their own zone. Kharlamov's phenomenon wasn't about just numbers or statistics. He wasn't a universal player but a unique one."

Just as Kharlamov awed North American defensemen with his speed and superb stickhandling, the acrobatic Tretiak drew raves from the sport's top goalies for his stunning saves. Los Angeles Kings goalie Rogie Vachon thought Tretiak had a totally different style for a European. "He was more Westernized," Vachon told writer Julie Cart of the *Los Angeles Times* in a 1987 article. "He'd challenge the shooter a lot more."

Vachon thought Tretiak was very quick: "He had great feet. He was able to be so quick and stay on his feet. His style was a combination of stand-up and butterfly. He'd go down in close range, and he'd stand up on the rush. He had a good glove hand. Of course, he had a tremendous team in front of him."

NHL players and coaches facing Tretiak for the first time in 1972 felt he survived on superior reflexes. By 1976, however, the NHL was impressed by how much Tretiak had developed his game. Flyers center Rick MacLeish believed Tretiak's size (6-foot-1, 203 pounds) allowed him to cover a large amount of ice in front of the net. Sinden said the star goalie had learned to play the angles much better. Tretiak's positional play, his ability to combine the elements of two styles of goaltending—classic stand-up and revolutionary butterfly—allowed him to take his craft to an entirely new level. Along with technique, Tretiak's improvement can be traced to his mental toughness. Defeat, he would say, made him physically ill. It was enough to drive Tretiak to win his first gold medal at age eighteen at the 1970 World Championships. It was the beginning of a career that would see him reign as Russia's top goalie until his retirement in 1984.

Physically gifted, Tretiak became renowned for his extraordinary work ethic. Long hours spent in practice produced an extremely high rate of consistent brilliance. Tretiak struck gold more times than a California miner, winning USSR gold thirteen times, world championship gold twelve times, and Olympic gold three times. He was MVP of the USSR League a record five times and a USSR All-Star from 1971 to 1984, receiving the USSR's prized Merited Master of Sport in 1971. Internationally, Tretiak's was named best goalie of the world championships four times and was a three-time IHF All-Star. He is the only player to have won the Gold Stick three times as the best player in European hockey.

Glenn Hall, known as "Mr. Goalie," is widely credited with being the first goalie to use the butterfly style, with the Detroit Red Wings from 1952 to 1957 and then with the Chicago Black Hawks from 1957 to 1967, and finally with the St. Louis Blues from 1967 to 1971. Tony Esposito, who followed Hall in Chicago, also employed the butterfly with great success, but it was Tretiak who combined the butterfly technique with the classic stand-up style.

Tretiak, who earned the Red Army rank of lieutenant colonel, would, as Cart wrote, become known in international hockey as the "Great

Intimidator." Yet it was Tretiak who was supposed to be intimidated when the Russians arrived in Canada in 1972 for Game 1 of the Summit Series. Jacques Plante, who had tutored the Flyers' Bernie Parent and helped him become, at the height of the Bullies' reign, the greatest goalie in the NHL, played a pivotal role in Tretiak's ascension to status as exalted as Parent. Prior to the 1972 Summit Series opener, Plante visited the Soviets' locker room to meet with Tretiak. Said to be feeling sorry for the young Russian, who was playing in juniors just three years prior and was about to be thrown to the NHL's wolves in front of a sellout crowd in the famed Montreal Forum, the aging Plante took pity on the twenty-year-old kid. Plante briefed Tretiak on the tendencies of Team Canada's stars and what offensive sets they would run. Photographer Denis Brodeur snapped an historic photo of the graying Plante and fresh-faced Tretiak posed together. Tretiak nodded politely to Plante when the NHL legend stood to leave, then headed to the ice for his greatest test.

Team Canada scored thirty seconds into the first period and scored again just before the seven-minute mark to make it 2–0. Hockey experts smiled knowingly. But then Tretiak, who had been hand-picked by Tarasov for just such a moment, began making saves in spectacular fashion, and by game's end the Soviets had stunned Team Canada and the experts, winning 7–3. The hockey world would come to know more about Tretiak. Fans of the sport, hungry to know more about the mysterious Russians, learned that Tretiak was born on April 25, 1952, and grew up in Dmitrivsky District in Moscow, that his father spent thirty-seven years as a pilot in the Soviet military, and that his mother was a middle school physical education teacher and a bandy player who gave her son his first lessons in ice skating.

Tretiak spent his childhood years excelling at several sports, including swimming and skiing, the former the preferred activity of his older brother. Tretiak was eleven years old when he first played hockey, entering the Children and Youth Sports School of the Central Sports Club of the Army. Vitaly Erfilov served as Tretiak's first trainer; young Vlad initially played a forward position and started playing goalie because he desired a CSKA sweater and no one else was willing to play the position.

Tretiak played the position well enough to attract the attention of Soviet officials and at age fifteen was allowed to practice with the Red Army club. By 1971, Tretiak was a familiar face in the Soviet Union, having been named to the Soviet's First All-Star Team. His international fame grew in 1972 with his gold medal play in the Winter Olympic Games and his performance against NHL players in the Summit Series. "I can't imagine a better goalie than Tretiak," says Chidlovski, who saw the Soviet star play in person in Russia.

Canadian scouts Bob Davidson and John McLelland underestimated Tretiak prior to the series, their in-person reports having been based on his poor performance in a single intrasquad game. Tretiak surrendered eight goals, but what wasn't considered by scouts was that he and his teammates had spent the previous night celebrating his impending marriage to his fiancée, Tatiana. By the end of the series, Tretiak had impressed several NHL owners enough that they wanted to sign him. Despite the Soviets being outshot in six of the eight 1972 Summit Series games, Tretiak stood tall throughout Team Canada's unrelenting attacks. The man dismissed by Canadian scouts seemed to be on his way to backstopping the Soviets to a series victory when Paul Henderson scored the goal heard around the hockey world, a rebound shot with thirty-four seconds remaining in regulation of Game 8 in Moscow. "God gave him that goal," Tretiak said, calling Henderson's score the "most maddening of all goals scored on me in hockey."

Having nearly won the series single-handedly for the Soviets, Tretiak emerged along with Kharlamov, Henderson, and Esposito as the heroes of the Summit Series. Considered the Russian version of Georges Vezina, Tretiak would become arguably the greatest goalie of his era. Like Kharlamov, Tretiak had a lasting and profound impact on Russian hockey. Gretzky calls Tretiak one of the best goalies ever, possibly the greatest.

Certainly, no goalie ever played under the same extreme pressure as Tretiak. While Team Canada alternated between Dryden and Tony O in the 1972 Summit Series, Tretiak was in net for all eight games. In 1974, Tretiak started in seven of the eight Summit Series games. Add in starting assignments in three Olympics, ten world championships, the four games of the 1976 Super Series, and three games in the 1979 Challenge

Cup, and it's clear Tretiak carried a heavy burden at the height of the Cold War.

Just as Ilya Kovalchuk and Evgeni Malkin paid homage to Kharlamov by wearing versions of his famed number 17 on their modern-day jerseys, NHL goalies Evgeni Nabokov and Ed Belfour honored Tretiak by donning hockey sweaters that bore his number 20 on the back. Kharlamov and Tretiak were twin towers for the Red Machine and are the only players to be immortalized in the Hockey Hall of Fame despite not having played in the NHL. In 2000, Tretiak was voted by the Russian Hockey Federation the best Russian hockey player of the twentieth century.

"Tretiak and Kharlamov were like movie stars in Russia," Chidlovski remembers. "Red Army fans idolized them." Hockey night in Moscow would see overflow crowds of fourteen thousand fans packed into the Palace of Sports of the Central Lenin Stadium for a game matching the Red Army and Spartak. The Palace of Sports was Moscow's answer to the Montreal Forum, and high-profile games were televised throughout the expansive Soviet Union in black and white.

The big-time hockey experience in the Soviet Union differed drastically from its counterpart in North America. On his visit to the Soviet Union in 1975, Mulvoy compared Russian hockey announcer Nikolai Ozerov to Howard Cosell, except that Ozerov's hair was silver and real, as opposed to Cosell's toupee. Ozerov called the game from a TV monitor stationed along the boards ringing the rink and was nattily dressed in a gray and black herringbone sport jacket that covered his blue sweat suit. Because Soviet TV did not carry commercials, there were no unnecessary breaks in the action. Mulvoy noted that unlike Cosell, Ozerov did not editorialize about the event; instead, he simply recited the names of the players involved in the action at the moment—Kharlamov, Tretiak, Mikhailov, Petrov, Yakushev.

"He was one of our favorite personalities," recalls Chidlovski. "In 1974 when Team Canada came to Russia, Ozerov gave me tickets to a game and told me, 'Today is your lucky day.' He was a great commentator. We had other great commentators in Russia, but Ozerov stood out."

Russian cameramen cut away from on-ice fights, and announcers diverted attention away from the occasional untidiness by reading soccer scores, some results from as much as two weeks prior. Attendees at Russian hockey games did not have to pay for program sheets, which cost $1.50 at the Montreal Forum, and for their arena seats they paid just a fraction of the cost NHL fans ponied up. Where seats at Madison Square Garden went for $12, a reserved sideline bench seat at the Palace of Sports cost but one ruble and twenty kopecks, the equivalent of $1.50. It was a single ruble for seats in the end zones, and youths who failed to sneak into the Palace paid ten to fifteen kopecks (fifteen to seventy-five cents) for a seat.

Mulvoy described the Palace of Sports as a "cold, drab building." The puck dropped for weeknight games at 7:30 p.m., and weekends featured doubleheaders starting at 1 and 4 p.m. Fans were supposed to leave the building between games, but those who knew where to hide did so to avoid paying the extra ruble or kopeck for the second game. Mulvoy found that a favored hiding spot was the private box of Leonid Brezhnev, the successor to Josef Stalin and Nikita Krushchev.

Palace patrons were not bothered by the noise pollution common to NHL arenas. Organ music and air horns were nonexistent inside Soviet arenas, and vendors did not block the view of the ice or hawk food and drink. Fans left their seats between periods to line up at concession stands, and for fifty kopecks could purchase a bargain meal of a sausage sandwich or hot dog, ice cream bar, and coffee or tea. Precisely five minutes before the game, players would exit their plain, and by NHL standards, poorly equipped locker rooms and enter a hallway adjacent to an area designated for visiting dignitaries dining on caviar and tea. The athletes lined up behind game officials and awaited the ringing of a bell that signaled the raising of a curtain. Their entrance onto the ice coincided with the recording of a Russian song with the title "Cowards Don't Play Hockey."

Attendance at games was largely male; Mulvoy estimated as much as 95 percent. Red Army supporters resembled fans of the all-conquering Yankees of the early 1960s. Many sat with stoic faces and arms crossed; their club's dominance was their due. Fans of teams like Spartak were

much more demonstrative and vocal, chanting their club's name—
Spar-tak!—for encouragement. Mulvoy attended a game between Spartak and Central Army at the Palace of Sports and thought it "spectacular."

Soviet coaches, wrote Mulvoy, did not think or act with independence; they were programmed by the hockey federation to operate prac-
tices and design game plans, and thus there was little to differentiate in
strategy in league games. Russian teams favored tic-tac-toe passes and
employed pick plays to isolate a forward for a high percentage shot. "In
essence," Mulvoy wrote, "four players simply move the puck around while
the fifth attempts to clear the route for that one good shot by picking
some defenseman and removing him from the play."

Soviet teams looked the same defensively as well. They largely dis-
regarded the North American tactics of forechecking and backchecking,
and the Russians did not skate into the corners with the same determination as North Americans—and certainly not with the ill humor of the
Broad Street Bullies. If two Soviet players were battling along the boards
for control of the puck, Russian officials would stop play lest the game
get too physical. Despite Russia's reputation as an aggressor nation, its
league stood in stark contrast to the warlike NHL. The Russian league
was similar to the NHL in that it, too, featured a galaxy of stars, and it
was Kharlamov and Tretiak who burned as bright and brilliant as any in
North America's constellation.

To a man, the Broad Street Bullies wondered how they were going
to cope with the Red Army's Mr. Go and Mr. No.

CHAPTER 5

Fire on Ice in Philly

JUST AS VALERI KHARLAMOV AND VLADISLAV TRETIAK REPRESENTED the top talents of the vaunted Red Army, Bobby Clarke and Dave Schultz were seen as the faces of the Flyers.

Clarke was, in the words of *Philadelphia Inquirer* sports columnist Bill Lyon, a "ruthless, toothless, rink rat." Kharlamov and the Central Red Army club agreed with that characterization. "Bobby Clarke," Arthur Chidlovski says, "is one of the least favorite players of Soviet hockey fans."

The reason for the Russians' animosity toward the Hall of Fame forward goes beyond his being the center of attention on the infamous Flyers teams. Before he bossed the team that became known as the Broad Street Bullies, Clarke became Public Enemy Number 1 in the Soviet Union for his slash that fractured the ankle of Valeri Kharlamov late in the 1972 Summit Series. Clarke didn't care what the Russians thought, since they hadn't played clean, either.

Flyers announcer Gene Hart called Clarke "one angry hockey player." The captain boasted a choirboy face and killer stickwork. Bob Nystrom of the dynastic late 1970s and early 1980s New York Islanders called Clarke the most tenacious player he'd ever seen. Clarke's tenacity was a trait that earned the respect of teammates, NHL coaches, executives, and opponents. Montreal coach Scotty Bowman screamed insults at Clarke from the bench but held him in such high regard that he believed if Bobby played for the Canadiens, Montreal would have won six or seven Cups in a row, instead of four.

Glen Sather lauded Clarke for his "hard work, class, and style." Islanders general manager Bill Torrey didn't think any team in NHL history had a better leader than Clarke. Future NHL president John Ziegler was an executive for Detroit when the Red Wings passed on taking Clarke, concerned about his diabetes. Ziegler called it the biggest mistake his team ever made. Clarke, Ziegler said, was the most intense competitor he'd ever seen, adding that one word always came to mind about Clarke: leadership. Clarke was a leader of men, said Ziegler.

The men Clarke led fed off their captain's intensity. "He was chippy on the ice and would never give up," recalls Andre Dupont. "He was our leader, and everybody followed him. We would never give up." Larry Goodenough calls Clarke "the hardest working hockey player I've ever seen. He was always the first one on the ice and the last one off." Bob Kelly says Clarke made his teammates work hard to get the best out of them. NHL writer Red Fisher thought the mention of Clarke's name made him think of words like intensity, dedication, loyalty, and winner. Bill Clement recalls Clarke's impact on the Flyers as immeasurable. "I don't believe there has ever been a leader in any sport as competitive as Bobby Clarke," he says. "He was a courageous leader, and he could have the tough conversations with teammates."

Clement recalls Clarke having a tough talk with second-line center Rick MacLeish. The Hawk was struggling in a playoff, and Clarke had seen enough. "Clarke and MacLeish were as good a one-two punch down the middle as any team in the NHL," says Clement. "Ricky was one of the most talented players, but he was also one of the most enigmatic. There were games where he seemed disinterested. We were in a Game 5 in the playoffs, and I was sitting between Clarke and MacLeish on the bench. Bobby leaned past me and said to Ricky, 'I sure hope you're saving it for Game 6!'"

Clement says Clarke was a player who was ruthless rather than dirty, comparing him to Mark Messier. "Bobby and Mark would do whatever it took to win," says Clement. Gordie Howe fit that mold as well, and Clement remembers an on-ice meeting with Howe during the 1979–1980 season, when Bill was thirty and Gordie fifty-two. "He put his arm around me and crushed me into the boards," recalls Clement. "I fell onto the ice and he said, 'You okay?' I said, 'Screw you, Gordie!'"

Clarke had a memorable on-ice encounter of his own with Howe, one that resulted in Bobby issuing an apology to the man he referred to as "Mr. Howe." It may have been the only apology the embattled Bobby ever offered on the ice. Clarke was born on August 13, 1949, in Flin Flon, a mining town in northern Manitoba whose moniker was "The City Built on Rocks." A smokestack eight hundred feet high served as the landmark for the town, its purpose being to propel the pollution and smoke from the mines as far away from the town's residents as possible. As Hart later wrote, Cliff Clarke instilled in his son a work ethic that became an edict: "You don't get nothin' for nothin.' Man was born to work, and if you're going to do a job, do it right."

It was the uncompromising and straightforward advice of a man whom Hart called "rough-hewn . . . a blue-collar worker with simple tastes and a simple way of life." In his approach to hockey and life, Cliff was much the same as the fathers of many Flyers who grew up in Canada. Bobby became enamored with hockey at a young age. He sometimes skipped school to play, lacing up hand-me-down skates to take to the ice on frozen ponds. Breathing steam and spitting ice, Clarke was known to play as much as forty minutes a game. He loved to get on the ice, loved to practice and play.

Summers saw Bobby working at Flin Flon's lone service station, his goal being to save enough money to buy new ice skates for a tryout with the junior Flin Flon Bombers. When he was sixteen, Clarke hitch-hiked to Brandon to see a shoemaker who made custom skates. It was a four-day round trip, but Clarke would do what was necessary to realize his dream of playing professional hockey. Flin Flon coach Pat Ginnell knew Clarke was diabetic, but he also knew Bobby played with what seemed to be an inexhaustible energy and possessed excellent instincts for the game. Clarke and Ginnell jelled, coach and player feeding off each other's hard work. To excel in the wild Western Canadian Junior Hockey League, Ginell made his team play with courage. Clarke was small, skinny, and not very powerful or fast. He was, however, very determined. That he twice led the Western Junior League in scoring and set records in points and assists proved he had learned how to handle himself against bigger, stronger opponents. His time with the Bombers led to Clarke's initial teaming with winger Reggie Leach; the pair would go on to greater fame with the Flyers.

To dispel doubts among NHL coaches and executives concerning Clarke's diabetes, Ginnell took Bobby to the Mayo Clinic. Doctors reported that Clarke could play at the highest level provided he took care of himself. Ginnell showed scouts the Mayo Clinic reports, yet NHL teams passed on Clarke in the opening round of the 1969 draft. As the second round got underway, Flyers scout Gerry Melnyk told the team's executives, "I don't give a damn if this kid's got one leg, he's the best player I've seen at this level. He'll right away be our best player."

Flyers brass contacted a Philadelphia-area doctor, who concurred with his colleagues at the Mayo Clinic. Satisfied that Clarke could play with diabetes, the Flyers selected him at number 17. That Clarke would never play a single game in the minors proved Melnyk was right. He was the Flyers' top performer, a fact attested to in a report from his first training camp: "The kid from Flin Flon is the best player."

Teammates called him "Clarkie," "Whitey" (for his pale skin), or "Angel." The latter, Hart surmised, was either an honest appraisal of his choirboy appearance or sarcasm for his demon brand of hockey. Upon arrival in Philadelphia, Clarke showed himself to be shy and almost silent. Hart recalled Clarke's vocabulary at that time to be largely limited to "yep" and "nope." Clarke was reluctant to talk about his diabetes. He didn't want his condition to be used as an excuse if he played poorly. "If I have a bad game," Clarke said at the time, "I want people to understand that it was because I was lousy, *not* because I was sick."

Clarke's rookie campaign resulted in 46 points in 76 games. He finished fourth in voting for Rookie of the Year, then upped his point total to 63 the following season and earned consideration for the Hart Trophy for league MVP. The 1970–1971 season, Clarke's third in the NHL, brought changes behind the Flyers bench, with Shero taking the reins. The new coach called his captain "a dream dressed in work clothes." Bobby was blue-collar in substance and style. While other stars celebrated their status with flashy cars and fashionable clothes, Bobby preferred blue jeans and a jeep. Under Shero's guidance, Clarke pushed his point total to 81 and received the Bill Masterton Trophy for dedication and perseverance. Clarke then headed to Canada for the historic 1972 Summit Series and his first confrontation with the Soviets.

At age twenty-three, Clarke was the youngest player on Team Canada's roster. Bob Kelly said Clarke went to Canada as the team's fifth center and was on the first line by the time he returned to Philadelphia. The Summit Series was Clarke's first time on a team with stars like Phil Esposito and Brad Park. The experience matured Clarke beyond his years. When he returned to Philadelphia, Shero honored him by making him the youngest player in NHL history at the time to wear the coveted captain's "C" on his jersey.

In 1972–1973 Clarke added another "first" to his résumé: Scoring 104 points, he became the first player from a non–Original Six team to produce 100 points in a season and the first from a post-1967 expansion team to receive the Hart Trophy. Clarke's superlative performance paved a path for the Flyers to post their first winning record (37–30–11), highest point total (85), highest finish (second in the West), and first playoff series victory. Philadelphia's season ended in the semifinals with a loss to eventual Stanley Cup champion Montreal, but the captain and his crew continued their ascendency. After improving by 19 points in the 1972–1973 season, they raised their point total 27 points in 1973–1974, embarking on another season of "firsts": Philadelphia won the West for the first time and finished only one point behind Boston (113) for the best overall record in the NHL. Teaming with Bill Flett and Bill Barber on the first line, Clarke posted 87 points.

The tenacity Nystrom spoke of was vividly illustrated in the 1974 Stanley Cup Finals against the Bruins. Film of Game 2 shows Clarke creating a turnover along the boards, then skating through the crease and taking a feed that led to his lifting a backhander toward Bruins goalie Gilles Gilbert. The shot was blocked, but Bobby collected the rebound, made a sharp pivot, and angled a forehand shot past the prone goalie. The captain's determination in digging out the puck to score the winning goal in overtime gave the Flyers their first victory at Boston Garden in seven years and the confidence they could beat an Original Six power.

Clarke's consistency in defeating Esposito in faceoffs proved pivotal in Philadelphia's becoming the first expansion club to celebrate a Stanley Cup victory. *Sports Illustrated* writer Mark Mulvoy declared that it was Clarke, "that tenacious, gap-toothed, diabetic rink rat, with the guts of ten dozen burglars, who destroyed Bobby Orr and the Bruins."

Esposito had paced the NHL during the regular season, with 145 points on 68 goals and 77 assists, but it was Clarke who won the battle between two of the league's top centers. Esposito thought it frustrating because he knew Clarke realized what Phil wanted to do, not only in that moment but a step or two beyond that. Bruins defenseman Carol Vadnais believed Clarke had everything one would want in an NHL player. Vadnais hated to play against Clarke, but he would have wanted him on his team. It was the biggest compliment Vadnais could give to an opponent.

With Clarke on their side, the Flyers won a second straight division title in 1974–1975. The captain again helped lead the way, his 89 assists setting an NHL record for a center as he teamed with Barber and the newly acquired Leach on the LCB Line. Clarke's 116 points represented a career best to that point, and the captain kept up with the brawling Bullies, posting 125 penalty minutes, as the Flyers returned to the Cup Finals. Clarke claimed his second Hart Trophy in three seasons and the first of his two consecutive NHL First Team All-Star selections. He was creating a legacy that would see him earn three Harts, eight All-Star Game appearances, the 1971–1972 Masterson Trophy for perseverance and dedication to the sport, the 1972–1973 Lester B. Pearson Award as league MVP as selected by NHL players, the 1979–1980 Lester Patrick Trophy for service to hockey in the United States, and the 1982–1983 Selke Trophy as the NHL's top defensive forward.

Clarke's will to excel made him an inspiration to diabetics around the world. Hart recalled a time when the Flyers were playing in Minnesota and Bobby was asked to speak to a group of diabetic children. Shy as he was, Clarke arranged with Flyers public relations manager Joe Kadlec to arrange for him to speak for no more than ten minutes. When one of the children said, "Mr. Clarke, I'm a diabetic, too," Bobby gave the child a warm smile and spoke for nearly an hour.

The Bullies had a benevolent side. Playing the Black Hawks in Chicago at Christmastime, Clarke asked a *Chicago Tribune* writer to meet him after the game in the visitors' locker room. Bobby and his Bullies had read an article in that morning's paper about a South Side mother who lacked money to purchase Christmas presents for her children or pay the heating bill for her apartment. The Bullies pooled their money and Clarke handed it to the reporter with instructions to give it to the struggling mom and her children. When the surprised reporter asked why the Broad Street Bullies would care about a Chicago family, Clarke smiled. "It's Christmas."

Clarke's generosity extended to his teammates. Rather than seeking extra ice time to pad his stats, he would play less in the third period of games in which the Flyers held sizable leads so that struggling teammates could have more playing time. While sparks fairly flew from Clarke on the ice, away from the game he was given to being humble and unassuming. He carefully monitored his blood sugar and administered his insulin shots, and his pregame ritual saw him dissolve three spoonsful of sugar into his Coca-Cola and drink it down. Between periods of a game, Clarke drank a half glass of orange juice; he drank a full glass in the postgame. Flyers' trainer Frank Lewis, recalling Bobby's two diabetic seizures in his first training camp, packed a tube of glucose and numerous chocolate bars in his equipment bag in case of emergency.

Just as Clarke's gap-toothed grimace represented the fearsome face of the Flyers, the flying fists of Dave Schultz provided the ferocious image of the Bullies of Broad Street. The Hammer was the Flyers' chief enforcer, but he was not alone. In an era when almost every NHL team employed at least one tough guy, the Bullies boasted four. Fronted by the Hammer, the quartet included Hound Kelly, Moose Dupont, and Big Bird Saleski. The Hammer, who became one of the NHL's more significant players of the 1970s, was unique. Hart thought that more than any player in the 1970s, Schultz "changed the face of the game while changing the faces of many of the game's players."

Schultz combined with Clarke to give the Flyers an identity. Hart thought Clarke gave the team character as a club of tenacious, hard workers, while Schultz provided the Bullies' arrogant, sneering demeanor.

Schultz's reputation spread as far as the Soviet Union. The Hammer was known by fans who lived under the flag of the Hammer and Sickle. "We knew about Dave Schultz, 'The Hammer,' and the Broad Street Bullies," Chidlovski says. "We had never seen anything like them."

When Shero visited the Soviet Union for a coaches' clinic following the Flyers' Stanley Cup victory in 1974, he brought back a sheaf of Soviet newspaper clippings about his team and about Schultz. *Sports Illustrated* writer Mark Mulvoy visited Russia in 1975 for a story on Soviet hockey and was asked by forward Aleksandr Yakushev about the Hammer. "This Schultz I keep reading about," Yakushev said to Mulvoy. "Is he really a good fighter?" That the "Big Yak," as the 6-foot-3, 200-pound Yakushev was known, would be concerned spoke volumes about Schultz's reputation. En route to battling their way to a second straight Stanley Cup title in 1975, the Bullies led the league in penalty minutes with 1,969, an average of nearly 25 minutes per game. When Soviet Wings coach Boris Kulagin learned of the Flyers' extraordinary penalty minutes, he shook his head in dismay.

Leading the way was Schultz, with an NHL record 472 penalty minutes. Opponents who roused the Hammer got nailed. Schultz's bad-boy behavior was celebrated in song and story. A 45 rpm titled "The Penalty Box" was played on Philadelphia radio stations and became the most requested song by the locals. Schultz's royalty was a nickel for every record sold. He recalled receiving a check for $795 and thinking, "That's a lot of records." *Philadelphia* magazine ran a cover story of Schultz wearing a World War II German helmet similar to Sergeant Schultz of *Hogan's Heroes* fame and holding a plucked daisy. The story was titled "This Is Dave Schultz: He Loves You Not."

The Bullies' brawling thrilled the Philly faithful and won them fans and games, but it left the writers covering their contests cold as ice. "Their games took forever with all the fights," remembered Lyon. "They were a horror to cover because of deadlines. One deadline after another passed and still there was no resolution. The Hammer is pounding some poor son of a bitch, Bob Kelly is still fighting, and Bobby Clarke is still instigating. And then you hear from your editor, 'Here's 30 minutes to write 500 words.'"

Schultz built a reputation for brawling, but the burly winger could also be a scoring threat. The Hammer's first NHL hat trick fueled a 4–2 win over the rival Rangers on Spectrum ice on January 3, 1974. Seven days later he recorded his second hat trick, this time against Minnesota. Schultz scored a career-best 20 regular-season goals in 1973–1974 and completed a quarterfinals series sweep of the Flames by slapping the puck past Phil Myre at 5:40 of overtime in Game 4. "Dave could fight, and he could also play hockey," Larry Goodenough recalls. "He could score, and he was a good enforcer." Clement agrees. "Dave would take off his gloves and fight like a man. He never hit anyone with his stick."

Shero credited Schultz's power game to creating a "vacuum" around him that few NHL players dared invade. "He scores goals from impossible places and it's only because a lot of players don't want to get too close to him," Shero said in a 1974 article in *Hockey Pictorial* magazine. Schultz knew his fisticuffs gave him room on the ice, and he used his reputation as a psychological weapon to intimidate opponents. "I've got an ability to fight," the Hammer told writer Dick Brown. "So why should I stop if I can help my team by fighting?"

Schultz's fighting was instrumental in the Flyers victory over the New York Rangers in the Stanley Cup semifinals in 1974, and the Hammer continued his belligerent ways in 1975. Schultz's army was not only the Flyers fans in the stands who adopted the Saskatchewan winger as their favorite Bully but also his teammates on the ice. Jerry "King Kong" Korab, a formidable physical presence for the Buffalo Sabres, said the Bullies didn't fight one-on-one. "They want to fight you nineteen-to-one." The Bullies' brawling was seen as a sign of team unity. No Broad Street Bully, Hart said, would have stood by while a teammate was battered bloody, as the Rangers did when Dale Rolfe was nailed by the Hammer. Film review shows Schultz landing twelve consecutive blows, and no Ranger rushed to Rolfe's side, even as he was being outpunched, 17–2. "The Rangers just watched, and I think that fight spelled the end of them," Lou Nolan, the Flyers' public address announcer at the time, told Sam Carchidi of the *Philadelphia Inquirer*. "That wouldn't have happened with our guys."

Shero singled out Schultz's row with Rolfe as the tipping point in the Flyers' 4–3 victory. "It took something out of them," Shero said of the Rangers. "They didn't do as much hitting after that." Schultz's pummeling of Rolfe resulted in the Bullies taking physical control of the contest and outshooting the Rangers, 46–34, in the deciding game, crashing the crease relentlessly. Ed Giacomin pointed to the Bullies' aggressiveness as the difference in Game 7: "They won because they were all over us all the time."

It was the second straight playoff series Schultz impacted, and he made it three straight in the finals against the Bruins. Having scored the series-clinching win in the quarterfinals against Atlanta and provided the emotional charge in the semis against the Rangers, Schultz played a key role in Game 2 in Boston. Two games after engaging in the most famous fight in Flyers history, Schultz pirated a pass to help set up the most iconic goal in franchise history: Clarke's overtime score.

The reputation of the fighting Flyers preceded them into every city, and sold-out arenas were waiting when the Bullies skated onto enemy ice. Fans hung the Hammer in effigy from balcony seats, threw sugar packets at the diabetic Clarke, and booed lustily when the Bullies were introduced in pregame ceremonies. Clarke and company weren't even spared at the NHL All-Star Game, where the crowd's loudest catcalls were reserved for the Flyers. The Bullies loved the boos; they loved the press clippings by writers in enemy cities proclaiming them "animals" and telling women and children to bar their doors because the enemy was at the gates. Hart, who traveled with the Flyers, thought the louder the boos, the more inspired the Bullies became.

No one was more inspired than Schultz, the Hammer's credo being that he would fight anyone or do anything to make certain nobody fooled with the Flyers. Schultz led the league in penalty minutes five times and set NHL records for PIMs in one season, in one playoff year, in one playoff series, and in one playoff game. If a "Gordie Howe Hat Trick" consisted of a goal, an assist, and a fight in the same game, writer Sergey Zikov suggested a "Dave Schultz Hat Trick" would be "a minor penalty, a fighting major, and a game misconduct." To top it off in a fashion befitting the Hammer, Zikov said the player who recorded a Dave Schultz

Hat Trick should give enemy fans the one-finger salute as he departed the ice.

The Hammer's fights were legendary. Schultz one-punched John Van Boxmeer of Montreal, battled Boston tough guy Terry O'Reilly eight times, duked it out with Detroit's Dennis Hextall Jr. (the father of future Flyers goalie and later general manager Ron Hextall), and collided with Clark Gillies of the Islanders. Schultz would sometimes start slowly, taking more than he gave. But then the Hammer would turn the tide, grabbing his opponent with his right arm and pummeling him with the most devastating left-handed punches delivered by a Philadelphian besides former heavyweight champion Joe Frazier. A typical Schultz fight would end with the opponent bloodied, the enemy team intimidated, the Bullies energized, the Spectrum electrified, and the Hammer banished from the ice. Schultz piled up 2,292 career penalty minutes and averaged 4.28 penalty minutes per game. "The Flyers used to get the hell kicked out of them," Schultz told writer Ben Olan at the time. "I'll be damned if that happens to any team I play on. I'll take on five or six guys at once if I have to."

Schultz's belligerence hit a historic high as the Flyers fought to defend their Stanley Cup title in 1974–1975. The Hammer eclipsed his own NHL record for PIMs in a season—set the season before at 348—piling up 472. He established career highs with fights in the regular season (26) and full season, including playoffs (34). The website Hockeyfights.com credits the Hammer with 130 NHL fights, 76 of those coming in his years as the Flyers' feared enforcer. Schultz's reputation as hockey's most ferocious fighter was such that *Hockey Illustrated* magazine ran an article comparing Schultz to legendary NHL tough guys Eddie Shore, Red Horner, Jack Stewart, Jimmy Orlando, Bill Ezinicki, Lou Fontinato, Reg Fleming, Howie Young, Ted Green, John Ferguson, and Ted Lindsay. "Maybe there are better fighters," Shero said at the time, "but nobody has ever defended a club the way he has." Clubs may be tough in their own rinks, said Shero, but "Schultz gave us courage on the road."

The road was rough for the Flyers, where the Bullies were greeted with banners reading "Kill Clarke" and "Broad Street Bull." Opposing fans heaped more vitriolic and vulgar verbal abuse on Clarke and Schultz than on any other players in the NHL. This reflected the attitude of hockey fans throughout North America, whose letters to national magazines referred to the Stanley Cup champions as the "dirtiest team in hockey," the "Filthydelphia Flyers," and the "most shameful excuse for a hockey team in history." One fan thought the champs a "mediocre team with a good goaltender and a quota of bloodthirsty muggers" whose hoisting of the Cup had Lord Stanley "rolling in his grave." Another fan thought Flyers hockey a "mirror image of roller derby." Clarke, in the eyes of enemy fans, was the sport's "dirtiest player"; Schultz was the "penalty-box king who mugged opponents."

Schultz had a soft side not known to many. Born October 14, 1949, in Waldheim, Saskatchewan, David William Schultz grew up in Rosetown, whose motto—"The Heart of the Wheat Belt"—reflects the fact that it is a rural agricultural community. Sitting seventy miles south of Saskatoon, Rosetown was home to some three thousand people at the height of Schultz's notoriety in the NHL. The locals worried that people were getting the wrong impression of Rosetown's most famous son. Dave's father, Edgar, who worked at the local Chrysler garage, often heard criticism of his son's wild and woolly ways on the ice. But when the Cup finals against the Bruins were aired in Rosetown, Edgar began hearing a differing opinion: "Hey, he can play hockey, too."

Phil Schell, president of the Rosetown Red Wings hockey club in the 1970s, told Dick Brown that people in town knew Dave could play "damn good hockey" and would rather have him known for his skill as a player than his prowess in punch-ups. "In Philadelphia they know Dave differently," Schell said. "Here [in Rosetown] he is the strong, quiet, clean-living kind of person." Schell's successor as Red Wings president, Irwin Sommerfield, figured hockey fans in the United States must have had the impression that Schultz went around all the time looking for fights.

It was Dave's mother who first helped her son into pair of skates at four years of age. As a boy, Schultz shied away from fights. His brother Raymond was bigger and more aggressive, and Dave was known mostly as a fast skater. Edgar refereed some of Dave's youth hockey games, and recalled that while Dave wasn't a brawler, he would stand up for himself.

Mostly, however, Dave backed away from fights, and he continued to do so while playing junior hockey for the Swift Current Broncos. Not until he joined the Sorel Black Hawks of the Quebec Junior Hockey League did Schultz begin to gain a reputation as a physical force. Edgar played a role in his son's on-ice transformation. "You're a winger, Dave," Edgar told him, "and if you want to get into the big time, you've got to be more aggressive in the corners."

Schultz became more aggressive. In a Junior B game, he staggered fellow future NHL player Butch Deadmarsh. Having been battered by the Blues in the 1969 postseason, the Flyers drafted Schultz in the fifth round and sent him to Salem-Roanoke, Virginia, in the Eastern Hockey League. The little kid who had been bullied was now the man who did the bullying. His 356 penalty minutes led the EHL in 1969–1970, and he followed the next season by pacing the American Hockey League with a then-record 382 PIMs while playing for Quebec. Schultz topped his own AHL mark the following season, amassing 392 PIMs.

Schultz's impact on the NHL was immediate. The Hammer led the league with 259 PIMs in 1972–1973, a record at the time for a forward. Fearful that a single punch might end his career, Schultz psyched himself before every game, like a fighter before a big bout. The Hammer took some heavy blows—in one game, Montreal's Pierre Bouchard had him hanging on until linesman John D'Amico intervened, and Gillies beat him in the 1975 Cup semis—but the thing he feared, the one-sided whipping that would wreck his confidence or lessen his value to the team, didn't happen.

Schultz became the lightning rod for the on-ice wars overwhelming the NHL in the mid-1970s. The Hammer and the Bullies were vilified by hockey purists for the vortex of violence engulfing their sport. Yet Schultz never felt completely comfortable in the role; preparing himself to be an enforcer prior to every game was not fun. It was, in fact, a nerve-racking experience. "It's hard to believe," he said once, "how I used to psych myself up to play that role." Once in the role of a strongman, Schultz found himself thinking, "My God, I can't get out." When he wasn't fighting or scoring the occasional goal, Schultz served as a third-line checker, teaming with Orest Kindrachuk and Don Saleski as the Flyers went in search of a second straight Stanley Cup.

Clarke set the tone for the campaign. The confetti from the two-million-strong crowd that celebrated the Flyers' title was still being swept from the parade route when Clarke told his teammates, "Boys, everyone is going to be gunning for us next season. This year won't mean a thing if we don't do it again. I want everybody to be ready to go. Be in shape to play."

The following September, Clarke rented a rink in South Jersey so he and his fellow champions could have ten days of on-ice workouts prior to starting training camp at the University of Pennsylvania. "Let's go, fellas," Clarke stated. "Give up the final ten days of your vacation and let's get back to work."

Pooling the money from the $19,000 check each player cashed for his Stanley Cup earnings, the Flyers covered the cost of their impromptu camp. The worth of their willingness to work was validated on September 15, 1973, when players reported for their physicals prior to the first day of formal training camp. Every member of the team was at or close to his playing weight, a significant accomplishment considering that in the mid-1970s players and teams did not stress diet and exercise to the extent they would in years to come. When training camp officially opened, Clarke issued another challenge to his team. "We won the Stanley Cup last year, but a lot of people think we just got lucky," he told them. "No one thinks we can do it again. I guess we better show them. We win it again this year, and no one can say last year was a fluke."

Shero backed up his captain's message, writing on the green chalkboard his first of many messages for the 1974–1975 season: *When the going gets tough, the tough get going.* The off-season had been anything but tough going for the Flyers. The Bullies had become a booming business, the subject of tee shirts, bumper stickers, books, beer mugs, bedsheets, calendars, clocks, and assorted other merchandise. A $2.95 record album titled *God Bless the Flyers*, containing highlights of radio calls from their 1974 Stanley Cup season, was produced. Flyers jerseys became such a hot commodity that supplier Mitchell & Ness took to answering phone calls by immediately stating they had sold out of Flyers jerseys.

Writer Edward Swift noted at the time that anyone in Philadelphia not wearing a Flyers shirt was "regarded with suspicion." The City of Brotherly Love loved its Flyers. When the franchise was founded in 1967, there were three ice rinks in Philadelphia; by 1976, there were twenty-two, and more were being built. Swift said street hockey was fast becoming Philadelphia's bicentennial pastime. The Flyers had introduced ice hockey to a city that had previously considered the American Hockey League's Hershey Bears as its home team, even though Hershey is one hundred miles from Philadelphia. The Flyers fueled the fans' passion, and each new rink built in the city came with a youth program that at times included girls' teams and players as young as four years old.

The Little Flyers were the city's top youth ice hockey organization, drawing tryouts for their five teams each September from the entire metropolitan area, South Jersey, and Delaware included. So keen was the competition for the Little Flyers that just one in five players qualified for one of the teams. Those who didn't qualify were able to play in leagues in Philadelphia, Cherry Hill, and Wilmington. Because the Little Flyers had an operating budget of only $50,000 for their teams, each player's family had to pay $300 to help support their team's seventy-game schedule. Those who couldn't pay in full received financial assistance.

The success of the Little Flyers mirrored that of the Bullies themselves. By 1975, Little Flyers teams had played for national championships. Their Squirt and Midget clubs won regional championships covering nineteen states. The city's hockey craze also extended to its high schools and colleges. The Intercounty Scholastic League went from six to thirty-four teams in just six years. Although school budgets were being cut, players and coaches willingly paid $250 apiece to finance their sport. The University of Pennsylvania played on one of the finest collegiate ice rinks in the country and boasted players who competed in both the Ivy League and an intramural program, as well as on a women's team, the Quakerettes. Villanova also boasted a men's ice hockey team, which was part of a league with Lafayette, Lehigh, Navy, and Rutgers.

The influence of the Bullies on Philadelphia's younger players was considerable. Fights and bench-clearing brawls in youth hockey games often followed televised Flyers games. Peewee players were reportedly coached at times to pull opponents' jerseys over their heads. Brawls became so common at the high school level in Philadelphia that the Intercounty Scholastic League instituted mandatory three-game suspensions for players penalized for fighting. Still, Swift noted in a November 1975 article in *Hockey* magazine that Philadelphia was growing more sophisticated in its understanding of hockey. Fighting was being played down, he wrote, "and hustle and close checking are cited as the real reason for the Flyers' success."

Those same attributes would fuel the Flyers' drive in 1975, yet it was a different Bullies club that took to Spectrum ice on October 10, 1974, for the first game of the season. Highly regarded defenseman Barry Ashbee was now behind the Flyers' bench as a coach following his career-ending eye injury in the semifinals against the Rangers the previous spring. Right winger Bill Flett had been traded to Toronto; the bearded Cowboy having seen his goal total drop from 43 in 1972–1973 to 17 in 1973–1974. Taking his place on the Clarke-Barber line was Leach, giving the Flyers the first "name" line in team history—the LCB Line.

Simon Nolet, an original Flyer from the first expansion season in 1967, was gone as well, having been taken by another expansion club, the Kansas City Scouts. Arriving from St. Louis were young goalie Wayne Stephenson and veteran defenseman Ted Harris. Harris teamed with Goodenough, a youthful defenseman who had been part of the trade with Toronto to bring Parent back to the Flyers. The Flyers looked different not only in personnel, but in uniform as well. To commemorate their championship, they wore on their jerseys black oval patches that bore an image of the Stanley Cup. It took just one game for the Flyers to feel uncomfortable wearing the patches. Clarke told management he and his teammates didn't like "flaunting" their title, and after the Bullies lost to the Los Angeles Kings, 5–3, in the opener, the patches were removed.

The first game of the season had been a disaster for the defending champs, the night belonging not to the kings of the NHL but to the Kings of LA. The Kings beat Parent twice in the first period for a quick 2–0 lead, and Schultz was sent to the penalty box four times, incurring two ten-minute misconducts, a five-minute penalty for fighting, and two minutes for slashing. The Bullies bounced back two days later with a dominant 6–1 win over Buffalo, their eventual opponents in the Cup finals. The Flyers rode a 4–0 victory over Pittsburgh on December 22 into the Christmas holiday, and New Year's Day brought a 2–0 blanking of the Canucks in Vancouver and a 25–7–5 mark. A five-game win streak in mid-January sent the Flyers sailing into February, and by the end of March the Bullies boasted a record of 49–18–10.

Throughout the long season the Flyers again sold out every game at the Spectrum, and thirty-one of forty road games. Hart and Don Earle provided colorful commentary of the campaign's highlights:

> Hart: "The Flyers are attacking with tremendous ferocity! Crisp scores for a case of Tastykakes!"

> Earle: "Bobby Clarke facing off . . . Jimmy Watson gets a shot . . . scores for a case of Tastykakes!"

Throughout their 1974–1975 campaign the Bullies built on their belligerent ways. Their 1,953 penalty minutes were even higher than the 1,728 they had amassed the winter before. Philadelphia had become the kind of town Frank Sinatra sang of—"a make-you town, or a break-you town and bring-you-down town." With three games remaining in their regular season, the Flyers were focused on breaking the franchise mark for victories in a season, set at 50 the year before. Parent backstopped a 4–1 win over the Islanders at Nassau Coliseum in the penultimate regular-season game on April 5 to tie the record. One day later the Flyers got goals from six different players in a 6–2 victory over Atlanta that gave Philadelphia its franchise record-setting 51st win. The Bullies had gone unbeaten in their final fourteen games and dropped just one decision in their final twenty games. The Flyers' furious push helped them tie the Sabres and Canadiens for the league lead in points, with 113. Philadelphia's 51 victories were two better than Buffalo and four better than Montreal, and for the first time in team history, the Flyers would have home-ice advantage throughout the postseason.

The first round of the playoffs followed a familiar script for the Flyers, Philadelphia winning four straight—this time against Toronto—and

Moose Dupont completing the sweep with an overtime goal in Game 4. MacLeish fueled the Flyers' offense with 4 goals and 6 points, while Parent paced the defense, pitching two shutouts.

The Flyers expected to play the Penguins—the last team to defeat Philadelphia in the regular season, 8–2, on March 8 in Civic Arena—in the semis. The Pens skated to a 3–0 series lead in their quarterfinal against the Isles, but New York rallied behind Gillies, Ed Westfall, Gary Howatt, and goalie Glenn "Chico" Resch to win four straight games. Having become just the second team in NHL history to win the final four games of a seven-game series, the Isles entered their first semifinal series in franchise history on a high note. They were quickly brought down in Game 1 in the Spectrum, with Stephenson recording the Flyers' third shutout in five games and Clarke, Barber, Saleski, and MacLeish scoring in a 4–0 final.

Clarke beat goalie Billy Smith in overtime in Game 2 for a 5–4 victory. It was Leach's turn in Game 3 at Nassau Coliseum, the Rifle's third-period goal the only score in a taut duel between Parent and Resch. An apparent Leach goal at the end of regulation in Game 4 seemed to have given Philadelphia a 4–3 victory and second straight series sweep, but referee Dave Newell ruled the Rifle's shot had crossed the goal line following the final buzzer. Gaining a reprieve, the Isles won in overtime on a goal by Jude Drouin.

Reclaiming their momentum from the Pittsburgh series, the Islanders made it two straight in Game 5 with a 5–1 thumping of the Bullies in the Spectrum. It was the Flyers' first loss on home ice since a 3–1 decision to the Rangers on February 6 and their first postseason defeat at the Spectrum in thirteen games. Lonsberry gave the Bullies a 1–0 lead with a first-period goal in Game 6 on Long Island, but Denis Potvin tied it in the second period and Gerry Hart netted the eventual winner in the third. New York's 2–1 win evened the series, and the Isles were working the same late-series magic against Philadelphia that they had against Pittsburgh. The Bullies' season now hanging in the balance, Kate Smith was summoned to the Spectrum for Game 7. The Flyers' good luck charm lifted her performance to meet the occasion. She stirred the fans, Hart thought, "to an overwhelming ovation."

Like Boston's Bobby Orr and Phil Esposito the year before, the Isles' Westfall and Resch sought to gain good luck for their team by presenting Smith with a bouquet of roses, but Dornhoefer's score on the game's first shot showed that Smith's good graces were reserved for the Flyers alone. MacLeish made it 2–0 with a power play goal off assists from Barber and Clarke, but Drouin answered with a power play score that eluded Parent and halved the Flyers' lead. The furious first-period action, which saw ten penalties assessed, escalated with MacLeish sending another power play goal past Resch to restore the Flyers' two-goal advantage. Parent and Resch settled down in a scoreless second period, and MacLeish's hat trick goal in the third gave Hawk his 10th goal of the playoffs and made it 4–1 Flyers. Parent made the lead stand up, the Spectrum's Sign Man Dave Leonardi flashed placards telling the Islanders to "HAVE A NICE SUMMER!" and the Bullies were back in the finals.

The 1975 finals were historic in that it was the first to match two expansion teams. Fronted by their famed French Connection line of Rene Robert, Gil Perreault, and Rick Martin, the Sabres blitzed Tony Esposito and the Black Hawks in five games in the quarterfinals and handled Ken Dryden and the Canadiens in six games in the semis. Orr considered the French Connection the greatest scoring line in the league; he also considered Parent the best goalie. For the second straight year, the Flyers defense faced a severe test. Buffalo ranked number 2 in the NHL in goals scored; Philadelphia was number 1 in fewest goals allowed.

The Sabres arrived in Philadelphia seeking their first victory inside the dreaded Spectrum. Downplaying his club's drought, Buffalo boss Floyd Smith boldly told reporters, "We'll beat the Flyers when we have to." The Bullies prepped for the most prolific first line they faced that season, the French Connection having inspired a song whose lyrics read in part:

Look out! Here comes the French Connection!
Look out! You better look out goalie!

Parent rarely looked better than in Game 1 when he limited the Sabres to a single goal in the Spectrum. The LCB Line got two goals from Barber and one from Clarke in a 4–1 final. Game 2 brought more of the same, the LCB Line getting one goal each from Leach and Clarke, with Parent yielding a single counter to Korab in a 2–1 win.

Ahead 2–0, the Bullies shuffled off to Buffalo and the Memorial Auditorium for Game 3. The Flyers jumped in front on goals by Dornhoefer and Saleski. The Bullies seemed assured of a three-game stranglehold on the series. Instead, the game took on an eerie setting more suited to *The Hound of the Baskervilles*. It was a warm day in Buffalo, and with no air conditioning in the Aud, the sweltering conditions in the smallish arena led to a thick mist rising from the melting ice. Play was periodically stopped so arena workers could take to the ice and wave towels in a desperate attempt to clear the air. "We didn't even see the puck in the fog," Dupont recalls.

The moor-like conditions seemed to favor a Flyers team whose coach's moniker was the Fog, but the Sabres seized the moment, battling back to tie the game three times and finally win in overtime on a French Connection specialty—Robert scoring off assists from linemates Perreault and Martin. The game was stopped briefly when a bat fluttered around the ice. Sabres forward Jim Lorentz high-sticked the bat to the ice, earning the moniker "Batman" from teammates. MacLeish then picked up the bat with a bare hand, raising howls of concern from teammates, and carried it to the penalty box. The "Fog Game" lives in the memories of Philadelphia fans, who would have a similar experience a decade later when the Eagles fell to the Bears in the "Fog Bowl" playoff game in Chicago on New Year's Eve 1988.

The Sabres continued their comeback story in Game 4, rallying from a 2–1 deficit in the second period to score three unanswered goals and win, 4–2. Tied at 2–2, the series returned to Philadelphia for Game 5. Stepping to the fore for the Flyers was Schultz. The Hammer produced the game's initial goal three minutes into the first period and closed out the Bullies' scoring with 9:56 left in the second in an eventual 5–1 win. The series went back to Buffalo for Game 6. Roger Crozier replaced Gerry Desjardins in net for the Sabres and dueled Parent through two scoreless periods. Eleven seconds into the third, Kelly outfought Korab for control of the puck behind the Buffalo net, then moved out in front and slipped the puck past Crozier. Some seventeen minutes later, Clement took a feed from Kindrachuk and scored the Stanley Cup–clinching goal. The Flyers won, 2–0, and became the ninth team in NHL history to claim consecutive crowns and the first to repeat since the 1968–1969 Canadiens.

"They had a good shooting team, and they had the French Connection," Dupont says. "But we had toughness and we had Bernie." As the Flyers carried the Cup aloft in the celebratory skate, Buffalo fans gave them a rousing ovation. Moved by the fans' splendid sportsmanship, Hart took their applause to mean, "Well done, Philadelphia. We didn't think you could do it, but you did it, and we applaud you for it." Dick Irvin Jr. recalls the ovation as particularly moving. "The fans in Buffalo were chanting 'Bernie . . . Bernie.' Parent had just beaten their team and they were cheering for him. I got tears in my eyes."

It wasn't only the Sabres' fans applauding the Flyers' accomplishment. The famed members of the French Connection felt the same appreciation for the champions' crowning achievement. Martin watched Clarke skate back to the Bullies' bench and thought there were times when it seemed Bobby was ready to collapse from fatigue, so exhausting was the effort he was putting forth. Yet minutes later, Martin saw Clarke summon energy from a seemingly inexhaustible reserve and return to the ice, then contribute a key play for his club. "Amazing," thought Martin.

Equally amazing was the extraordinary effort the Flyers put forth in defending their title. Having proved that their first Stanley Cup was not a fluke, the Flyers took their place among the great teams in NHL history. "People used to talk about the Bullies, and I would say, 'Hold on. That's a heck of a hockey team,'" Irvin remembers. "There's no doubt they were good."

The Flyers were the NHL's best, but were they the best in the world? Super Series '76 and the much-anticipated meeting with the Red Army would provide the answer.

Philadelphia Flyers founder Ed Snider celebrated consecutive Stanley Cup titles in 1974 and 1975. Snider served as one of the architects in the building of the Broad Street Bullies, who terrorized the NHL in the 1970s with their talent and toughness. (PEETLESNUMBER1 VIA WIKIMEDIA COMMONS)

The Flyers' first title in May 1974 has been immortalized in many ways, including this statue of Hall of Famers Bernie Parent, left, and Bobby Clarke, right, hoisting the Stanley Cup.
(ALAN BASS WRITING VIA WIKIMEDIA COMMONS)

Flyers forward Dave Schultz, "The Hammer," was the NHL's chief enforcer in the 1970s. Known for his physical play, Schultz could also score, as evidenced by his two career hat tricks and twenty-goal season in the Broad Street Bullies' 1973–1974 Stanley Cup season.
(ROBERT B. SHAYER, PUBLIC DOMAIN VIA WIKIMEDIA COMMONS)

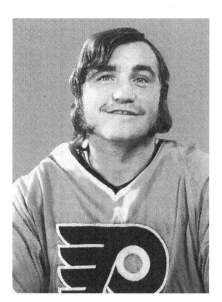

Rick MacLeish, "The Hawk," was called by Broad Street Bullies captain Bobby Clarke the Flyers' most talented player in the 1970s. MacLeish was a clutch player who paced the Stanley Cup champions in goals and points in 1974 and 1975.
(PHILADELPHIA FLYERS/NHL VIA WIKIMEDIA COMMONS)

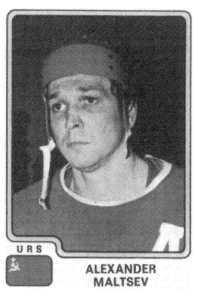

ALEXANDER MALTSEV

Aleksandr Maltsev is one of the top forwards in the history of Russian hockey. A six-time Soviet All-Star for Dynamo Moscow, Maltsev struck Olympic gold in 1972 and 1976.

BORIS MIKHAJLOV

Central Red Army forward Boris Mikhailov teamed with Valeri Kharlamov and Vladimir Petrov to form one of hockey's greatest lines.

Valeri Kharlamov was one of the top wingers in the world when the feared Soviet Red Army club arrived in Philadelphia to take on the Stanley Cup champion Flyers in the final game of Super Series '76.
(S. ULYANOVSKY, PUBLIC DOMAIN VIA WIKIMEDIA COMMONS)

Vladislav Tretiak is considered by some hockey historians to be the greatest goalie in history.
(LEO MEDVEDEV VIA WIKIMEDIA COMMONS)

Flyers forward Don "Big Bird" Saleski battles Soviet Red Army defenseman Vladimir Lokotko in the showdown game of Super Series '76.

Russian sportscaster Nikolai Ozerov, second from left, broadcasts back to the Soviet Union that the Red Army team is leaving the ice in protest of the Flyers' punishing play in the first period of the climactic game of Super Series '76. Red Army coach Konstantin Loktev stands next to Ozerov with his back to the camera. (AP PHOTO)

Flyers defenseman Joe Watson works to control the puck in front of Soviet Red Army goalie Vladislav Tretiak in Super Series '76.
(COURTESY OF FLYERS ARCHIVES)

Flyers Joe Watson (foreground) and Bill Barber shake hands with Soviet Red Army goalies Vladislav Tretiak and Nikolai Adonin following the Broad Street Bullies' 4–1 win in the climactic game of Super Series '76.
(COURTESY OF FLYERS ARCHIVES)

CHAPTER 6

Super Series '76

VLADISLAV TRETIAK STOOD ATOP SOVIET HOCKEY IN 1975–1976. His career was reaching new heights, and he had been named by Russian sports writers as the USSR's best goalie. In recognition of his success with Central Red Army, Tretiak was feted in the Kremlin and awarded Russia's prestigious Order of the Badge of Honor, an award given to civilians by the Soviet Union for outstanding achievements.

Tretiak's fame was global. Letters addressed to him arrived from all around the world, offering congratulations, seeking requests, and asking questions about Russian hockey. Questions concerning Soviet hockey had arisen as well among sports fans and hockey insiders as the USSR's Red Army club, coached by Konstantin Loktev, and Soviet Wings, headed by Boris Kulagin, departed for North America and their eagerly awaited Super Series '76 against National Hockey League teams.

North American players, coaches, and owners believed they had suffered in 1972 and again in 1974 from the unfamiliarity of playing together on an all-star team. By contrast, they noted, players on the Soviet national team were accustomed to each other's styles and thus had a sizable advantage in a short series. NHL adherents also noted that the two previous Summit Series had been played in the league's traditional preseason, when North American players were still working to get themselves in shape for the season ahead.

Let NHL teams play the Soviets, North Americans suggested, and see what happens. Word of the North Americans' confidence reached the Russians. In his autobiography, Tretiak wrote that at the time of Super

Series '76, Canadians were asserting that NHL clubs "were a lot stronger than any national team."

Strength was indeed at a premium in the NHL. While the Russians had developed their game from the Canadian style of precision stickhandling and slick skating, the NHL had moved to an American model that hockey writer Shirley Fischler said had won two world wars and made Vince Lombardi a legend: "Get them as big as you can, and then intimidate the opposition from playing its own game." This thinking had led to the physically intimidating Big, Bad Bruins and Broad Street Bullies and would confront the swift Soviets in their meetings with NHL clubs.

Super Series '76 would prove historic since Soviet teams in previous competition against North American professionals had faced all-star teams. Now, as Tretiak noted, the Russians for the first time were to face the "strongest clubs of the NHL." Those clubs included the Flyers and the Sabres, who had met in the Stanley Cup Finals the previous spring; the 1974 finalist Boston Bruins; the 1973 champion Montreal Canadiens and runner-up Chicago Black Hawks; and 1975 playoff teams in the Pittsburgh Penguins and New York Islanders. The latter, along with the Canadiens, had been Stanley Cup semifinalists the season before. The inclusion of the Islanders and Penguins surprised some, but these were young clubs who played a memorable seven-game series in the preceding year's Stanley Cup quarterfinals; the Pens pounded out a 3–0 series lead before the Isles rallied to sweep the next four games.

Each of the eight teams were in the northeast. Two notable exclusions to the list of NHL clubs were Original Six teams Detroit and Toronto. The reason for the Red Wings was obvious; Detroit had totaled just 58 points the previous season. The Maple Leafs' exception was more complicated. They were a playoff team in 1974–1975, but club owner Harold Ballard would not allow Russian teams to skate on Maple Leaf Gardens ice. Massive media attention and fan expectations surrounded Super Series '76 in North America and Europe. Phil Esposito, traded from the Boston Bruins to the New York Rangers and wearing the captain's "C" on his jersey, was concerned about the possible implications of Super Series '76.

"I hope it doesn't become a political thing," Esposito was quoted by Norm MacLean in an article for the *Hockey News*. This was precisely what had happened in 1972, when the teams were used by their respective governments as, in Esposito's words, "political footballs."

Super Series '76 promised more of the same. The Cold War was ongoing, and the Soviet's tour of NHL cities roused intense interest on both sides of the Atlantic. "The Russians have been preparing for this since 1948 when they started playing hockey," Esposito told MacLean. He believed that when North Americans played the Soviets, it was political war being waged on ice. "We had to win—at all costs, no matter what," he said. Esposito's determined play in the 1972 Summit Series so impressed a young Wayne Gretzky, watching on TV, that Gretzky said later he has never seen a better performance in a single series.

Esposito thought back to 1972 while preparing to face the Soviets a second time. "The last time we played them we didn't know how good their goalie [Tretiak] was, or how good they could skate or shoot," he told MacLean. "We had a bad scouting report. . . . I think they will be rougher this time, but I don't think the series will get dirty with high sticks or anything like that."

Esposito was disappointed when he learned the Red Army and Soviet Wings had been allowed by the NHL to bolster their formidable clubs with players from other Soviet squads. "We give in too much, all the time," he said. The Rangers' captain noted that Russian negotiators had gotten their North American counterparts to agree to allow the Red Army to add Aleksandr Maltsev and Valeri Vasiliev from Dynamo Moscow and Slava Solodukhin from SKA Leningrad. The Soviet Wings brought aboard what one observer called "four ringers" from Spartak Moscow—Alexandr Yakushev, Sergei Glukhov, Vladimir Shadrin, and Viktor Shalimov. Esposito shook his head at the news: "Why can't we add [Los Angeles Kings star] Marcel Dionne?"

Espo's former teammate in Boston, the swashbuckling Derek Sanderson, offered his services in mercenary fashion to NHL teams who would be facing the Soviets. Sanderson had been dealt from the Rangers to the St. Louis Blues eight games into the 1975–1976 season, and because the Blues would not be playing in the Super Series, the Turk offered to rejoin the Rangers or any NHL team for their game against the Soviets. "If the Rangers, or whoever, are willing to pay me, then I'll play against the Russians," Sanderson said.

NHL executive director Brian O'Neill said the league drew a line in the sand for additional dealings with the Soviets. "In the future," he said at the time, "this series will be conducted on a club basis, with no extra players being added to any of the Soviet teams."

Writing for *Hockey World* magazine in January 1976, Barry Wilner stated that for NHL teams, the Super Series would "be a matter of personal pride and satisfaction to do well against the Soviets, especially in light of the inconclusive Team Canada '72 results. None of the NHL contingents want to let their fans, the league, or themselves down." Wilner warned readers not to believe that NHL players weren't looking forward to facing the Soviets. NHL fans were also eagerly awaiting the confrontation between their hockey heroes and the mysterious Soviets. Wilner wrote that fans "in all eight metropolises are pointing their interest to the brief encounter their favorites will have with the Russians."

From the NHL's point of view, there was one more possibility to consider, and for league president Clarence Campbell, it was a chilling notion: Suppose the Soviets defeat the eventual 1975–1976 Stanley Cup champion? "What will that do to the credibility of the NHL titleholders," Wilner asked, "and the Cup itself?"

On the Soviet side, Wilner wondered if the players skating for the Soviet Olympic team would go all out in the Super Series and risk injury one month prior to the Games? "And will the Soviet brass accept a few losses in order to present a façade of weakness to the world prior to the Games?" Tune in, Wilner advised, as "these things should either be straightened out or muddled beyond repair. But it ought to be fun, anyway."

This series against NHL teams was unprecedented, and Tretiak recalled the Russians feeling uncomfortable when they arrived in Montreal. He and his teammates ached physically and were extremely tired. Quartered at the Queen Elizabeth Hotel, the Russians found themselves besieged by the media. The Soviets knew of the Canadians' love for hockey but found that their attitude toward visitors had changed.

Russian players sightseeing on the streets of Montreal were greeted with smiles from Canadian hockey fans. Even Harry Sinden, head coach of Team Canada four years earlier and a man whom Tretiak recalled as being hostile to the Soviet national team, had a change of heart. The Russians read articles in which Sinden said Soviet teams excelled because they had strong individuals who executed carefully crafted strategies and played together as a team.

Sinden compared Valeri Kharlamov to Rick Martin of the Sabres and used the comparison to draw a distinction between the Soviets and NHL that favored the Russians. Sinden knew that besides Kharlamov, the Russians had many strong individual players. Yet he wondered how many Rick Martins the NHL had.

Unlike the 1972 Summit Series, Super Series '76 was not being projected by North American sportswriters to be a one-sided event. Though most media members believed the NHL would triumph, there were dissenters. Tretiak wrote that he and his fellow Russians were surprised when a sportswriter for *Le Journal de Montréal* predicted the Soviets would win the eight-game series, 5–2–1.

Sportscaster Tim Ryan, the voice of the NHL broadcasts on NBC's Game of the Week and the play-by-play man for the Islanders, considered North American teams to be the clear favorite. "NHL teams will win five of the eight games," Ryan said in the *Hockey News*. "I think the Islanders, Buffalo, Chicago, Philadelphia, and Montreal will win." Gary Bergman, who played for Team Canada in 1972, believed NHL teams could beat the Soviets but that victories weren't going to be easy. "If our guys dig and work, they can win the series," he said. "But they have to work."

Following a Christmas Eve reception in the Montreal Forum, the Red Army and Soviet Wings met the media. The *New York Times* noted that Soviet players dressed "with a bit more taste than the typical NHL player and with less expense, the Soviet team members also comported themselves in conservative fashion at first, acknowledging greetings from the press and Canadian hockey dignitaries with nods and firm handshakes, but nary a smile." The *Times* reported that the Russians ordered

Coca-Cola at the bar and returned to their tables, where they sat stoically amid the glare of TV lights and the stares of a curious media.

When the Russians held a practice, it was attended by the Montreal Canadiens, and Tretiak noted that the professionals watched every Russian player and wrote copious notes. "Their expressions," he recalled in his autobiography, "were a blend of respect and enthusiasm." Tretiak found the difference between 1972 and 1976 striking. NHL players who had formerly met their Russian counterparts with what Tretiak thought was "arrogance, haughtiness, and disregard" were now studying them intently and taking notes.

The Red Army began its four-game Super Series in New York against the Rangers. Tretiak thought the reception for his team left much to be desired. There was difficulty in finding a hotel for the Russians, and there were delays in getting them dinner. It was enough to leave Tretiak and his teammates wondering if the NHL was trying to make them angry. Still, the Soviets were given new skates, and a Madison Square Garden employee sewed nameplates on the red sweaters of Central Army. The Rangers wore a commemorative patch on their white jerseys. The special adornment celebrated their fiftieth anniversary and was only the second patch the club had worn to that point, the first in a quarter century.

A new day in hockey history dawned on Sunday, December 28, 1975, when the Red Army skated onto Madison Square Garden ice. Cigarette and cigar smoke hung like fog and added to the mystery of the event as John Condon, the voice of MSG, welcomed a sellout crowd of 17,500 fans for this historic first meeting between a Soviet League team and an NHL club:

On behalf of the National Hockey League and the New York Rangers, and in the spirit of good sportsmanship, Madison Square Garden is proud to present this evening a premier attraction of international hockey, as the 1975 champions of the Soviet Union, the Soviet Army team, meet the New York Rangers. This will be the first time a Soviet club has competed against a team from the National Hockey League, certainly an historic event. Let us now meet the champions of Russia.

Though the Russians were introduced to the crowd according to their uniform numbers, Kharlamov (17) and Tretiak (20) were brought out last, receiving the loudest ovations accorded to the Red Army club. Sinden joined Canadian Broadcasting Company sportscasters Dick Irvin Jr. and Bob Cole and told the huge viewing audience there was "a lot of excitement here tonight."

Rangers fans were anxious to see how their Broadway Blueshirts—newly acquired Esposito and Carol Vadnais from the Bruins, veteran Rangers Rod Gilbert and Steve Vickers, and scoring leader Rick Middleton—would fare against the Red Army. Rangers coach Ron Stewart was 1–1 in previous meetings with the Russians, having lost while with Portland in the Western Hockey League and won with Springfield. "This is my rubber match with them," Stewart told reporters. "I hear we start off with the Russian referee [Yury Karandin]. I wonder what that will mean."

It didn't take long to find out. The Blueshirts blitzed the Soviets early, Vickers getting assists from Esposito and Gilbert and backhanding the puck past Tretiak twenty-one seconds into the game. Renewing acquaintances with Esposito, the Russians soon learned that while he was not as fast on his skates as he had been, Espo's trademarks—what Treitak called "his superb ability to control the puck, his powerful game in front of the net, and his astounding intuition"—remained. Esposito's skills helped the Rangers to a rousing start. "We came out in the first four minutes (flying) and they waited to see what was going to happen," he said. "We absolutely dazzled them."

It was a fast start similar to Game 1 of the 1972 Summit Series, when it took Team Canada just thirty seconds to score the first goal. But just as they had four years earlier, the Russians retaliated. Tretiak believed the Rangers' quick score excited the Soviet forwards. He watched teammates take the play to the Rangers with fast, intense hockey. The Red Army's attack against goalie John Davidson had the Russians believing the Rangers couldn't comprehend what they were dealing with as the Soviets scored three unanswered goals. Watching from behind the Blueshirts' bench, Stewart saw a scenario unfolding that he had been wary of. Because the Soviets could move the puck so well, Stewart knew Espo,

Gilbert, Vadnais, Vickers, and company would have to take on Kharlamov, Mikhailov, Petrov, and their swift-skating mates in one-on-one situations.

Trying to keep pace with the Red Army players proved to be a problem for the Rangers, who were shorthanded, as they were whistled for three first-period minors. Boris Alexandrov, twenty years old and the youngest Red Army team member, tied the game at 4:04 of the first with a power play goal. Vladimir Vikulov scored just over a minute later to give the Russians a lead they would not relinquish. The Soviets struck again with eighteen seconds left in the period, when Kharlamov scored another power play goal for a 3–1 lead. It wasn't until the second period that Karandin called a penalty on the Soviets, and the partisan Rangers fans rose as one to give the Russian referee a sarcastic standing ovation.

With the Rangers reeling, the Red Army iced matters in the second period with three unanswered goals from Petrov, Vikulov, and Mikhailov. Tretiak thought Davidson appeared bewildered, "in a state of confusion." Tretiak heard later that Rangers forward Pete Stemkowski said it seemed as if the Russians were on a merry-go-round. Wes Gaffer of the New York *Daily News* watched the carnage and thought Russian players were choreographed rather than coached. Tapping his typewriter keys, he described the Soviets as "whirling in elaborate circular patterns that utterly confused the Rangers and made the annual ice show a superfluous offering at the Garden."

Loktev thought the Red Army's play wasn't as dominant as it appeared, but he did believe the Blueshirts had a weight problem and that gave his Red Army skaters a big advantage. From where he stood behind the Red Army bench, Loktev could see the Rangers were not as fast as his team and that New York needed to improve its conditioning if it hoped to ever beat the Soviets.

As the Red Army dominated, a rotten egg was thrown at Tretiak from the stands. It hit the ice not far from him, causing Tretiak to look up and see a police officer taking hold of a fan who turned out to be a member of the Jewish Defense League protesting the Soviet government's treatment of the Jews. Petrov's power play goal 3:16 into the third was the Soviets' third with the man advantage and made it 7–1. New York answered with late goals from Gilbert and Esposito to close out the scoring at 7–3. The only battle the Blueshirts won was in shots taken—41–29. Alexandrov, who ignited the Red Army offense with a goal and two assists, was said by one reporter to have "showed the Rangers what hockey is all about."

Kharlamov added a goal and 3 assists, Petrov 2 goals and 2 assists; Tretiak turned away 38 shots and played with, as one observer remarked, "lightning-quick reflexes and X-ray eyes." The Soviets' Broadway show drew rave reviews. So impressive was the performance that one North American news story suggested it wasn't the Canadians who invented hockey, but the Russians. At least it seemed that way, the report read, on the ice of Madison Square Garden.

Campbell wasn't convinced. With Montreal, Buffalo, and Philadelphia on the Soviets' schedule, Campbell was quoted in the *Hockey News* as being optimistic about the NHL's chances. "I think they can beat them."

Sinden, however, sounded a cautionary note. The Rangers, he said, made all the mistakes opponents can't make against the Russians, including taking cheap penalties. If other NHL teams do the same, he warned they'll be handled by the Soviets. "It's that simple," Sinden said in the *Hockey News*, "and in a way, that tragic."

The Red Army's romp over the Rangers shocked many, and not only those on Madison Avenue. It was the initial test case of how one of the NHL's flagship franchises would fare against the Soviets. "I warmed my teammates to watch out for the Russians," Esposito said after the rout. Even Rangers vets like Gilbert sounded shaken. "I thought we were high enough for the game," he said. "I also thought that most of us played our best. But it wasn't nearly good enough." As the first NHL club to get a firsthand look at the Red Army, the Rangers provided a personal scouting report. Defenseman Doug Jarrett said the Soviets were like a team of Yvon Cournoyers, with Gordie Howe's hit.

Jarrett's remark was testament to the Red Army's immense speed and strength. More of the same was on display the next night when the Soviet Wings won in Pittsburgh by the nearly identical score of 7–4. Reporting for the *New York Times*, Robin Herman wrote, "Using the same magic with which their Soviet Army comrades hypnotized the Rangers last night, the Wings of the Soviet beat the Pittsburgh Penguins. . . . The

Russians' eccentric style, their weaving patterns that neutralize the traditional NHL wing-on-wing defense, and their quick passes from forehand or backhand, cast a spell on the Penguins so that they gave up four goals in the opening period."

A crowd of 13,218 in the Pittsburgh Civic Arena watched in silence as the Soviet Wings scored four unanswered goals in the first period and made it 5–0 just over a minute into the second on Shadrin's second goal. The Soviet center was a legend in Russian hockey. He helped the Soviets win gold in the 1972 Olympics, producing points on 3 goals and 5 assists. One of four players on loan to the Wings from Spartak Moscow, Shadrin had been instrumental in Spartak's interrupting the Red Army's domination of Soviet hockey. Shadrin played for Spartak from 1965 to 1979 and helped his club win league titles in 1967, 1969, and 1976. Shadrin ranked second on the Soviet national team in the 1972 Summit Series, and his impact on Russian hockey in domestic and international competition was explained by Russian coach Anatoly Tarasov.

Tarasov thought Shadrin useful both for Spartak and the national team. He believed Shadrin had a highly developed sense of the pass and gave teammates the puck subtly and skillfully, and at the right time and in line with their moves. Taraov considered Shadrin fluent in the art of passing and a master of shooting, stickhandling, checking.

Yakushev, Shadrin's teammate on Spartak Moscow, also scored against Penguins goalie Michel Plasse, who faced 35 shots. It wasn't until the second period that the Penguins resembled the playoff team they had been the previous spring, peppering Wings goalie Alexander Sidelnikov and scoring three times. Otherwise, wrote Herman, the Soviets played "a superb fast-skating game and also showed that Russians know how to check."

Yakushev loomed large over the proceedings. He was the Soviets' top physical threat offensively and effectively wielded his sickle-shaped blade, allowed because the NHL was not enforcing its stick-curvature regulations in the Super Series. The Big Yak told reporters his teammates let up after taking a 4–0 lead in the first period. "It is the matter of psychology," Yakushev said. "They thought the game had already been won."

The Soviet Wings started each period with a quick strike. Yuri Liapkin, an offensive defenseman, had two goals. He added two assists for the Wings' top line of Yakushev, Shadrin, and Shalimov. Penguins left winger Vic Hadfield, a former Ranger who had played against the Soviets in 1972, said the Pens tried tough hits and ankle slaps, but nothing fazed the Russians. "Like they had iron legs or something," Hadfield said. "And once we found we couldn't hurt them we started playing our game again. We took out the man instead. We went back to interference, skating, and checking. That's our game. If we were able to get over those first 10 minutes, we might have been able to do it."

Two nights later, on New Year's Eve, the Red Army took to Montreal Forum ice to face the Canadiens. The Habs were riding high at 26–5–6, and a festive holiday crowd of 18,975 packed the Forum, an arena Tretiak and his teammates held in high esteem. "A hockey palace," Tretiak called it. Looking at the arena from the outside, Tretiak thought it lacked any special attributes or architectural inspiration. Instead, it looked to Tretiak like a cube of concrete that resembled several faceless buildings. One could walk past the Forum, Tretiak thought, and not realize it is a "holy place" of Canadian hockey. Once inside the Forum, the Red Army realized it was a mecca, one of hockey's holiest shrines, where thousands of hockey fans could, in Tretiak's words, "worship their divinity, hockey."

The Russians learned that trips to hockey's promised land came with a cost. Tickets were priced at $6, but good seats cost $17.50 apiece, exorbitant at the time. Some 2,500, the cream of Canadiens fans, had season tickets. These coveted seats were inherited and passed down from one generation to the next, so season tickets often stayed in the same family for decades. Becoming a season ticket holder, Tretiak found out, was as difficult as becoming a member of the Parliament of Canada.

As the Red Army entered the visitors' locker room, they passed walls covered with photographs of legendary Canadiens players. Over the photos was a sign that read: "To you from failing hands we throw the torch . . ." The Russians saw another wall with a list, inscribed in gold, of members of Canadiens teams through the years. The photos, the signs, the inscriptions impressed upon Tretiak and the Russians that the Canadiens were a club that valued their gilt-edged legacy. That the Canadiens took this game with the Red Army extremely seriously was given voice by defenseman Guy Lapointe. Pointing to the walls of the Forum, Lapointe told reporters, "We must show the world that the best hockey players are playing within these walls."

Wilner and fellow hockey writer Joel Blumberg ranked the Montreal Forum as one of the top hockey arenas in North America. Viewed from the outside, the Forum could be mistaken for just another office building, but when fans entered the arena, that perception changed, and fans found themselves soaking in history and nostalgia. The lobby's photos and words celebrated the Canadiens' glory years, and pennants hung from the rafters recalling each of the franchise's seventeen title teams. Even the outdated hard wooden chairs failed to dampen fans' belief that they were inside hockey's Taj Mahal. Their allegiance to their team was unyielding, and, as Blumberg and Wilner noted, fans were "never satisfied with anything less than perfection from their *bleu, blanc et rouge* skaters."

As game time drew near, Tretiak believed all of Montreal was "electrified." The appearance of the Russians and Canadiens on the same ice shook the Forum, a sellout crowd screaming as one. Tretiak thought it a "thunderous roar" the likes of which he had never heard. It was Tretiak's habit to try to help teammates during a game by shouting instructions from his goal crease. But he knew it would be useless to shout instruction this night.

Like the Rangers, the Canadiens started fast, forward Steve Shutt sending the puck past Tretiak 3:16 into the game. Just over four minutes later, left winger Yvon Lambert beat Tretiak to make it 2–0. The Canadiens clamped down, allowing only four shots on goal against Ken Dryden. This was a Montreal team on the verge of a dynasty, a nearly incomparable club that would win the next four Stanley Cups. The Soviets left the ice at the end of the first period greatly concerned. Tretiak could see that the Canadiens were breaking the Red Army's defense; Russian forwards were unable to organize a counterattack. The Canadiens outshot the Soviets, 11–4, in the first period, but the Russians refused to panic. In the visitors' locker room, Loktev and fellow coaches Anatoli Firsov and Veniamin Aleksandrov told their team to skate faster and be more accurate with their passing. "Everything," Loktev insisted, "will be okay."

The Red Army appreciated their coaches' calm approach. Even in the heat of battle, Loktev and his coaching staff maintained a calculating manner. It was their belief that to yell at a player during a game was to break the player's concentration. The Soviets started the second period shorthanded when center Viktor Zhluktov was sent to the penalty box for two minutes. With a man advantage, Montreal made the Red Army work, sending one shot after another on goal. Tretiak later recalled that each shot was "hard and accurate."

The Russians cut their deficit to 2–1 at 3:54 when Mikhailov scored on an assist from Vasiliev. Four minutes later, penalties on Solodukhin and Aleksandr Gusev resulted in another Montreal power play, and this time the Canadiens capitalized. Cournoyer's goal off assists from Guy Lafleur and Jacques Lemaire restored the two-goal lead. Tretiak recalled it as an "extremely hard shot" that found the net despite attempts by three Red Army players to block it. Just under four minutes remained in the second period when Kharlamov, off assists from Mikhailov and Petrov, put the puck past Dryden. Tretiak saw Kharlamov's goal and thought, "What a beauty!"

Tretiak detailed what he witnessed of his fellow superstar's score: "Breaking the sound barrier, he went through two defensemen, made a smart move on Dryden, and completed his staggering raid with an accurate shot."

Dryden faced just three shots in the second period, but the Soviets scored on two of them. The third period saw Montreal regain the offensive. These were two great teams at the peak of their powers, playing hockey at a high level. The Canadiens put the pressure on, firing 16 shots at Tretiak in the third while only allowing Dryden to deal with 6 counters. Yet with 4:04 gone in the third period, it was the Red Army that scored, Boris Alexandrov tying the game at 3–3. The score stuck, and the Russians and Canadiens left the ice knowing they had just played one of the great games in hockey history.

Tretiak believed the New Year's Eve game in Montreal made a lasting impression on the Russians. As far as they were concerned, this was how hockey should be played— "fast, full of combinations, rough (but not rude), with an exciting plot." The Canadiens dominated the stat sheet, owning a 38–13 advantage in shots on goal. Habs coach Scotty Bowman said after the game that Tretiak saved the Red Army from a rout: "This Russian lieutenant stole the victory away from us." Despite the universal acclaim for the game, Dick Irvin Jr. dissented. "I didn't think it was that great a game," he said. "It was very one-sided, even though the teams tied."

As the calendar flipped to 1976, the Soviet Wings arrived in Buffalo to take on the Sabres. On January 4, an audience of 16,433 braved the cold and crowded into Memorial Auditorium. What they witnessed was a scoring spree that led to Sidelnikov and Aleksandr Kulikov and their opposite, Gerry Desjardins, desperately trying to survive a fusillade of shots.

Aware of the social and political situation surrounding the Super Series, players and fans knew this was a big night. When the Sabres took the ice, the noise from the crowd lasted several minutes and reverberated throughout the building. Buffalo general manager Punch Imlach's strategy for the Wings foreshadowed what Fred Shero and the Flyers were planning for the Red Army. To make the most of the Sabres' size advantage—defensemen Jerry Korab, Bill Hajt, and Jocelyn Guevremont all stood at least 6-foot-2 and weighed more than 200 pounds apiece—Buffalo's players were told to take the body at every opportunity, to ground the high-flying Wings with hard body checks. Studying film of the Wings' win in Pittsburgh helped the Sabres prepare. "The films changed our whole game plan," Sabres center Peter McNab told reporters. "Our defensemen weren't allowed to come out past our blue line."

Buffalo's bulky defensemen and high-flying French Connection line made their presence felt early. Korab and company pounded the Soviets, and Guevremont scored the game's first goal at 6:10 of the opening period. Gil Perreault and Rick Martin combined for three more first-period goals as the Sabres stormed Sidelnikov for a 4–2 lead. Herman reported that the "Sabres forechecked the visitors into helplessness and broke up their formations at center ice."

In 2020, forward Jim Lorentz, who scored Buffalo's fifth goal, told Chris Ryndak of Sabres.com that the Sabres were motivated by intense emotion and that there was a "genuine hatred" for the Russians. Lorentz thought it a feeling that seemed to "permeate throughout the NHL and not just with Buffalo."

When the Wings managed to maneuver the puck into the Sabres' end of the ice, Buffalo's defense broke up the plays with what Herman wrote was "some of its best physical work in weeks." Sergei Kapustin's score at the end of the period kept the Wings in the game, and the fire-wagon hockey continued in the second period as the third member of the French Connection, René Robert, scored for a 6–2 lead. Sidelnikov had been replaced by Kulikov when the score reached 5–2; Kulagin said the move was made to give his goalie "a chance to relax and think it over."

Sidelnikov returned after Vladimir Repnyev and Korab traded goals, but the scoring surge continued. After Shalimov scored to make it 7–4, Danny Gare and McNab added goals, and by the end of the second period Buffalo led, 9–4. While the French Connection ran wild, Korab was tasked with shutting down the Wings' top line of Yaksuhev, Shadrin, and Shalimov. Each time Yakushev looked to weave his way down the left side or breach Buffalo's defense for one of his patented shovel shots, Korab would bounce the Big Yak into the boards. "I figured if I can stop a guy like him I can slow down the whole team," Korab told reporters.

Yakushev praised Korab's play to Robin Herman: "Korab *kharasho* (good)." Kapustin recorded his second goal of the game early in the third period, and Fred Stanfield answered for Buffalo. Yuri Lebedev scored for the Soviets before Gare's second goal of the night fourteen minutes into the third made it 11–6. Brian Spencer's power play score at 18:04 closed the scoring at 12–6.

The offensive explosion led to a combined 71 shots on goal. Buffalo outshot the Wings, 46–25, and the Sabres made history by becoming the first NHL team to defeat a Russian club. The Soviet Wings likewise made history in that game, the loss being the worst ever by a Russian hockey club in international competition. Imlach called the one-sided win the "all-time high point for the Sabres" and a highlight of his Hall of Fame career. The victory was so well received by NHL fans that the

Sabres received a standing ovation in Montreal prior to playing the Canadiens. Dick Irvin Jr., who broadcast the game, remains moved by what he witnessed: "I don't think any other visiting team has ever received a standing ovation in Montreal Forum."

Martin had never been so fired up as he was for the Wings, and it showed in his performance, producing a team-best 5 points on 2 goals and 3 assists. Gare later told Sabres.com, "There was a lot of controversy going on in the global aspect of it, but that was a special night." Just how special is reflected in Lorentz's comments. "When we played the Soviet team, that was like the seventh game of the Stanley Cup," Lorentz said. "That's the way we approached it."

Kulagin claimed overconfidence played a role in his club's loss. Buffalo was 21–11–5 but had been struggling, winning just five of their previous seventeen games and going winless in their three prior outings. The Wings were in attendance on New Year's Day when the Sabres lost to the Los Angeles Kings, 9–6. "Seeing the Los Angeles-Buffalo game did not help," Kulagin remarked to reporters. "Our players were overconfident."

Sidelnikov said the Sabres appeared to be worse than the Penguins team the Wings had routed. Buffalo coach Floyd Smith believed his team's victory could help other NHL teams deal successfully with the Soviets. "They have one style," Smith said. "Play around for the break. We set the style for the other clubs. I think the Islanders, Bruins, Chicago will know what to do now." Kulagin wasn't convinced. "I want to add that this series of games are not over," he told Herman. "Our score is one to one."

Having been humbled by an offensive onslaught in Buffalo, the Soviet Wings looked to bounce back against the defense-minded Black Hawks in Chicago on Wednesday, January 7. Where the Sabres had featured the French Connection, the Black Hawks boasted goalie Tony Esposito. Backstopped by Tony O, Chicago was 16–10–13, and the Black Hawks had not been beaten since December 19. Opposite Esposito was Sidelnikov, who, despite his poor showing against the Sabres, was a skilled goalie whose game was founded upon a quick mind, correct anticipation of opponent's tactics, and fast reflexes.

Sidelnikov was a central figure in Krylya Sovetov's national championship in 1974 and was Tretiak's backup on Team USSR from 1972 to 1977. Sidelnikov had played center in Russian junior hockey, and when he became a goalie, he would move out from the net to intercept passes. Russian coaches taught Sidelnikov to stay in the crease, but he was eventually allowed to play his own style.

Chicago's scouting report on Sidelnikov was that the Soviet goalie stayed within the crease, but the Black Hawks found out different when play began at historic Chicago Stadium, nicknamed the "Madhouse on Madison," where the noise level was known to intensify to the point that the broadcast booth would rock as the crowd cheered on the Black Hawks. Blumberg and Wilner considered Chicago Stadium one of the top arenas, noting that it had been called everything "from an 'over-sized barn' to an 'indoor Comiskey Park' to 'a furnace with seats.'" Stadium seats were built not outward but upward, "an engineering stroke of brilliance," according to Blumberg and Wilner. "No matter where you sit, you are almost above, yet near the ice." Two beloved fixtures of Chicago Stadium were the Great Depression–era scoreboard and the world's largest stadium pipe organ. The pipes, ranging from six feet in diameter to the size of a pencil, added to the massive sound reverberations that Blumberg and Wilner said made "20,000 fans sound like 20 million."

The Soviet Wings' accoutrement was truly international. On their heads were red helmets manufactured by Jofa, the result of a recent deal with the Swedish company. They wore blue Czechoslovakian sweaters with white letters KC (translated to KS for Krylya Sovetov) and Soviet-made baggy blue hockey shorts. Victor Kuznetsov wore green and gold skates courtesy of Charles O. Finley's California Golden Seals.

"Most of our equipment is imported," Vyacheslav Koloskov, head of the Russian aggregation, told curious reporters. Black Hawks general manager Tommy Ivan recalled that when the Soviet national team first arrived in North America for the 1972 Summit Series, he sneaked a look into their locker to check out their equipment and was surprised. "They had almost nothing," he said.

The Russians' ragged appearance, their ripped socks and scraped skates, had brought derision and laughter from NHL supporters during the 1972 Summit Series, but the Soviets were better dressed for Super Series '76. Bauer salesmen greeted the two Russian championship teams upon their arrival in Montreal and measured each player for complimentary skates. Sidelnikov and Tretiak wore Cooper leg pads, and Red Army players pulled on Cooper hockey shorts they had obtained on one of their previous trips to North America. Sidelnikov hefted a Cooper hockey stick, while Tretiak preferred a Soviet stick called a "Montreal Special." At every stop in an NHL city, team equipment managers supplied Soviet players with various items. In Buffalo, Yakushev shocked Sabres equipment managers when he took virtually every roll of tape.

The Big Yak played a part in the Soviet Wings' strong start in Chicago Stadium. The Soviets struck first, Yuri Terekhin beating Tony O following assists from Yakushev and Krikunov. The power play goal, which came 8:46 into the opening period, set the tone for what was to follow. Russian referee Yury Karandin, who had worked the Red Army's win over the Rangers at MSG and drawn criticism for what was deemed by New York's players and fans as biased officiating, would be criticized again by Black Hawks team members and fans. Chicago had been shorthanded on Terekhin's goal, and all four penalties called in the first period were on the Black Hawks.

To the enjoyment of 18,500 roaring fans, Dick Redmond tied the game at 9:11 of the first period, but the Soviets ramped up their intensity in the second period, overwhelming Esposito with three goals, two of which came on power plays as the Black Hawks continually found themselves shorthanded due to penalties. Kapustin's goal at 4:03 gave the Wings a lead they would not lose. Four minutes later, forward Viktor Shalimov made it 3–1 with a power play goal, and at 17:13 Liapkin pushed the Soviet advantage to 4–1 with yet another power play score, assists coming from Yuri Turin and Yakushev.

Seven minutes into the third period, Dennis Hull stirred Chicago Stadium when he got assists from Stan Mikita and Grant Mulvey and pushed the puck past Sidelnikov. The Soviet goalie did not surrender another score, and the Wings claimed their second win of the series, 4–2. Chicago put 18 shots on goal, compared to 30 for the Soviets, and the Russians benefited from penalties that presented power play opportunities. Three of the four Wings' scores came on a man advantage, the Black Hawks being whistled for fourteen penalties to the Russians' four.

The Red Army returned to action on Thursday, January 8, in another fabled arena: Boston Garden. Tretiak considered the meeting with the Bruins one of the most important games of the Super Series. The Red Army was aware of the recent success of the Bruins, one of the NHL's Original Six teams, who had won two Stanley Cups in three years from 1970 to 1972. Tretiak called the Bruins "one of the strongest and most famous clubs."

The Red Army believed Boston would be inspired by Buffalo's victory over the Soviet Wings, and would also benefit from Sinden following the Russians from city to city for scouting purposes. The Bruins GM also took his players to watch the Soviets practice. Tretiak saw them lined up along the boards, studying every Soviet player. It made the Russians realize the importance of the game.

The Soviets hoped to play against Bobby Orr, knowing that every game Orr played was considered an event. A knee injury had prevented Orr from facing them in 1972, and before a Red Army practice he told Tretiak he had dreamed of playing in Super Series '76. But a recurring injury to his left knee sidelined Orr. Though the Russians had never played Boston, Tretiak thought it possible to visualize how the game would go, since the Bruins were, in his view, "a colorful representative of the traditional Canadian school." Tretiak believed Boston would seek to seize momentum from the start, storm the Red Army, and bombard them with pucks to crush them quickly. Entering Boston Garden, the Soviets found the old building a huge, gloomy place. The best they could say was that the ice surface was large, like the international rinks they were accustomed to.

Blumberg and Wilner believed Boston Garden to be one of hockey's best arenas. Called the "Snake Pit" or "The Zoo," the Garden sat atop North Station. Like Montreal Forum, it had wooden seats, many of which were near the ice. Sightlines varied, and fans seated below the upper balcony had to deal with the overhang, which partially obstructed the view of the scoreboard. The upper balcony provided the best view and housed the more vocal fans. John Kiley's organ music greeted early arrivals, and Blumberg and Wilner wrote that Kiley's "stirring rendition of 'Paree' as the Bruins skate onto the ice is as much a part of the Boston hockey scene as Bobby Orr."

The game began as the Soviets expected. The Bruins were strong; there was a reason coach Don Cherry's club was 21–9–9. They applied what Tretiak called "furious pressure" as Boston bombarded him with 19 shots in the first period. Kharlamov and Mikhailov pressured Boston goalie Gilles Gilbert, but the first period ended scoreless. Tretiak thought the fluid movement of the players was poetry in motion. Left wing Dave Forbes provided the game's first goal, sending a long shot that ticked off Tretiak's pad and skittered into the net. Coming at 2:54 of the second period, the 1–0 lead brought a roar from the big crowd.

Kharlamov tied it two minutes later on a power play goal following an assist from Maltsev, and the two combined again to make it 2–1 at the eleven-minute mark. Maltsev's score two minutes later increased the Red Army's lead to 3–1, but Bruins' center Jean Ratelle scored a power play goal on an assist from Ken Hodge near the end of the second period. Their lead trimmed to 3–2, the Red Army regained momentum 43 seconds into the third period on a goal by defenseman Gennadi Tsygankov. Eight minutes later, forward Boris Aleksandrov beat Gilbert to finish the scoring at 5–2. As had been the trend in the Super Series, the Russians were outshot, this time by 40–19, and Cherry pointed to goaltending as a key difference. "Tretiak," said Cherry, "is incredible." Having outscored the Bruins, Canadiens, and Rangers by a combined 15–8, the Red Army looked confidently toward their finale in Philadelphia. "We are in good shape," Tretiak told reporters.

The Soviet Wings were also flying high as they headed to the Nassau Coliseum on Saturday, January 10, for the final game of their series against the New York Islanders. The announced crowd of 14,865 filed into the Coliseum to see if the Isles could salvage some of the NHL's prestige and take down the Wings. The Isles, 21–12–7 heading into their meeting with the Russians, were putting together pieces of a dynasty that would produce four consecutive Stanley Cups from 1980 to 1983 and five straight appearances in the finals. Chico Resch, Billy Smith,

Denis Potvin, Bryan Trottier, Clark Gillies, Bobby Nystrom, and company would play for the Islanders when their Cup run got underway in 1979–1980.

Fresh from his goalie duel with Tony O, Sidelnikov now matched up with the Isles' colorful netminder, Resch. Following a scoreless first period, the Soviets took a 1–0 lead on forward Viktor Shalimov's short-handed score six minutes into the second. Trottier tied it at 14:59 with assists from Potvin and Gillies. Just fourteen seconds remained in the period when forward Vyacheslav Anisin beat Resch. Despite owning the best power play in the NHL, the Islanders went one-for-eight in man advantages. New York played a strong game defensively, but the Wings' quirky goals were the difference. Sidelnikov made the 2–1 lead stand up, giving Krylya Sovetov a 3–1 mark against NHL teams. The Russians led Super Series '76 by 5–1–1, and a concerned NHL now looked to its league champion to save its sinking reputation.

Knowing this, Shero considered the coming confrontation with Central Red Army a contest more important than either of the Flyers' two Stanley Cup victories. Bobby Clarke knew that what would take place on Spectrum ice was more than a hockey game. Fans around the world agreed, and would tune in by the millions to watch the Stanley Cup champion and international champion battle for bragging rights of their sport. "It was a big story for the NHL," Joe Watson recalls, "and for hockey."

The Bullies' throwdown with the Red Army represented not only a clash of cultures but a collision of political systems and playing styles. Hunkered down in his office, Shero studied film—"fillum," in his lingo—of the Soviets. What he witnessed was classic Red Army hockey, the Russians regrouping in the neutral zone before attacking with all five skaters. Shero saw the influence of Tarasov, the Soviet hockey master's interest in ballet, chess, and literature leaving fingerprints on the Red Army's style.

Shero never coached against Tarasov, but the styles of two legendary leaders would clash when the Red Army took on the Broad Street Bullies. Shero respected Russian hockey, but he also saw its flaws. Bill Clement had seen enough of the Soviets to know what style they were taking to the Spectrum. "They would overload one side, use drop passes, crossing patterns," he recalls. "That style doesn't work without superior skills. They had the philosophy that if they took a shot and it didn't work, they were turning the puck over."

A student of hockey history, Shero devised a strategy for the Soviets: make the past serve as prologue. Reaching back to Hap Day's Toronto Maple Leafs Stanley Cup title teams of the 1940s, Shero, Mike Nykoluk, and Barry Ashbee crafted a game plan imbued with NHL history. Day's Toronto teams were forerunners to Shero's Flyers. Strong and physical, the Leafs played a scheme in which their forwards stood up at their blue line and dared opponents to break through their interior lines. Shero's Flyers would follow suit. He told his team not to chase the Russians as the Rangers and Bruins had done, but to fall back to their blue line in a 1–4 alignment and body check the Red Army when it advanced. The Flyers' 1–4 alignment amounted to a neutral-zone trap that had the centerman pressuring the puck carrier while two wingers and two defensemen defended the blue line in front of goalie Wayne Stephenson. This would counter the Soviets' strategy of forcing the Flyers into difficult decisions while trying to contend with two-on-one situations in open ice. Thus, just as Loktev was employing the strategy of Tarasov, Shero was channeling Day.

"I think it was important for my father [to defeat the Soviets] regardless of how the other teams fared," Ray Shero says. "The Russians were another way to judge how good his team was. My father had a long respect for the Russian game, systems, tactics, and training."

The Fog had gone to the Soviet Union twice to study the intricacies of Russian hockey. It wasn't coincidence that his visits coincided with Stanley Cup titles. Now Shero would put into practice the tactics and training methods he had learned from the Soviets. The Red Army wasn't convinced this would work. Tretiak told reporters in Boston that if the Flyers played "a fair game," the result would be much the same as it had been against the Bruins and Rangers. Still, the Soviets were wary of the Broad Street Bullies' reputation for rowdy play. When the Russians and Flyers gathered at a goodwill get-together before the game, the Soviets studied Schultz at length. The atmosphere was tense, and there were no goodwill gestures as there had been when the Russians met with the Canadiens in Montreal and the Bruins in Boston.

"Bobby Clarke's team," *Sports Illustrated* writer Mark Mulvoy told the Red Army, "does not play 'friendlies' with anyone." Perhaps knowing that to be true, the Soviets had added Vasiliev, who knew about Schultz and was fond of physical play, to the Red Army roster. While Central Army wasn't known for fighting, the Wings were the most penalized team in the Soviet League, averaging more than eight penalty minutes per game—a paltry sum compared to the Broad Street Bullies, who averaged more than twenty-five penalty minutes per game. "Is that why you've added Vasiliev to the Army Club's roster?" Mulvoy asked Kulagin. When Kulagin expressed surprise at the question, Mulvoy stated the obvious. "The Army Club plays in Philadelphia."

The Red Army watched the Flyers practice, and Jimmy Watson remembers Shero putting his team through a variety of drills. "We were like fish out of water," he says. "The Russians were watching us, and they must have been thinking, 'What are we watching?' We were having a spectacular year, so we were very confident. There was some apprehension, some nervousness, but we were going to play with poise. As the game neared, we got ourselves ready to play. Our focus kicked in."

The game was billed as an exhibition, but everyone knew better. "It was no ordinary exhibition game," Gene Hart later wrote. The meeting had been much anticipated since the schedule was announced, and the Flyers had no difficulty selling out the Spectrum for their game against the Red Army. Ashbee told writers when the Super Series was first announced that most NHL players "want badly" to play the Russians.

No one wanted to play the Soviets more than the Bullies, who heard from Clarke how tough and talented the Russians had been in 1972. Clarke considered Tretiak a top goalie and believed that if Kharlamov played in the NHL he would win a Hart Trophy and that Maltsev and Petrov would be NHL stars. The best Soviet hockey players, Clarke thought, were as good as the top NHL players. And while the NHL was vastly different than Soviet hockey, Clarke was confident the Russians would adapt. The Soviets, he said, "feared nothing."

When the Red Army arrived in Philadelphia, the Russians had already won the Super Series. The Soviet Wings had lost only once and Central Army was undefeated. The Red Army took a break from its winter campaign on January 9 to watch the previous summer's blockbuster movie, *Jaws*. That they had not yet defeated one of the NHL's top teams had fans feeling skeptical about the Soviets' performances.

The climactic confrontation matching the champions of the NHL and the Soviet league would settle the matter. The same night that the Red Army mauled the Bruins, the Bullies battered the Los Angeles Kings, 6–4, in typical fashion, racking up 12 penalties and 30 penalty minutes. Having dispatched the Kings of LA, Shero and his squad set their sights on the kings of international hockey. Hart recalled later how quiet the Flyers' dressing room was following the win over LA. He attributed the apprehension to several factors, most notably that the Bullies knew that the Red Army was a great club and that they would face the Army attack without Bernie Parent in goal.

Apprehension was evident on both sides during the luncheon in the Spectrum's Blue Line Club, when the Red Army and the Bullies were face-to-face for the first time. Polite applause greeted the introduction of each player, but when Schultz's name was announced, the Russians "perked up," recalls Joe Watson. "They were wondering what they were in for." Hart spoke Russian, and prior to the luncheon Ed Snider asked for a favor. "Gene, come up with a Russian phrase or something that I can say at the end of my speech on Friday." Hart instructed Snider to welcome the Soviets with a Russian phrase that translated to "Good luck to all on Sunday."

The luncheon got off to a disastrous start, the Russians arriving a half hour late. Clarke said the Flyers offered the Soviets gifts, but the Russians rejected them. Tretiak recalled it differently, saying the Flyers made it clear they had no intention of associating with the Soviets. "The Stanley Cup winners were highly unfriendly, if not hostile," Tretiak wrote. "Nobody came over to welcome us." Tretiak said that even the Philadelphia press was stunned by what he called the Flyers' "blatant inhospitality." Reggie Leach recalled the two teams staying on their respective sides of the room, sizing up one another.

The Russians had high regard for Shero. They respected the fact that this North American coach traveled to the USSR to learn Soviet hockey. Tarasov liked Shero and visited him in the United States. Flyers statistician Bruce "Scoop" Cooper thought the friendship between Shero and Tarasov a perfect one. Referencing the Fog's sometimes shrouded statements, Cooper joked that neither Shero nor Tarasov spoke English.

All jokes aside, there were concerns among the Russians about the rough style Shero's squad employed. Soviet hockey official Alexander Gresko later wondered why Shero, an advocate of the Russian style, allowed his team to "indulge in so much muscle." Since the Bullies were successful, Gresko supposed the end justified the means, but he still thought it a contradiction.

At the luncheon, Loktev approached his counterpart. Would the Flyers, the Red Army coach asked, agree to play a clean, honest game? The Bullies' boss must have choked back a chuckle at the question. Shero knew his team would intimidate opponents if they could, it was part of the game. He had a team that liked to fight, so he let them fight. Shero told Loktev it was difficult coaching the Bullies, and two players in particular—Schultz and Bob Kelly—since he never knew what they would do at any given moment.

In truth, the Fog's game plan had already been formulated, and it contained a fair amount of physical play. Shero dissected the Soviets—their breakouts, special teams, and defense—and was aware of the strategies employed by the Penguins, Canadiens, and Sabres. The Flyers would send their centerman into the Soviet zone to forecheck and would drop their other four players back to the blue line. As author Lawrence Martin wrote in his book *The Red Machine*, Shero's strategy for the Soviets was to employ "team discipline and passing (with an overlay of violence)."

Clarke knew that NHL teams that tried to follow the Soviets' style had been embarrassed. The Flyers weren't about to do that. They would stand back and use their blue line alignment to force turnovers and counterattack. Offensively, the Bullies' blueprint was to put pucks on goal and force Tretiak to secure shots and rebounds. The Soviets' strategy was also set. Psychological warfare would get the Bullies riled up, causing them to take out their anger on the ice. Penalties would ensue, giving the Red

Army numerous power play opportunities. Owning man advantages, the swift Soviet skaters would flash past the outnumbered Flyers.

Loktev, however, was concerned; Martin wrote that the Soviet coach was "a politically scared man." With the Winter Olympics approaching, Loktev felt pressure to keep his team healthy. He believed that even if the Red Army beat Philadelphia but returned home with injuries, he would have to answer for it. Fearing punishment from the politburo, Loktev sought assurance from Shero that the Flyers would play "honestly and cleanly." Instead, the Red Army was going to find out firsthand what it was like to face a Broad Street Bullies' squad backed by frenzied fans in a sold-out Spectrum.

As the tense luncheon proceeded, Hart stood and issued a few words in Russian, introducing the players and coaches of the Red Army and the Flyers and finding enjoyment in pronouncing "all those wonderful Russian names." When Hart introduced Schultz, the Soviets stirred at the imposing sight of the Hammer. A member of the Soviet contingent boasted to Hart, "We are not timid." Seeking to impress the sportscaster, the Russian remarked that one Soviet player already had "40 penalty minutes!"

Hart smiled but refrained from telling the Russian that Schultz sometimes had 40 penalty minutes in a *game*. When it came time to speak, Snider stared at the Soviets, issued some brief remarks and a terse "Thank you very much," and abruptly sat down. Hart was surprised; the Flyers owner omitted the Russian phrase for goodwill. Following the failed luncheon, Snider approached Hart with what the announcer recalled as "more fire in his eyes than usual."

"I want to tell you, Gene, I appreciate what you did, and I wanted to let you know that I didn't forget it," Snider said. "It's just that I looked at those cold sons of bitches, and I couldn't say to them, 'Good luck on Sunday.'"

Clarke shared Snider's feelings. By his own admission at the time, Clarke "really hated those bastards." The Bullies took umbrage at the Russians' attitude. "They don't like anything," Clarke said. "They always complain of something and whine all the time." It was part of the Soviets' psychological warfare. "They always try to play with our minds," said

Clarke, who then lightened the mood a bit. "But that won't work with our club. We've got 20 guys without brains."

While Shero saw the Red Army as a formidable but flawed team, he spoke favorably of the Russians. "This will be a great opportunity for us to learn from them and to compete with them on a more suitable basis than an All-Star team arrangement," he told the media. "The fans have wanted a team versus team series for a long time, at least since the 1972 series."

Bill Barber agreed. The Flyers' star forward told reporters before the game he would have preferred to play the Red Army in a series. But, Barber added, he didn't want to sound unhappy with the single-game arrangement; he was excited about meeting the Soviets. "I haven't played against them and from what I hear from Bobby Clarke and other guys, it's a great competitive feeling being on the ice with them," said Barber. "They're the best in the world. Players and fans want to see how we match up."

Clarke believed the Flyers would match up well. "We'll play our regular system," he said at the time, "and if we do that properly we've got the personnel to beat them."

The captain told the media that one thing seemed certain. The NHL's series against the Soviets, he said, was creating a heightened interest in hockey.

Heightened interest, and for the NHL, increased anxiety. Evidence of the latter was Campbell and Scotty Morrison visiting the Flyers locker room before the Red Army game and telling the Bullies the NHL was going to let them play their style against the Soviets.

"They made it quite clear to us," Jimmy Watson remembers. "We said, 'Thank you very much.' This game was different; it was very political. We *had* to beat these guys."

Dick Irvin Jr. says the NHL's bold decision was telling. "Emotions were running high," he remembers.

Hockey's coldest war was about to begin. It would be a winner-take-all contest to decide the world championship, a Cold War conflict on ice. What followed was a game that had everything—pulsating plays, great goaltending, hard hits, and enough controversy to render détente doubtful.

CHAPTER 7

Realpolitik, Spectrum Style

As Central Red Army approached the Spectrum on game day, players saw an arena sitting amid a sports complex that included Veterans Stadium and John F. Kennedy Stadium. The parking lots surrounding the Spectrum were filling with the cars of thousands of fans who would pack an arena ranked as one of the six best in America. In 1976, writers Joel Blumberg and Barry Wilner called the home of the Stanley Cup titlists "among the champs of NHL arenas . . . a marvelous arena in which to watch a game."

Spectrum doormen outfitted in blue uniforms took tickets at each entrance from fans who would fill every upholstered seat in the Spectrum. Blumberg and Wilner warned visitors not to root against the Bullies. "Abuse is gratuitously heaped upon the enemy," they wrote, by Flyers fans who were "noisier than a Boeing 747 readying for takeoff." Game day against the Soviets saw the Spectrum alive with noise and intensity, the meeting of hockey's superpowers garnering global attention. Philadelphia sportswriter Bill Fleischman thought the game between the Flyers and the USSR champions was receiving more attention than a Stanley Cup Final—more even than the Super Bowl. Worldwide sports coverage that day, Fleishman wrote, was "focused on the Spectrum."

An explosion of crowd noise accompanied the entrance of the icemen. Few sights in North American sports were more unnerving to opponents than the Broad Street Bullies bursting forth from their locker room. Nor was there any vision in international sports more intimidating than the Red Army lining up to the sound of the State Anthem of the

Soviet Union. The temperature inside the Spectrum was set at 60 degrees but would rise several degrees due to the intensity of players and fans. The Red Army were already in a heated state when they took the ice for their pregame skate and saw protest banners ("God Bless America, God Save Jewry"). The feeling among many inside the standing-room-only Spectrum was that the charged-up atmosphere surpassed that of a Stanley Cup Game 7. "It was electric," Flyers defenseman Larry Goodenough remembers.

The setting was unique in hockey history, the first meeting of the champions of North American and European hockey. Not only was world hockey supremacy at stake. This was capitalism colliding with communism, North America versus the Eastern Bloc, democracy taking on dictatorship, free society opposite the Iron Curtain. "We were the Stanley Cup champs and they were the world champs," says Goodenough. "I was so wired for that game."

The Spectrum lights were dimmed for the anthems, then blared in all their brilliance as the long-awaited game was finally at hand. Montreal goalie Ken Dryden was among those who felt the playing of Kate Smith's "God Bless America" created "a tremendously exciting atmosphere, tangible electricity." Dryden didn't doubt that Smith's song could have an intimidating effect on a team the first time they heard it. He could imagine the devastating effect it had on the Russians, "the whole Hollywood atmosphere with the spotlights and all."

And here we go, the final chapter in Super Series '76 about to be written. Lloyd Gilmour goes to center ice, and there is Bobby Clarke against Maltsev . . .

Canadian Broadcasting Company announcer Bob Cole's statement at the start of play for the showdown between the Red Army and Philadelphia Flyers was broadcast to a huge international viewing audience. Cole was joined in the CBC broadcast booth by Dick Irvin Jr. and New York Islanders defenseman Denis Potvin. As Clarke bent forward in his faceoff stance and eyed his Soviet opposite Aleksandr Maltsev for the game-opening puck drop at center ice in the rocking arena, the Red

Army represented to the Flyers and the NHL nothing less than the most dangerous hockey team on the planet.

In the view of a league whose reputation would be determined by this game, CSKA Moscow was the most awesome threat it had ever encountered. The Red Army club was not just army by name, but also army by nature, as Shane McNeil would later write in TSN. He called the Red Army "the most dangerous team of a generation."

"To the Soviets sports were, in a way, a kind of warfare," Cold War–era journalist Vladimir Pozner said in the Oscar-nominated and Emmy Award-winning documentary Red Army. "The game for them wasn't just a game, it was also part of what you would call propaganda making it very clear that: 'We're the best. And we're the best because of the Soviet system.'"

In a 2015 *Esquire* article on *Red Army*, Ryan Bort wrote that when North Americans thought of the Central Army club, the image was of "a villainous, Goliath-like red machine." Soviet players, Bort added, were "faceless, emotionless, socialist robots programmed to crush the west with ruthless efficiency. They represented all that was evil in the world, their very existence was a threat to our freedom."

The Broad Street Bullies versus this Red Machine transcended sports. In the larger picture it was about politics—East versus West. The Flyers knew this game, played at the height of the Cold War, was about beating the Soviet system. Gabe Polsky, director of the *Red Army* documentary, told writer Emily St. James in 2019 that Soviet versus North American hockey was a culture clash as much a clash about how hockey should be played. The Russians wanted to be the best in the world, and because sports were politicized the Soviets, Polsky stated, were "indirectly spreading the ideas of Communism."

The Red Army's comrades, the Soviet Wings, had successfully concluded their North American schedule the night before with a victory over a talented Islanders team. The Russians had painted the NHL red, and the proud pros were reeling. The Red Army, however, had one challenge still to be dealt with—the Broad Street Bullies.

Amped up by owner Ed Snider's strong dislike of the Soviets, the Bullies became hell-bent on proving they were the best hockey team in the world. To do so, the Flyers would have to solve the riddle that was Vladislav Tretiak. Arguably the top goalie in the sport, Tretiak's play befuddled the best of international competition as he compiled a sterling 1.78 goals-against average. Nine times he led the Russians to European championships, and he amassed more than ninety medals in all. A recipient of the Order of Lenin, Tretiak would go undefeated in forty-five consecutive world championship games.

Such was the challenge that awaited the Flyers. During their Stanley Cup years, the Bullies had defeated the best goalies in the NHL—Ken Dryden, Tony Esposito, Ed Giacomin, Rogie Vachon—yet Tretiak presented a unique challenge. The Russians knew it, and they knew the Bullies' reputation for doing what it took to win. Alexandr Yakushev called Clarke's shattering of Valeri Kharlamov's ankle "intentional and horrible." Wary as the Russians were, the Soviets steamrolled into the Spectrum boasting a lineup that included four of the top ten players in Russian hockey history: Maltsev, Kharlamov, Tretiak, and Valeri Vasiliev.

To the 17,077 fans packed into the Spectrum on this cold Sunday afternoon, the visitors from the East were as exotic and mysterious as Mother Russia. Arriving from behind the Iron Curtain, they were regarded with as much curiosity as if they were from another world. Unlike most NHL players at the time, the Soviets wore helmets, bright red Jofa headgear that reflected the glare of the Spectrum lights. They represented a lifestyle and brand of hockey completely foreign to Philadelphia fans. Snider stared at the Soviets and thought of the harsh treatment of Jews in Russia. "Sons of bitches," he spat.

The Russians wore red uniforms with UCKA across the front in white block letters. The Cyrillic characters on their sweaters translated to CSKA, Central Sports Club of the Army, the players sponsored by the Soviet state. Soviet uniforms were typically spartan in appearance, plain red sweaters with white names and numbers and minimal striping. For Super Series '76, the Red Army sweater bore blue nameplates with the players' surnames stitched in white lettering and spelled in English. As they had since 1970, the Flyers wore white sweaters trimmed in orange and black. A large "Flying P" in black adorned the front of the jersey, while the back of each sweater carried the player's number. Player's nameplates had been added to the back of the sweaters in 1972. Black shorts and white socks with a single horizontal orange stripe completed the Flyers' uniform.

Red, white, and blue bunting hung from the rafters of the Spectrum for this game, adding to the atmosphere of a championship contest. The crowd booed the introduction of each Red Army player and stood in stony silence during the playing of the Soviet anthem. When Kate Smith's "God Bless America" followed, frenzied cheers drowned out the song's ending. From his seat high in the press box above the gleaming white ice, sportswriter Bill Lyon of the *Philadelphia Inquirer* studied the Soviets for signs of the Philly Flu. "What was wrong with them," Lyon remembered, "was that they would look across the ice and know that Dave Schultz was ready to pound the hell out of them."

Standing behind the Flyers' bench, Fred Shero stared out at the ice from behind his glasses. A year before facing the Red Army, the Fog broke down the Soviet style of play in his autobiography, *Shero: The Man Behind the System*:

> *In the last thirty years, since the beginning of the red line, we have done nothing in center ice. Every other team does the same thing: They get the puck over to the center; if the wings are covered, they shoot it in. The Russians have advanced beyond that stage. Instead of shooting the puck, they will create openings. . . . The Russians are creating openings even in their own zone. They will weave and cut to get away from the wings and create openings.*

The Red Army had mastered the weave, and Shero's response would be the Flyers' disciplined defense and 1–4 alignment. Joe Watson remembers this game not being the first time Shero employed his blue line scheme. "Any time we had the lead and there were ten minutes or less to play," he says, "we would use the 1–4." The Flyers emphasized their blue line defense in practice in the days leading up to meeting the Red Army. The Bullies were further instructed by Shero to play their normal physical game, but to use their aggression with discretion. He didn't want his team to spend too much time in the penalty box. Take the body on Red Army players, Shero told his team, but do it cleanly.

The worth of Shero's strategy would be on display for the world to see. Wilner, writing in *Hockey World* in January 1976, opined that of the four NHL teams that would face the Red Army, Shero's Bullies had the best chance to win. Wilner felt the Flyers "should match up as well as any club against the Soviets, and not just because they are Stanley Cup champions. Shero's willingness to adopt Russian techniques will make that matchup more intriguing than most of the other contests."

It was critical for the NHL that Shero's strategy work. Gene Hart noted at the time that league officials and players who had condemned the Flyers for their ferocious play were cheering them on. Those who belittled the Bullies even though Philadelphia had won more than one hundred games and two Stanley Cups in the past two seasons were calling on them to save the NHL. Hart recalled team owners, players, coaches, and fans imploring the Bullies to "win it for the league!"

"Screw the league!" Joe Watson thought. "We're going to win it for ourselves!" The Flyers believed that being the first NHL team to defeat the Red Army would prove to the world that they were a talented club coached by one of the game's greats.

Shero and his coaching opposite, Konstantin Loktev, matched strengths from the start and sent their top lines to center ice. Maltsev was flanked by fellow forwards Kharlamov and Mikhailov and backed by defensemen Vasiliev and Aleksandr Gusev, with Tretiak in goal. Clarke anchored the LCB Line, with Bill Barber to his left and Reggie Leach on his right. Defensemen Jimmy Watson and Ed Van Impe fronted goalie Wayne Stephenson. The line matches meant much to afficionados of the sport, as Barber, believed by many to be the NHL's top left winger, was opposite Mikhailov, the captain and inspirational leader of the Red Army. Barber was eager for the challenge, since he believed he could skate with any wing, big or small, speedy or muscular.

Leach, one of the league's top snipers, was on the Flyers' right wing and going against Kharlamov, who was known to leave opponents in his exhaust fumes. The Flyers took the ice looking to make an immediate impression on the Red Army. "We feel we're the NHL's best, so people are looking to us to beat the Russians," Barber said before the game. "I'd rather play them in a best-of-seven series. That would really prove something. But if we only have one shot, we want it to be our best."

Clarke stole a sidewise glance at Kharlamov. The Bullies' captain knew that what Kharlamov could do with the puck was pure artistry. As Maltsev crouched opposite Clarke, the Russian forward looked into the face of the Flyers' captain and saw what the rest of the NHL was accustomed to seeing, what Bryan Trottier of the New York Islanders had seen in his rookie season. Clarke, Trottier once said, had "that look in his eye, that toothless half-smile/half-sneer that made you feel as though he could stare right inside of you."

The unmistakable message Clarke's grin issued to Maltsev mirrored the lyrics of the metal band Nazareth's hit song "Hair of the Dog," released one year earlier, and it was that the Red Army was now messing with a son of a bitch.

Clarke was a faceoff specialist whom Trottier called "the most intense competitor I've ever faced off against, and the one I respected the most." Maltsev had earned the same respect among his Soviet peers, and players on both sides leaned forward at this opening confrontation between two of the greatest players in the histories of their respective leagues. Maltsev's 321 games played and 213 goals scored are Soviet standards for international competition. He would help Soviet national teams win two gold medals and a silver in the Winter Olympics. A six-time Soviet all-star, Maltsev was lightning fast, and few players in the world could keep up with him when he was flying at full speed. In 530 career games in the Soviet League, Maltsev produced 321 goals and 552 points.

Maltsev was called on by Loktev to replace Vladimir Petrov, who was missing his second straight game with a groin injury after having played so well against the Rangers and Canadiens, on the Red Army's top line. The loss of Petrov was significant, since he was a certified star in the Soviet League. From 1965 to 1983, Petrov produced 839 points and 435 goals in 677 games, was twice named Soviet League Player of the Year, and led the league in scoring five times. Petrov proved just as dominant in international competition, helping lead the Soviets to six world championship gold medals and emerging as the leading scorer four times. He also won two Olympic gold medals and one silver medal. In addition to Petrov, the Red Machine was also missing from its lineup defenseman Gennadi Tsygankov (concussion) and forward Victor Shluktov (fever). The Flyers were absent nonpareil goalie Bernie Parent.

From the Flyers' bench, teammate Terry Crisp studied the drop of the puck to start this historic game. Crisp considered himself a very good faceoff man, but he believed Bobby to be the best. Clarke bent low in his crouch and slid one gloved hand down the blade of his stick. Once Gilmour dropped the puck, Crisp knew that Clarke would use his stick, his arms, his legs—his entire body, if necessary—to tie Maltsev into knots. The Bullies' captain knew taking on Maltsev was no easy task. He had played Maltsev in the Summit Series four years earlier and considered the Soviet center a "tough son of a bitch." When the series ended, Clarke's opinion of Maltsev was, "Man, that's a hockey player."

In this meeting between the best faceoff man in international play and the best in the NHL, Maltsev controlled the faceoff against Clarke.

Cole: "This game is underway!"

Skating free of the faceoff circle, Gilmour was referee for a crew that included linesmen Matt Pavelich and Yury Karandin. It was a stellar group, as all three would be elected to halls of fame for their work as officials. As far as some NHL players and fans were concerned, Karandin was the most controversial member of the crew. His work as referee in the first game of Super Series '76, the Red Army's victory over the Rangers, was criticized as too favorable to the Soviets. It was Karandin's considered opinion that the games between the Soviets and NHL were more of a benefit to the North Americans. "I can only state the obvious," Karandin once remarked. "Canadians took all the best from Soviet hockey; we took all the worst from Canadian hockey."

Karandin's opinion was shared by others, including Boris Kulagin. The coach of Krylya Sovetov told *Sports Illustrated*'s Mark Mulvoy in 1975 that outbreaks of violence in the Soviet League had been on the rise following the 1972 Summit Series. "It has been terrible," Kulagin said.

"Since that 1972 Summit Series against Team Canada we have played more dirty in every game. The professional influence is hurting us."

There was concern among some how close a game Karandin would call, considering the reputation of the Broad Street Bullies. No one doubted his credentials, however. Karandin began his officiating career in 1961 and would continue through 1987. His career in the Soviet Union saw him officiate 876 games, and the quality of his work was such that he was selected as a top-ten Soviet referee twenty-three times in his twenty-six seasons. Among his career highlights, Karandin was the first Soviet referee selected to officiate games involving NHL teams when he was assigned to Super Series '76. His experience in international competition would see him officiate 268 games, including six world championships, four Super Series, two Winter Olympics, and two Canada Cup competitions. In the 1969 Soviet championship game, Karandin disallowed a late second-period goal by the Red Army in its game with Spartak because the official timekeeper's watch expired. Red Army coach Anatoly Tarasov argued Karandin's call because one second remained on the scoreboard clock. Tarasov's protest delayed the game for forty minutes, but Karandin's call stood, and Spartak went on to win, 3–1.

For Super Series '76, Karandin recalled being "urgently summoned" to Moscow to apply for a Canadian travel visa. To travel abroad, he was excused from his domestic duties by Soviet administrators. Karandin earned $10,000 for his work in Super Series '76 and called the event one that altered his destiny. For that he expressed gratitude to the NHL. Though some criticized his performance as referee of the Red Army's game against the Rangers, New York captain Phil Esposito praised him. Karandin then served as a linesman in the Red Army's New Year's Eve classic in Montreal before traveling to Philadelphia for the series finale against the Flyers. In 2004, Karandin would join many of the players on the ice this day in Philadelphia when he was inducted into both the Russian Hockey Hall of Fame and the IIHF Hall of Fame.

Like Karandin, Pavelich was a well-respected official. Two months away from turning forty-two years old, Pavelich was on his way to becoming the first NHL linesman selected for induction in the Hockey Hall of Fame, an honor he would receive in 1987. Pavelich's career as an official began in his teen years; he was fourteen when he started offici-ating minor games in Sault Ste. Marie, Ontario. He advanced through the ranks and six years later was the Northern Michigan Intermediate League's referee-in-chief. At age twenty-two, Pavelich officiated the 1955–1956 season in the American Hockey League. He impressed the NHL's referee-in-chief Carl Voss, and in October 1956, Pavelich made his NHL debut. Together with his brother Marty, who played for the Detroit Red Wings, the two became the first official/player brother com-bination in league history.

Because he was the junior official in the three-man crews, Pavelich often performed the most unpleasant duties, such as clearing the ice of items thrown by fans. In Detroit's famed Olympia Stadium, Pavelich had to pick up the numerous octopi pitched down from the stands. From 1956 to his eventual retirement in 1979, Pavelich worked 1,727 regu-lar season games, 245 Stanley Cup playoff contests, 10 NHL All-Star Games, and 7 Stanley Cup Finals. His regular-season and playoff game totals stood second only to Neil Armstrong and John D'Amico, respec-tively. Following his retirement as an NHL linesman, Pavelich became the NHL's supervisor of officials under referee-in-chief Scotty Morrison.

A 1964 *New York Times* article stated that a hockey official was "a man with iron in his soul." At that time, Pavelich was part of a group of five full-time referees and four linesmen who traveled on a rotating, cross-league schedule. Pavelich, then thirty years old, thought the lone-liness of the road was offset by hard-core hockey fans. Pick up a piece of paper from the ice and a fan would yell, "Garbageman, you're getting good practice for your next job!"

Pavelich and his officiating mates, Gilmour and Karandin, would hear plenty of verbal sniping in this game. The Bullies and the Red Army were known for taunts and criticisms, and Spectrum fans were among the more verbal in the NHL. As the Soviets took initial control of the puck, Shero's game plan was revealed. Rather than give chase, as other NHL teams had done, the Flyers employed their 1–4 defense, with only the centerman, Clarke, in pursuit of the puck carrier. The Flyers' neutral-zone trap could be effective in stopping the Soviets from carrying the puck in, but it was not without risk, since the Russians' speed could lead to breakaways. As the Red Army wingers worked in concert to create space, the Bullies stood astride their blue line, determined to deny open ice.

"When the [first] puck was dropped, the Red Army won the face-off and proceeded to make three or four tic-tac-toe passes," Ray Shero remembers. "But the Flyer forwards never moved. They never got into chasing the puck. It was [the Flyers'] form of the 'trap' for that game." Says Flyers forward Bob Kelly, "Freddy caught them off-guard. We confused them." Jimmy Watson agrees: "I was on the ice for the opening draw, and after five or six passes, I could see the puzzlement on their faces. Freddy came up with a tremendous scheme. And Bobby was such a great leader. He told us, 'Stay patient, don't run around.'"

Faced with the trap, the Red Army regrouped, then displayed its famed circular skating and precision passing. Polsky would call the Soviets' weaving and constant movement "collective brilliance." Every time the Russians touched the puck, Polsky told St. James, "they did something interesting." Larry Goodenough had played against the Russians in Junior hockey and was familiar with their style. "They would skate, pass, and break," he remembers. "They were successful with that system." Like Goodenough, Leach had played the Soviets before. He faced them when he was with Flin Flon and the Bombers met a Moscow Selects team and again when he was added to the roster of the national squad for its games against a Russian touring team. Now taking on the Red Army, he found them impressive. He thought each of their three lines excellent and believed the Red Army's third line would have been a second line in the NHL. Like Clarke, Leach realized the Russians were physically strong men. The difference was that the Soviets didn't play a physical style, and the Bullies were hockey's most physical team.

Kharlamov took control of the puck and was immediately confronted by Clarke. It was their first on-ice meeting since the Summit Series. The Soviet legend had not forgotten. "I remember Clarke," Kharlamov told Mark Mulvoy. "Anything can happen in a game, but I try to keep no grudge. He was not a sportsman in that game, but it is over." Kharlamov passed the puck into the Soviet zone, where the Russians proceeded with their tic-tac-toe passes, each covering some twenty feet of ice. Clarke forechecked to a resounding roar from the Flyers faithful, then Gusev stickhandled past the Bullies' captain and headed up ice on the Red Army's first attacking move.

Cole: "Gusev got away from [Clarke] and they're on the move!"

The Soviets, Polsky remarked, "played more of a possession game." The Red Army's first shot was to Stephenson's left and off target. Barber chased down the puck, passed it behind the net, then regained control before running into Vasiliev at the Russians' blue line. Not known as one of the Bullies' muscle men, Barber raised his stick high to Vasiliev's shoulder.

In the booth, Irvin remarked to Potvin that the NHL had heard much about the swift-skating Soviets and wondered if the Islanders had problems keeping pace. "I think the Soviet Wings showed us skating ability we probably hadn't seen before," Potvin said. The Red Army was seeking to show the Flyers the same, but to Philadelphia fans, the Russians seemed robotic in their movements, playing the game in an unfamiliar manner. Seeing the Soviets skating in elaborate patterns, confronting for the first time the Red Army weave, the Flyers stood firm at their blue line. Clarke told teammates the Soviets would skate back into their own zone and try to lure the Flyers out of position.

"We were well prepared," Dupont says. "We just had to stay calm and do what Freddy said. The system we used, the 1–4, [the Russians] didn't have a clue how to play it. You had to dump the puck in and go after it, but they didn't want to do that."

As the Red Army advanced and the Bullies took the body for the first time, they realized the Soviets did not play as NHL teams did. Rather than send the puck deep into the Flyers' end of the ice and then race to regain control, the Russians weaved in intricate patterns and circled back to regroup.

"Freddy had us well prepared for the Russians," Goodenough remembers. "They would come out of their end and go into weaves and crisscrosses. Freddy told us, 'Don't leave your lanes.' It was very simple what Freddy laid out for us. We stayed along the boards and stood four-strong at the blue line."

Arthur Chidlovski recalls his fascination at seeing the Red Army on the same ice as the Broad Street Bullies. "I was on winter break from school and watched the game live on TV. We had read about Schultz, Clarke, and Shero. The Flyers put up a concrete wall on their blue line. We couldn't penetrate it. We didn't have any answers for that. I don't think we were intimidated by it. We were just not ready for the wall they built on the blue line."

The blue line wall on Broad Street was proving as daunting as the wall in Berlin. "We were going to show them where the best hockey is played," recalls Joe Watson. "We were going to show them our style of play. They weren't used to getting bumped. When they came to our blue line, we were waiting for them."

Roger Kahn wrote that the Russians started the game with "a razzle-dazzle Icecapadeski" in their end of the ice. The Bullies ignored it, and Kahn credited Crisp and the Flyers with forechecking "beautifully." Facing the Red Army, Flyers defensemen took what Kahn called "their customary inhospitable view of rival forwards." The Soviets, Kahn noted, "could neither control the puck nor the flow of the game."

Taking the offensive, the Flyers' first shot came courtesy of Barber and was handled by Tretiak. Barber followed with another shot to Tretiak's stick side, and the goalie brushed it aside. The Red Army broke out and sent a shot that Stephenson deflected. Wayne was glad to be tested early by the Soviets; he went into games hoping to be challenged at the outset, as it helped him to relax. He was also comforted by the knowledge that the Flyers were an outstanding team that excelled in home games; they were, in fact, in the process of putting together a home ice win streak of twenty games that tied the mark set by the 1929–1930 Boston Bruins. By the end of the regular season, the Flyers would go 36–2–2 in the Spectrum.

The Bullies kept the pressure on, Barber again making his presence felt as he peeled back to take down Mikhailov with a body check. Barber aimed another shot at Tretiak, who kicked it aside. Line changes followed, Rick MacLeish replacing Clarke and taking over the role as the Flyers' foremost forechecker. The game's first penalty occurred at 2:24, when Boris Aleksandrov was called for interference on Gary Dornhoefer at center ice. The Flyers used the man advantage to bombard Tretiak as Leach and Barber forced the Red Army goalie to make three acrobatic saves.

Orest Kindrachuk's speed and stickhandling turned the Soviet defense around, bringing a roar from the crowd. Tretiak smothered a shot in close from Kindrachuk, eliciting a reaction from the CBC booth. "Tretiak has been the number one story on this trip," Irvin commented. "He looks brilliant right now." Potvin said the Soviet goalie "seems to be doing everything amazingly well. What I've noticed is that he seems to move from side to side better than any goaltender I've ever seen."

Bob Kelly tried to jam in a shot from the crease, but Tretiak held firm. A brief scrum broke out in front of the Russians' net, Kelly being tripped up and falling to the ice and Mel Bridgman muscling Mikhailov. The Flyers' flurry gave them 10 shots on goal at the 15:31 mark to just two for the Red Army. Irvin said that when Tretiak had to make heart-stopping saves, he proved able. "He did it in Montreal," Irvin informed viewers, "and he's doing it again."

The Flyers stepped up their physical game, prompting Cole to remark that the Flyers were "taking it to this Red Army team!" The Bullies shifted into beast mode. Don Saleski battled Vladimir Lutchenko along the boards, Big Bird ending the exchange with an elbow to the jaw and a raised stick. Feeling icy toward the Soviets, the Flyers were hot for a cold war. Ross Lonsberry had promised reporters that the Bullies would deliver "some brutal hits." Leach said the Flyers realized that if they banged the Russians around, the Soviets wouldn't like it. Joe Watson recalls the Flyers knowing they had to hit the Red Army at every opportunity. Let the Soviets slate around and play "dipsy doodle" with the puck, and they would be a problem. Hit them hard, Joe Watson says, and the vaunted Red Army would play like an ordinary team. Covering the game for *Sports Illustrated*, Mark Mulvoy wrote that the Flyers didn't just hit the Soviets, "they assaulted them."

Irvin: "I think a lot of people wondered what might happen from a physical standpoint, the Flyers noted for same."

Encouragement for the Bullies to play physical against the Soviets came from unlikely sources—Lloyd Gilmour, NHL president Clarence Campbell, and Scotty Morrison. The Flyers' bullish play was producing scoring opportunities. Irvin noted that Philadelphia had sent 18 shots toward the goal, 10 of them on target against Tretiak. The Red Army, meanwhile, had been limited to three shots, two on Stephenson.

The player the Russians were most wary of made his initial on-ice appearance at the six-minute mark. Dave Schultz immediately made his presence felt, rubbing his gloved left hand across the face of Mikhailov following a pileup in front of Tretiak. Schultz and Mikhailov glared at each other, and the Hammer then collided in a corner with the Red Army's most physical player, Vasiliev.

Dupont's high-sticking penalty put the Russians on a power play at the twelve-minute mark, but the Flyers killed it without surrendering a shot. Analyzing the Flyers' play from the booth, Potvin said the Bullies were neutralizing the way the Soviets come out of their own zone. "Those long passes aren't working for the Soviets," he said. "The Flyers have got them leery about the fact that they're going to hit them at center ice, and they're not as anxious to go for that puck as they should be."

The Flyers forced a turnover in their end of the ice and Clarke and Barber took off on a two-man break. Vasiliev had other ideas, dropping the Bullies' captain to the ice with a resounding body check. Cole remarked that Clarke was "belted hard by Vasiliev," and Irvin added that Vasiliev "threw quite a jolt" into the Bullies' captain.

Vasiliev's crunching hit on Clarke reinforced his status as the best body checker in European hockey. His physical style earned renown and he was named captain of the Soviet Union's national team. In his thirteen years of international competition, Vasiliev contributed to two Olympic gold medals and eight world championships. During the Soviet League season, he starred for HC Dynamo Moscow and earned eight Soviet All-Star selections.

Born in Volkhov, Russia, Vasiliev grew up in a tough section of Gorky, now known as Nizhny Novgorod. Vasiliev played for Gorky's top club, Torpedo, but was then signed by Dynamo Moscow. He would play a record 619 Soviet League games over the next seventeen seasons.

By the time he faced the Flyers, the twenty-six-year-old Vasiliev was considered the top defenseman in international play. Being named the best defenseman at three world championships reinforced the belief that Vasiliev's resilient, stay-at-home style made him a player without peer at his position.

Vasiliev was tough physically and mentally. He would play through a heart attack in 1978, and he overcame his belief that he was responsible for the Soviets losing the 1972 Summit Series on Paul Henderson's dramatic goal late in Game 8. Vasiliev said years later that Henderson's goal remained etched in his memory. Vasiliev had hesitated for a moment, the puck jumped off the blade of his stick, and Henderson immediately stuffed it into the goal. In the dressing room afterward, Soviet national team coach Vsevolod Bobrov said nothing to him, but later, during a team training session, Bobrov told Vasiliev to stop blaming himself.

"Don't doubt yourself," Bobrov said. "Know that you're a player on our most important hockey team, and that you deserve to be here."

Just as Maltsev played in more games at the international level than any Soviet forward, Vasiliev played more international games than any Russian defenseman. A predecessor to great Russian defensemen Slava Fetisov and Alexei Kasatonov. Vasiliev would captain the Russians' 1981 club that claimed the Canada Cup championship.

Vasiliev's decking of Clarke stopped the Flyers' offensive. Seeing his captain dropped to the ice, Van Impe answered for the Flyers, picking up a penalty for hooking Maltsev. Taking advantage of a power play, the Red Army rallied. A shot clanged loudly off the lower post to Stephenson's glove side. Joe Watson held up Maltsev at the Flyers' blue line, but the Russians regained control and circled back into their own zone. Kharlamov and Clarke matched up on open ice, and Valeri brought a reaction from the fans when he stickhandled past Bobby, turning the captain around in the process. Still owning a man advantage, the Red Army rampaged toward the Flyers' blue line. The Bullies stood their ground, and what took place over the next minute was furious mayhem. It began with the bulky Dupont dropping Gusev at the blue line, causing the Spectrum's noise level to nearly drown out Cole's call.

Cole: "Gusev is belted hard by Dupont! What a check at the blue line!"

"They weren't used to getting hit," Dupont recalls. "But we were there to play our game, not theirs." The Moose was one of the biggest and baddest members of the Broad Street Bullies. His expressionless face and bone-rattling hits were signature traits, as was his celebratory "Moose Shuffle" when he scored a goal, a takeoff on the elaborate NFL end zone dances of the 1970s.

One of the few NHL players at the time to wear a helmet, Dupont was a product of Trois-Rivières, Quebec, and was originally signed by the New York Rangers, who drafted him eighth overall in 1969. Playing for the Rangers' Nebraska farm team, the Omaha Knights, and their coach Fred Shero, the Moose made himself known immediately and claimed Central Hockey League Rookie of the Year honors by scoring 11 goals and recording 37 points. He followed up by sharing the CHL's Most Valuable Player his second season after producing 15 goals and 46 points. While he was earning CHL hardware, Dupont was becoming known as an enforcer, racking up penalty minutes in startling fashion—258 in his rookie campaign and 308 the following season.

As a young player in the Montreal Juniors, the Moose had lived up to his moniker by packing 250 pounds on his 6-foot-1 frame. Hart joked about Dupont's lack of mobility, saying, "Two guys used to carry him out to the blue line, and he'd slash people as they skated by." The hefty Dupont referred to himself as "de Mooze," but he was mobile enough to appear in three consecutive Memorial Cups with three different clubs and won the 1969 cup with the Montreal Junior Canadiens.

Realizing he needed to shed weight to achieve his goal of playing in the NHL, Dupont dieted down to 205 pounds, which would remain his playing weight over the course of his pro career. He credited retired hockey player Roger Bedard with straightening him out. "He made me lose 40 pounds and get ready to turn pro," Moose once said. Dupont played sparingly for the Rangers, appearing in just seven games in the 1970–1971 season before being dealt to the St. Louis Blues. Over the next two seasons Moose became more of a fixture in the lineup, gaining the starting nod in eighty-five games. Dealt to Philadelphia, Dupont was reunited with Shero, his coach at Omaha. The Fog, a fan of the Moose's physical play, had pushed for the trade.

Though no longer with St. Louis, Dupont continued to leave opponents with the blues. Following a brawl in Vancouver in which Dupont and eight other Flyers were charged by the police for a melee that saw players brawling with fans in the stands, the Moose sat at his locker, naked except for the black helmet on his sandy, sweat-soaked hair, and took a deep drag on a cigarette. "Great trip for us," Dupont told bemused reporters. "We don't go to jail. We beat up their chicken forwards. We win. And now de Mooze drink beer."

Hart thought Dupont's wild side surfaced at strange times. Sometimes, the Moose's victims were his own teammates. When the Flyers obtained Vancouver's Dennis Ververgaert, the forward was going through the pregame skate when Moose cross-checked him and nearly sent the 185-pounder over the boards. Seeing Ververgaert's surprise, Dupont rumbled, "That was just to show you're not with them pansies anymore in Vancouver!"

But the Moose saved his best hits for opponents. Playing Toronto, Dupont chided a Maple Leafs player, "Hey, Swiss Cheese!" When Dornhoefer asked who "Swiss Cheese" was, Moose pointed to Borje Salming. Dornhoefer told Dupont the Toronto defenseman was Swedish and not Swiss. "Same thing," Moose said, and continued to chide Salming: "Hey, Swiss Cheese!"

The Moose was on the receiving end of pain as well. Suffering a dislocated thumb and having it jammed into place by the Flyers' team doctor, Dupont looked more pale than usual. Clarke, seeing Moose in pain, jokingly asked, "Hey, Doc, did Moose cry?" Responding before the doctor could, Dupont remarked, "No, but de Mooze make faces!"

Now it was Gusev making a face following Moose's body blow. "Moose delivered a big hit," remembers Goodenough. "Running into Moose was like running into a brick wall." Dupont's hit registered on the arena's Richter scale and got fans "Flyered" up. Dana T. Graf wrote a year earlier that Sunday crowds at the Spectrum had once been more relaxed and less knowledgeable than the boisterous blue-collar crowds that took over the building for Thursday night games. The Flyers' Stanley Cup seasons changed that, wrote Graf, the crowds becoming "very homogenous." Barber threw another charge into the crowd when he followed Vasiliev into the corner and hammered him into the boards.

Cole told viewers Barber knocked Vasiliev "flying." Barber turned and caught Kharlamov along the boards and sent the Soviet star sailing skates over helmet with a high forearm. "We knew it was going to be rough," Chidlovski says of the Bullies' play. "It wasn't going to be a ballet on ice."

Cole told his audience the Flyers were "getting physical. Kharlamov is really belted by Barber! Kharlamov is still dizzy from that check!"

Tom Bladon told Philadelphia sportswriter Jay Greenberg that the Flyers' bullying of the Soviets wasn't planned. The Stanley Cup champions were wound up emotionally due to the enormous pressure they were under to save the NHL. Peter White of the *Globe and Mail* agreed with Bladon and thought the Flyers were playing on "high emotion." He also believed the Soviets to be startled by the preliminaries, which saw the dimming of arena lights for introductions, the players at the center of spotlights, Kate Smith's "God Bless America," and the booing of Russian players. The Soviets, White wrote, had not seen or heard anything in Super Series '76 like what they were experiencing in the Spectrum.

Mulvoy wrote in *Sports Illustrated* that Schultz "rubbed his glove in Boris Mikhailov's face. . . . Dupont waved his stick under Mikhailov's nose. . . . Van Impe tattooed the stomachs of Alexander Maltsev and Boris Alexandrov. Bill Barber rearranged Valery Vasiliev's helmet. And Clarke reintroduced his hockey stick to Valery Kharlamov's ankle." Dave Anderson of the *New York Times* thought the temperature inside the Spectrum as cold as the atmosphere, "as if somebody had left a window open in Siberia somewhere."

The Bullies were anxious to deal with the Soviets, and the most damaging hit, the hit heard round the hockey world, was soon to be delivered. Van Impe charged out of the penalty box, the tough defenseman drawing a bead on Kharlamov, who was streaking down the right wing. "If Ed Van Impe is on the ice," Lyon recalled, "you had to have your head on a swivel." Kharlamov didn't, and as he skated deep into the Flyers' zone to take a pass from Mikhailov to the left of Stephenson, the unsuspecting winger was dropped by the raised right shoulder and right elbow of Van Impe. Kharlamov was looking down to pick up the puck. "And when he looked up," said Van Impe, "I was there." Van Impe thought a Soviet winger had made "a sucker pass" that forced Kharlamov to turn his head to find the puck. At the same time the puck connected with Kharlamov, Van Impe connected with the Soviet star. "And flattened him," said Van Impe, who said he was just welcoming Kharlamov to Philadelphia.

"Kharlamov ran into Eddie's elbow," says Goodenough, who also spoke to the aggressiveness of a teammate sometimes called Zorro for his educated stickwork. "Ed Van Impe was the only guy who would come back to our bench with hair on his stick."

Cole remarked that Kharlamov was "really belted by Van Impe and he's prostrated on the ice! The Soviets are all standing, they want a penalty! But that was a solid check, and I didn't see much wrong with it." Potvin agreed, adding that the Bullies had the Soviets "leery of them."

Kharlamov lay prone, his gloved hands holding his helmeted head. Kharlamov lay face down, "as if he had been guillotined," wrote Lawrence Martin in *The Red Machine*. Loktev had seen enough. Gesturing toward Gilmour, Loktev shouted, "We never play against such animal hockey!" Gilmour disagreed: "It was a helluva check. A clean check."

Loktev saw the Bullies' play as an intention to damage Red Army players. Irvin said the Bullies were engaging in the roughest exchange of the Super Series. The Soviets' bench demanded Van Impe be penalized, but Gilmour refused and hit the Russians with a two-minute penalty for delay of game. Mikhailov and Loktev waved their gloved hands dismissively at the referee. From his seat in the broadcast booth, where he was doing the national TV telecast with Rangers announcer Marv Albert, Hart thought Kharlamov collapsed "as if he'd been shot."

"I was on the ice when Eddie hit Kharlamov," Jimmy Watson remembers. "Kharlamov tried to cut up ice and Eddie hit him." Van Impe said the fact that Kharlamov had his head down left him vulnerable. When Kharlamov looked up to see where the puck was, Van Impe hit the Russian on the side of the head with his shoulder. "It was perfectly legal," said Van Impe, who saw no reason why Kharlamov should roll around on the ice "looking dead." Jimmy Watson didn't see any reason for

Kharlamov's reaction either. Skating over to the downed Russian, Jimmy told him, "Get up!" Watson then heard Mikhailov, the Red Army's vocal leader, yelling at him, "Be quiet!" Dupont thought Kharlamov was acting more hurt than he was. To the Moose, Kharlamov was Hamlet.

Bill Clement recalls talking with Van Impe and asking about the hit on Kharlamov. "Eddie said, 'I barely touched him. I grazed him and he folded up like a $2 suitcase.'" Hart noted that Barber had delivered a harder blow to a Red Army defenseman and no theatrics had ensued. Clement watched the game on TV and recalls "cheering like hell" for his former teammates. "It was Us against Them," he says of the NHL versus the Soviets. Jimmy Watson says the Flyers were motivated by the belief that the Russian players represented the Soviet Union: "They were the famous Red Army. But you could see that they didn't know what they were dealing with."

Known to his Flyers teammates as "Fast Eddie," a joking reference to his limited skating ability, Van Impe was like so many other members of the Bullies who weren't among the most talented players in the league but were a big asset to their team because they played to their capabilities. For Van Impe, playing to his capabilities meant playing with pain and with a sizable chip on his shoulder. Playing the Oakland Seals in Philadelphia, Van Impe sacrificed his body, dropping down to block a slap shot as Wayne Muloin wound up. The shot drilled Van Impe, and blood splattered on his face and jersey. Van Impe, his jaw stitched up by the Flyers' team doctor, returned to the ice for his next shift and played the remainder of the game. It wasn't known until the next day that Van Impe had continued to play with seven teeth from his upper jaw and three more from his lower jaw sheared off. After the game, Eddie's wife, Diane, drove her husband to Lankenau Hospital. Surgeons removed his shattered teeth, his jaw was wired shut, and Van Impe returned to the Flyers' lineup.

Hart called Van Impe a classic example of a journeyman player who attained a level far above what he might otherwise have achieved due to the intensity of his play, pride in his game, and a work ethic that rivaled Clarke's. Hart thought Van Impe a prototypical Flyer from that era—tough and unyielding, yet with a sense of humor, integrity, and character.

Van Impe was, in Hart's words, "smart, tough, mean, and unbending in front of the net." Hart believed if one word could be used to describe Van Impe's play, it was "mean." Against Vancouver during the 1974–1975 season, Fast Eddie followed who he thought was forward Don Tannahill into a corner and leveled him. Skating past Parent, Van Impe shouted, "I guess that takes care of Tannahill!"

"That wasn't Tannahill," Parent shouted through his goalie mask. "It was [Chris] Oddleifson!" Van Impe shrugged. He might zap the wrong guy, but he would, in Hart's words, "zap *somebody*."

Van Impe's zapping of Kharlamov brought the Spectrum crowd to its feet, but Fast Eddie had not always been a favorite of Philadelphia fans. Second to Boston's Bobby Orr in the 1966 NHL Rookie of the Year voting, the Chicago Black Hawk had balked at being selected by the fledgling Flyers in the 1967 expansion draft. The Saskatoon, Saskatchewan, native struggled along with the rest of the team through the Flyers' growing pains. He was a rock on defense and a rough competitor, averaging 123 penalty minutes in his first three years in Philadelphia. As Van Impe was often on the ice during difficult situations, he became a focal point of the fans' displeasure. Frequently booed by the Spectrum patrons, Fast Eddie persevered, and the catcalls eventually turned to cheers when Van Impe stopped a shot or carried the puck into the attacking zone.

"Eddie could barely skate, barely shoot, and he used his stick like Zorro," says Clement. He also used his elbows, and the Soviets took issue with Van Impe's hit. Loktev, fearing for his players' safety, ordered his team off the ice. Tretiak wrote later that he and his comrades were in full agreement with Loktev's decision. "The game could not go on under such conditions," according to Tretiak, and when the Red Army left the ice, they didn't believe they would return.

"No Red Army player wanted to play against the Flyers," Tretiak wrote. "Each of us believed we could be hit from behind, cross-checked, kicked." Tretiak wondered what kind of sport this was. Whatever it was, he believed it had nothing in common with hockey. Compounding the problem from the Soviet point of view was that in less than a month they would begin training for the Olympics. Tretiak said the Soviet coaches had forbidden their players to fight. The Russians were looking to return home healthy, not injured.

Van Impe scoffed at the Soviets' concerns. His hit on Kharlamov had been within the rules, he said, and Valeri's prone position on the ice was an act. Clement believes the Red Army was intimidated by the Flyers. "They wanted to get the hell out of Philadelphia," he says. "Even before they stepped on the ice they were intimidated by Schultz, Saleski, and Kelly. They were intimidated by the Broad Street Bullies."

CBC cameras caught Loktev screaming at Gilmour and Pavelich (the latter understood Ukranian), in protest of the Flyers' ferocious hits. An angered Gilmour skated away from Red Army coaches and defiantly penalized the Soviets' bench. The forty-two-year-old Gilmour thought he had seen it all in his nineteen-year career as an NHL referee, but this bizarre turn of events was new even for him. A native of Cumberland, British Columbia, Gilmour had wanted to be an NHL player, but his career path was decided by an injury. He grew up dreaming of a career in the NHL, and his play with the Nanaimo Clippers captured the attention of New York Rangers scouts. As a nineteen-year-old prospect, Gilmour suffered debilitating injuries in a logging accident in 1950. The accident caused injuries to his back, hips, legs, and pelvis and put him in the hospital for six months. Though some thought he would never play hockey again, Gilmour returned to the ice. He realized, however, that his injuries would prevent him from being the player he had been, and two months later, he altered his career goals and turned his focus from playing to officiating.

Gilmour began his career as a linesman in 1952 in the Okanagan Senior Amateur Hockey League, then moved up two years later to the Western Hockey League. In the 1950s and early 1960s, he officiated hundreds of minor-league games. Gilmour's goal of a career in the NHL became reality in the early 1960s. His first game took place in the historic Maple Leaf Gardens. He had an up close and personal view of the NHL's expansion from a six-team league to one with eighteen teams, was on the ice for the Vancouver Canucks' first NHL game in 1970, was a fixture in big games, and was respected by coaches and players for being consistent in his play calls.

Gilmour was on the ice for several strange occurrences, including the "Fog Game" in Buffalo in the 1975 Flyers-Sabres Stanley Cup finals. Yet no game in his career was more strange or memorable than the Red Army–Flyers game he was now officiating. That Gilmour was in charge was fitting, since *Sports Illustrated* would call him "the NHL's best official because he is virtually an invisible man on the ice."

Gilmour, however, was very visible in standing up to the Russians. As the Soviets screamed that the Bullies were playing like animals, Flyers superfan Dave Leonardi, who earned national fame as Philadelphia's Sign Man, held up a white placard with the words "TELL IT TO THE CZAR!" in bold black letters. Leonardi's sign was a play on words of his usual "TELL IT TO THE JUDGE!" sign, which he used to taunt visiting coaches and players who complained about the Bullies' play.

With 8:39 remaining in the opening period, an animated Loktev waved his players back to the visitors' locker room, leading the CBC team to express surprise at the Soviets' actions. "The Soviets are leaving!" Irvin exclaimed, prompting Potvin to express disbelief. The Russians, he said, were "acting like a very frustrated hockey club. I think they're displaying very poor sportsmanship."

Those familiar with the Soviets' decades-long practice of Realpolitik—decisions and actions based on practicality rather than ideology—saw irony in the Red Army's protest. The Flyers were playing a style practical for them, not the style the Russians wanted. "We confused them instead of them confusing us," remembers Goodenough. "It was head games."

Throughout the years, the Bullies had been penalized, hung in effigy, hauled into criminal court, brought before NHL brass, and battled fans in the stands. What's an international incident, they thought, compared to years of hell-raising? Shero stood stoically behind the Bullies' bench. He had seen Tarasov wave his team from the ice in dispute during international games. "It's a tactic they use sometimes when the game isn't going their way," he said once. "They always come back."

Joe Watson wasn't so certain. "I honestly didn't know if they would come back," he says. "I think at that point they were looking for a way out. We got aggressive with them, and they wanted out." Dupont remembers being "quite surprised" at the sight of the Soviets skating off the ice. "I thought, 'What the hell is that?' I had never seen a team leave the ice. That game was different. [The Red Army] had a different style, but Freddy was ready for them. They were really confused."

Jimmy Watson recalls that "all hell broke loose. We're only ten minutes into the game and they're leaving. Clarkie said, 'Don't worry. They'll come back.'"

Some saw the Soviet walkout as proof of the claim by the Sabres' Rick Martin that the Russians were machinelike in their play but lacked the heart of NHL players. Leach wasn't so sure. The NHL in the 1970s was "rough and tumble," he wrote in his autobiography. The Russians weren't used to that style of play and had difficulty dealing with it. On the US broadcast, Hart, who was doing the play-by-play, discussed the international incident with Marv Albert. Hart said that while he didn't want to "get political," the Soviets' walkout "doesn't show me a great deal." Albert called the scene "incredible."

Cole issued a call that is among the more memorable in NHL history, telling startled viewers the Red Army was "going home! Yeah, they're going home!"

The forty-three-year-old Cole's career in broadcasting was the result of an unfortunate knee injury suffered playing soccer as a youth. Forced to spend six months in the hospital, Cole passed the time listening to Canadian sportscaster Foster Hewitt calling NHL games on the radio. An interest in sportscasting led Cole to Hewitt's office, where he presented the broadcasting giant an audition tape. Hewitt brought Cole to his office, listened to the tape, and spent two hours talking to his grateful visitor.

Inspired by Hewitt's complimentary words, Cole began his broadcasting career calling hockey games on VOCM radio in St. John's, Newfoundland. He moved to CBC Radio in 1969 and four years later moved on to television and the prestigious *Hockey Night in Canada*. Cole became the lead play-by-play announcer for *Hockey Night in Canada* and a familiar hockey voice in America as well. He would become associated with Toronto Maple Leafs games as well as Stanley Cup contests. He became known for "Coleisms," including "What a dandy!" and "I leaveno to Betsy!"

As Cole, Irvin, and Potvin discussed the Soviets' abrupt departure from the ice, Irvin picked up on Potvin's observation that the Russians were frustrated, pointing out that "they were certainly being outplayed." Irvin remembers what he calls the "famous walkout" and that the Red Army were no angels themselves. "I heard all about their beautiful play and all that crap," he recalls. "The dirtiest game I've ever seen was the Russians versus the Czechs in the 1960s." During the fifteen-minute delay that followed, Campbell huddled with Snider, NHL Players' Association chief Alan Eagleson, and Morrison. They then raced to the Russians' locker room, where they encountered an enraged Loktev.

"We play no more!" Loktev yelled. "Your team the Flyers damage our players!" Loktev told Campbell he wanted to take his players back to Russia in one piece, "not on stretchers!" Campbell was no stranger to tough negotiations. Before becoming NHL president, he had been a lawyer so distinguished he helped represent the Allies against Nazi war criminals at the post–World War II Nuremberg Trials. Charges and countercharges flew fast and furious as Campbell and Loktev argued their cases. Interpreter Adolf "Aggie" Kukulowicz, known as the "Henry Kissinger of hockey" served as interpreter. Kukulowicz was a former New York Ranger who moved to Moscow in 1965 and spoke Russian, Polish, Czech, and Ukrainian. Writer Charles Mandel described him as a "giant of a man who punished his opponents with ease. Off ice, he was a gregarious man who made everyone feel like his best friend." Kukulowicz served as an interpreter during the 1972 Summit Series and is credited with helping make that series a success.

Morrison believed the Soviets were trying to intimidate the NHL into calling a different type of game. The man responsible for assigning NHL referees to games had a long history with the Bullies and their aggressive play. He knew officials "had to be prepared for anything" when working Flyers' games. One night the Flyers would play great hockey and the next night they would come out fighting, leaving officials to wonder, "What the hell's going on here?" The biggest complaint Morrison got from the Bullies was that officials hurt them because their best penalty killers were also their best scorers, and they tired themselves out killing penalties. "That's their own fault," said Morrison.

The NHL's referee-in-chief had little sympathy for the Flyers, but he was also aware that two years earlier, in a game in New Haven, Connecticut, between the Soviet Wings and the New Haven Tomahawks of the AHL, Soviet coach Boris Kulagin had pulled his team from the ice and forced the reversal of a penalty call. In Philadelphia, Morrison and the NHL held firm. According to some, Campbell reminded the Russians they were getting paid $200,000. The NHL president warned Loktev that if the Soviets continued their protest, "then you won't get any money." Kukulowicz translated the Soviet demand that the Bullies change their style of play. "No way!" Morrison snapped. Goodenough recalls standing a few feet away from the talks and hearing Snider shout at the Soviets, "No play, no pay!"

"When Ed Snider told them that, they said, 'Okay,'" Goodenough says. Hart heard that Loktev thought over the ultimatum and relented: "With all the money, we fix the damage."

The Soviets' version of events deep in the Spectrum differed greatly. Loktev told Lawrence Martin the Russians had received their payment upon arrival in North America, "so how could they not pay us?" He reportedly told Snider, Campbell, and Eagleson the Soviets would play, but they had not come to Philadelphia to be part of a boxing match. He stopped the game to show the NHL that this was not hockey as it was meant to be played.

Loktev knew this was a serious step to take, but he didn't want his first line injured. He proposed to Eagleson that the Soviets remove Kharlamov, Mikhailov, and Maltsev and the Flyers sit Clarke, Leach, and Barber to preserve them from injury. If the remaining players on both sides wanted to play rough and fight, so be it. The Red Army agreed to play, the Soviet version goes, after receiving a promise from the NHL that the Flyers' rage would be reined in. Tretiak wrote that only after "prolonged assurances" from the NHL that the game would be played according to the rules did the Red Army agree to play. Loktev warned the NHL that his team would not continue in this type of physical game. Yet it was reported by the CBC during the game that Flyers general manager Keith

Allen angrily retorted that he did not want his team to have to change its style to suit the Soviets.

"Red Army thought the Super Series was over and wanted to get out of Philadelphia as soon as possible and not get injured," Chidlovski recalls. "They didn't want to play this kind of hockey. The Flyers were a team of enforcers. The Russians didn't have players like that on their team. We didn't understand why the Flyers tried to injure Kharlamov. They didn't have to do that."

Loktev argued for the delay of game penalty to be dismissed. Campbell refused, telling the Russians, "You can't change the rules in the middle of the game!" The two-minute bench minor would be enforced, and the Flyers would be on the power play when the game resumed. Irvin thought it "a very dicey moment on the international hockey scene."

"Loktev pulled his team off the ice, and it was said that they were scared, they were chickens," remembers Chidlovski. "But the call by Loktev was justified because of the Olympics. After the Soviets won in New York and Boston and tied in Montreal, from the Russian perspective we had won the Super Series."

Clarke thought the walkout reflected poorly on the Red Army and was bad for Soviet hockey. It appeared as if the Russians were afraid of the Flyers, and Clarke knew that was not the case. The Russians, he said once, were not cowards. On top of that, he didn't feel the Flyers were playing dirty. The Bullies were tough, but that's allowed. It looked to Clarke like Van Impe checked Kharlamov cleanly. Clarke dismissed the Soviets' claim that the Bullies were trying to intimidate them. "You can intimidate only those who allow themselves to be intimidated," the captain said. During the walkout, Clarke met with Brian McFarlane of the CBC for an on-ice interview. Clarke said the Flyers were prepared for such an event because they had met with Eagleson the previous week in Toronto. "Don't be surprised if they walk off the ice or show up half an hour late for the game," Eagleson told the Flyers. "They're going to do all these little things to try and throw you off your game. They try to mess with your mind. They're going to play, so just keep your cool."

Clarke said Shero told his team the Soviets wanted the money, so not to worry about the walkout. Clarke brought up the Russians' actions during their pregame luncheon at the Spectrum: "They're staying five minutes from the Spectrum, and they're half an hour late for the lunch, and we're sitting there like fools. It makes us late for our practice. They tell us the gifts we got for them, they don't want them. They say they've got one stick for each player, and they need sticks. We offer them sticks, and they say our sticks are no good, and they don't want them. They're always doing crazy little things like that, and that's what I hate about them." McFarlane brought up the difference between playing the Soviets and playing the Canadiens or Bruins. "Those other teams have a little class," Clarke said. "The Russians don't."

Van Impe thought it ridiculous for the Soviets to leave the ice, and Barber thought the Red Army might retreat for good. Howie Meeker, a former NHL star and colorful sportscaster, said on the air that if the Russian players didn't return, they should never again be allowed in North America.

The Flyers believed that the Red Army was finding out about the Bullies' brute skill. Philadelphia was controlling the pace of play, and the Soviets were struggling to adapt. "They were so dominant they never had to adjust," Joe Watson says. Goodenough knew the Russians were disciplined, but the Flyers were just as disciplined. "We were beating them at their own game," he says. "As far as the physical aspect of that game, that's how we played. We worked hard and were aggressive." Dupont says the Flyers were simply playing their system, playing their game.

Watching the game in his Moscow home, Chidlovski was amazed at what he saw. "It's still very fresh in my mind," he says. "I knew about the Broad Street Bullies, but I never saw something like this. They intimidated us from the very beginning. It was like hitting a brick wall."

During the lengthy intermission, Hart and Albert filled up air time on their telecast by discussing the various signs they were seeing inside the packed Spectrum: "Soviets, go home!" "Flyers will emerge victorious!" "Flyers are the best in the world!"

The Red Army returned to the ice, in the words of Tretiak, "totally frustrated. Everything was turned inside-out." Some thirty seconds after play resumed, Leach lived up to his reputation as the Rifle. Skating to Tretiak's stick side as Barber wound up, Leach deflected the puck into the net. Potvin noted that Leach "has a habit of coming in from behind the net and standing in front when the shot is taken." Leach, Potvin added, provided a "perfect deflection, and Tretiak never had a chance."

Leach's power play goal came at 11:38, Barber gaining an assist. Leach showed once again the acumen of Keith "The Thief" Allen when it came to building the Bullies. In Leach's two seasons with the California Golden Seals prior to joining the Flyers, he totaled 45 goals. The Rifle matched that mark in his first season in Philadelphia and was on his way to a league-high 61 by the end of the 1976 regular season. Hart believed no Flyer ever shot like the Rifle. "Reggie," Hart wrote, "was the ultimate sniper."

For a player boasting such a big shot, the Rifle preferred a small stick and blade. "The smaller the stick," Leach said once, "the better the control." Hart credited the Rifle with popularizing the now-common phrase "five hole" to describe the area between the goalie's legs. Leach designated the upper left and upper right corners of the net as the number one and number two holes, respectively. The number three and number four holes were the lower left and lower right corners. Leach knew the goalie had to move left or right or come out, and it was while he was moving that he was most vulnerable between the pads.

Along with being nicknamed the Rifle, Leach was also known as "The Chief" due to his Indigenous heritage. Reggie was active in his offseason association with fellow Indgigenous peoples, and was involved in a Billings, Montana, junior hockey club. While the Rifle fired up the Flyers' offense, the Bullies' aggressive forechecking frustrated the Russians' hopes of countering. Cole thought the Soviets were "completely disorganized" by the Flyers.

The Bullies were in high gear, hitting every Soviet player in sight and forechecking ferociously. As the intensity ratcheted up, tempers flared. Jimmy Watson was dropped to the ice, and Lutchenko was battered at the Bullies' blue line. Vasiliev battled Bridgman and Dornhoefer along the boards, and Clarke barreled into Solodukhin in the Soviet end. The Red Army and Broad Street Bullies had elbows up and were playing hard through the whistles, leading to extracurriculars along the boards and in the corners.

Near the end of the period, the Flyers got a partial breakaway when the Red Army got caught up ice. MacLeish outskated the Soviets, swooping in on Tretiak and, taking advantage of Dornhoefer running interference, wristing a shot past Tretiak's upraised left shoulder.

Potvin: "Tretiak made the move down and MacLeish put it in the top corner. Beautiful!"

The score came at 17:37, with an assist going to Lonsberry, and the Flyers' 2–0 lead left the cradle of liberty rocking. That MacLeish would score a clutch goal surprised no one in the Spectrum. "MacLeish was the most talented player on our team," Goodenough states. He was also the target for some of Clarke's verbal jabs. Goodenough recalled Clarke approaching MacLeish before a game and snapping, "Hey, Hawk, can you at least break a freakin' sweat tonight and score a couple goals?" Giving as good as he got, the Hawk snapped back. "Screw you, Clarkie!" Goodenough remembers what happened next: "MacLeish went out, scored a couple of goals, and we won."

The Hawk was the Flyers' first big goal scorer and point producer. MacLeish's trademark was to skate down the right side, cut to his left past the slot, and unload what Hart called "that fabulous wrist shot." MacLeish rarely showed emotion, be it elation or pain. Instead, he would wipe his hand across his face, a move Hart took to mean the Hawk was wiping away an expression along with his sweat. As the Flyers' second-line center, MacLeish anchored a line that was as complementary to his talents as the LCB Line was to Clarke's. Flanked by wingers Lonsberry and Dornhoefer, the Flyers' second line impressed with their abilities. Hart considered the second line "a wonderful contrast to the feeding center and scoring wings" of the LCB Line.

The contrast in the Bullies' top two lines could be traced to the contrast in the centermen. Clarke and MacLeish were great centers and competitors, and while neither was physically imposing, both were extremely strong from the waist down. Hart said that while Clarke used his tremendous leg drive to grind away, MacLeish used his to glide away.

Where Clarke's additional strength was in his mind, the added strength of MacLeish was in his huge wrists.

Humble and shy, the Hawk was also tough. MacLeish so battered and bloodied Red Wing Hank Boucha in Detroit that few opponents would physically challenge the Hawk again. MacLeish could take physical punishment as well. In a game in the Los Angeles Forum, the Hawk slipped and fell to the ice in front of Marcel Dionne. Though it appeared that the Kings' forward tripped over the fallen Flyer, it became apparent when MacLeish failed to rise that something was wrong. Dionne's razor-sharp skate had sliced MacLeish's neck just a fraction of an inch from his jugular vein. It was the Hawk's great fortune that Everett Borghesani, the Flyers' oral surgeon, happened to be making his first trip to the West Coast with the club. Grabbing his suture kit, Borghesani raced to MacLeish's aid and closed the wound with eighty-eight stitches. With MacLeish out of danger, the Flyers hung a sign in their locker room reading, "What's the difference between Hawk MacLeish and Frankenstein's monster? Two stitches."

MacLeish's score allowed the Bullies to carry a 2–0 lead into the first intermission. As the period ended, Flyers fans showed their appreciation with a standing ovation. The Bullies' domination of the first twenty minutes was reflected not only on the scoreboard but also in the stat sheet. The Flyers averaged nearly a shot a minute and owned a 17–2 advantage over a Red Army team that was trying to figure out Shero's Iron Curtain. If they expected the kind of rout they had achieved against the Rangers and Bruins, the Russians were experiencing a reality check. The Flyers had taken away the Soviets' downhill leverage, Shero's defense representing a Rubik's Cube the Russians couldn't comprehend. Spaced along their blue line, the Flyers were going chest-to-chest with the Russians, the Bullies' big bodies blunting the breakout patterns that were signatures of the Soviet style.

Ted Lindsay thought a lot of people were fooled by the Flyers. "They think of the Flyers only as a muscle club," he said at the time to writer Frank Bertucci. "They are a disciplined club. They play the way most of the teams used to play."

The old-school Flyers were beating the new-school Soviets, and Tim Burke of the *Montreal Gazette* thought that what was taking place on Spectrum ice was "one of the most remarkable displays of preparedness, discipline, and unflappability in the annals of sport." The Flyers' play, Burke wrote, was "elevating Shero's systematic approach to the game beyond question."

The Red Army was frustrated, but the Flyers found it difficult to tell how much. Like other NHL players, the Bullies wondered what manner of men the Russians were. "It's impossible to tell," Sabres center Peter McNab said after facing the Soviet Wings. "They have no emotion at all."

The start of the second period would see emotions run high as the Soviets sought to take control, and the Bullies battled to keep it. "We knew," Jimmy Watson remembers, "they had the ability to come back."

CHAPTER 8

The Soviets Strike Back

TENSION WAS MOUNTING WITH EACH PASSING MINUTE IN THE EPIC encounter between Central Red Army and the Philadelphia Flyers. By the start of the second period, it was becoming clear that the Broad Street Bullies had succeeded in seizing physical control of the contest from the Soviets. As Bobby Clarke and Aleksandr Maltsev returned to center ice for the faceoff and puck drop by Lloyd Gilmour, a big question on the minds of the more than seventeen thousand fans shoehorned into the Spectrum and the millions watching worldwide was, how would the Russians respond?

The first period had seen the Soviets put off their game by the strategy of Fred Shero and the rough play of his Bullies. Vladislav Tretiak later wrote of the Russians' bewilderment at what they were facing: "We didn't know that a pack of barbarians could put on skates and get away with hunting hockey players in front of thousands of spectators." What the Flyers had demonstrated, he said, was their usual style. He knew that even among NHL players the Bullies were considered "monstrously brutal."

Red Army coach Konstantin Loktev pulled no punches in describing with disgust the Bullies' style of play. "Animal hockey," he spat. Yet there was more to Shero's game plan than extracurricular activities. Larry Goodenough notes that along with their 1–4 alignment the Flyers also employed a 2–1–2 scheme, the latter differing from the former in that two Philly wingers were at the top of the circles and two were near the goal line. The Flyers' wingers up front sought to force their Soviet counterparts to either side, while the defenders down low controlled their corners. The Flyers' centerman was in a supportive role, assisting where needed.

Shero knew his Keystone State neighbors, the Pittsburgh Penguins, overcame their confusion over how to play the Soviet Wings and adjusted in the second period. Rather than chase the puck and fall prey to the Russians' elaborate skating, the Pens took the body. Down 5–0, Pittsburgh's punishing forechecking led to a 4–2 scoring advantage the rest of the game. The film of the Pittsburgh game proved beneficial to Buffalo, who scripted their game plan to keep their defensemen at their own blue line. The Sabres' pugnacious general manager, Punch Imlach, told his burly defensemen to pound the Soviets and wear them down, to hit them hard and often. Taking advantage of Memorial Auditorium's smallish surroundings and shrinking it further with big bodies, the Sabres shored up the neutral zone; at the same time, their French Connection line took the play to the Soviet defensemen. By the game's end, the Stanley Cup finalists from the season before skated to a 12–6 win. In Montreal, the Canadiens likewise built on the Pens' plan and pursued the Russian puck carrier. The Habs outplayed the Red Army, but Tretiak's superior play was a prime factor in the 3–3 tie.

The Bullies' blueprint incorporated elements from the success of the Penguins, Sabres, and Canadiens. Like the Habs, Shero sent in his centerman to forecheck. In a style similar to the Sabres, the Flyers manned their blue line rather than pursue the puck carrier. And in a manner consistent with both Buffalo and Pittsburgh, the Bullies took the body, physically punishing the Russians. "The Flyers were like freedom fighters in that game," remembers Arthur Chidlovski.

The Spectrum had become a house of horrors for the Soviets, and in an interview with reporters between periods, Ed Snider stated that intimidation was the Flyers' way, it was the NHL way, and that the Bullies were better than the Russians. The Flyers' physical play tipped the ice in their favor. Clarke won the second-period face-off from Maltsev, and Jimmy Watson fed Reggie Leach for a one-timer from the right wing. The shot went wide and was retrieved by Bill Barber along the boards. The winger fed his captain behind the net, but Clarke lost the puck to

Aleksandr Gusev, who sailed it up ice and into the Flyers' zone. Moments later, the Red Army had the puck in their zone, and Bob Cole described on Canadian Broadcasting Company television the precision passing that was the Soviets' signature.

Cole: "They set up the box in their own zone and try to get this system moving . . ."

Boris Mikhailov and Valeri Kharlamov played keep-away from Rick MacLeish. When Gary Dornhoefer pressured Gusev, the Soviets saw their opening. Mikhailov took control of the puck and threaded a pass through the Flyers' defense and onto the tape of a streaking Kharlamov. The Russian rocketed past Andre Dupont and zeroed in on goalie Wayne Stephenson. Unable to keep pace with Kharlamov, the Moose used his stick to catch the right skate of the Russian winger from behind and send him airborne. Knocked flying by the Flyers again, Kharlamov landed on the seat of his red hockey shorts and slid into the end boards.

Dupont headed to the penalty box for two minutes for hooking, and at the 18:52 mark the Red Army had a man advantage. Clarke and Maltsev lined up in the face-off circle to Stephenson's left, and once again the Flyers' captain won the draw. Barber nearly broke in on Tretiak, but Guzev bodied him off the puck. Jimmy Watson took aim on Guzev in the open ice, but the Soviet sidestepped him. Out on the flanks, Barber's matchups with Mikhailov and Kharlamov fascinated fans and media. Cole commented that Barber was watching Kharlamov "very closely."

Maltsev took a pass from Valeri Vasiliev and carried the puck past center ice but lost it when he leapt to avoid the imposing figure of Ed Van Impe. Maltsev arose covered in ice chips and looked toward the Soviet zone to see Mikhailov knock the puck away from Clarke. The Russians regrouped, and Kharlamov led a charge past the Bullies' blue line. The Flyers took control, and Orest Kindrachuck delivered to Don Saleski. Big Bird got around Gusev and took aim at Tretiak, wristing a shot to the goalie's stick side. Kindrachuk fired another quick shot, but Tretiak kicked the puck away and the Red Army went on the offensive.

Boris Aleksandrov's pass to Vladimir Vikulov in the crease went awry when Vikulov whiffed on his shot. The puck went into the corner, and Tom Bladon took over for the Flyers. He passed to Saleski along the boards, and Big Bird found Kindrachuk at center ice. In a classic give-and-go, Kindrachuk sent the puck back to Saleski, who was barreling in on Tretiak from the right wing.

Saleski's blast was blocked by Tretiak, but the puck remained free as Joe Watson, trailing the play, drove the net and took the advice of Spectrum Sign Man Dave Leonardi, positioned behind Tretiak, to "INSERT HERE!"

Cole: "Rebound! He scores! Joe Watson!"

The hard-charging defenseman backhanded a rebound past Tretiak, who had fallen and couldn't control the puck. It was the first shorthanded goal scored against the Red Army in Super Series '76 and came on assists from Saleski and Kindrachuk. Watson's goal also marked just the second time in sixteen games an NHL player scored a shorthanded goal against the Soviets; the first was Pete Mahovlich's goal in 1972.

Watson's score was particularly satisfying to Kindrachuk. Nicknamed "Oscar the Grouch" after the *Sesame Street* character, the cranky Kindrachuk had Ukrainian grandparents who suffered under Soviet rule. In the booth, Dick Irvin Jr. remarked to viewers that the Bullies were "flying" up ice, and Denis Potvin added that "the Soviets were caught with only one man back."

The Red Army's weakness was its defense; the club was not as strong in that area as other teams in Soviet hockey—namely, Dynamo Moscow and Spartak. "A couple of teams in Soviet hockey played strong defense," Chidlovski says, "but Red Army was known for its offense. That was its forte."

Shero saw additional flaws in the Soviets' style. The Russians, he thought, weren't very good on face-offs, and they did a lot of unnecessary skating, a lot of retreating, looking to get defenders to leave their position. But the Bullies wouldn't be enticed out of position. It took patience to beat the Soviets, and the Flyers were playing a patient game. The Red

Army's lack of defense was apparent on Joe Watson's goal. "I would get across center ice maybe a couple of times each season," he recalls. "After the game, Freddy [Shero] told me I set the Russian hockey program back twenty years with that goal."

Flyers teammates called Joe Watson "Thundermouth." Gene Hart wrote that as a child Joe must have been vaccinated with a phonograph needle. "He had that rare ability to chatter on incessantly," Hart said, "no matter where he was." Hart called Joe "the vocal conscience" of the Flyers. He saw him as possibly the "first overt tell-it-like-it-is player" on the Flyers, and that helped make him an asset to his team. If the Bullies won a game that was poorly played, Joe told reporters, "We won, but we shouldn't have. We stunk."

During a fight-filled playoff game in Toronto in 1976 that spilled over into the crowd, Joe swung his stick over the glass of the penalty box and accidentally hit a Toronto police constable. Following the game, Thundermouth joked, "If I go to jail, I hope I get Harold's old cell!"—a reference to Maple Leafs owner Harold Ballard's recent confinement. Before Thundermouth could say anymore that might raise the ire of Toronto authorities, Dupont warned him, "Don't kid, Joe."

Earlier in his career, Joe had been so unhappy with the Flyers' struggles that he considered retirement. He was talked out of it, and he proved hugely beneficial to the Flyers. It was Joe who talked his brother Jimmy into picking Philadelphia and the NHL over Calgary of the rival World Hockey Association. Without the Watson brothers and their defensive skills, Hart said, the Flyers might not have won Stanley Cups in 1974 and 1975.

That he was a defense-minded defenseman made Joe Watson's score against Tretiak more surprising. It came 2:44 into the second period, and Leonardi captured the heady feeling among frenzied Flyers fans in the Spectrum, holding up a placard reading "BEST IN THE WORLD." Leonardi arrived at the Spectrum that afternoon prepared, as he once recalled, "for a hard-fought game." Like everyone else, he never expected the Russians to walk out as they did in the first period. He added to the raucous atmosphere inside the Spectrum when he taunted the Soviets with signs reading "CHICKEN" and "TELL IT TO THE CZAR!"

Leonardi began bringing signs to Flyers games in 1972. Sign Man's professionally printed placards coincided with the action on the ice and captured both the mood of the game and the attention of Flyers fans and players—as well as opposing players and NHL officials working the game. Leonardi's signs usually brought smiling acknowledgments, even from enemy players and officials. Yet on one occasion in the early 1970s, Leonardi's placard of an eye chart for the officiating crew received an unfavorable response. Interestingly, it involved Matt Pavelich, the same linesman working the Flyers' game with the Soviets. When Pavelich saw Leonardi's eye chart sign, he skated past Sign Man and barked, "You're a horsebleep artist, too!" Leonardi stressed that Pavelich did indeed say, "Horsebleep."

Leonardi's fame spread to the point that he was included with Derek Sanderson, Dave Williams, Don Cherry, and Peter Puck in a Hockey Hall of Fame time capsule capturing notable characters from the 1970s. His signs were sometimes tailored to the sentiments of his fellow fans inside the Spectrum and were welcomed by fans because they reflected what many were thinking. Each placard measured 19 by 22 inches, and he reportedly brought one hundred signs to each game. Another three hundred signs were kept in his home.

Among the more favored placards held up by Leonardi included:

TELL IT TO THE CZAR (Message to the Russians)

OUTTA SIGHT (When Stephenson or Bernie Parent made a great save)

BC SUPERSTAR (Bobby Clarke)

TKO SCHULTZ (Celebrating another knockout victory by the Hammer)

NEXT GOALIE (Heralding the opponent's change of goalies in a Flyers rout)

REF CHART (Eye chart)

START THE BUS (Used when the Flyers were closing in on a win)

HAVE A NICE SUMMER (To opponents eliminated in the playoffs)

Irvin thought Sign Man one of the stars of the Spectrum show. Leonardi was often included in pregame meetings with the network televising the game so producers could be aware of what signs he brought and when he expected to use them. Network cameramen trained their cameras on Sign Man at the appropriate time during the game. Irvin's favorite sign came in 1975, in the Flyers' Stanley Cup Final against the Sabres, and it did not involve Leonardi. In the famous "Fog Game" in Buffalo, a bat fluttered amid the players until Jim Lorentz batted it to the ice with his stick. Kate Smith was the Flyers' good-luck charm, and when the two teams returned to Buffalo for Game 6, one Buffalo fan had a sign inside Memorial Auditorium reading, "THE FLYERS HAVE KATE SMITH AND WE HAVE AN OLD BAT TOO." Irvin chuckled at the sign. "That one," he said, "is tough to top."

The Flyers enjoyed Sign Man's work. Leach loved Leonardi's signs and looked forward to each one. The Rifle spotted Sign Man in the crowd in the game against the Soviets, his dark mustache framing a frown at the Red Army.

Clarke once again won the faceoff from Maltsev, and the short-handed Flyers got off another shot, this one a blast by Barber from the left circle that was blocked by Tretiak. The Soviets sought to mount an offensive, but Vikulov was bounced off the puck by Van Impe. The Flyers continually disrupted the Soviets' stickhandling, deterring their planned attack and forcing the Red Army to regroup. The Red Machine was sputtering; defenseman Sergei Glazov finally sent a long shot in on Stephenson, a drive completely out of character for the Soviets.

The crowd cheered Stephenson's save, then cheered even louder when Bob Kelly rushed onto the ice and began a prolonged battle with Glazov. Kelly's high-octane offense sent Glazov sprawling, and Kelly turned his attention to Alexei Volchenkov.

Cole: "Kelly's all over the place!"

"Hound was like a pinball machine," Goodenough recalls. "He was all over the ice. That was his turf. He owned it."

Dana T. Graf thought Kelly's "physical rabble-rousing and overall drive" caused Shero to "scrap his highly acclaimed system of positional hockey" and employ a "box and one" scheme similar to basketball. A "four-man zone," wrote Graf, "with Bob going after whoever has the puck. It's really fun to watch." Kelly's pinball play amped up the intensity, and players on both sides were picking themselves up off the ice. This was the Bullies' type of game.

Cole: "The Soviets, completely disorganized in their own zone. The Flyers are all over them . . ."

The Russians had a scoring opportunity, but Joe Watson made another big play, tying up Vladimir Popov in front of the net and preventing the forward from taking a pass from Maltsev. Dave Schultz carried the puck along the boards and into the Soviet zone, and moments later Kharlamov had possession of the puck and was racing to the Flyers' end. Van Impe muscled Mikhailov in the corner to Stephenson's right, and after the Flyers iced the puck, Clarke won another faceoff, this time in the left face-off circle. The CBC crew noted the captain's popularity. Irvin said Clarke "won the applause meter award for the largest ovation."

Irvin was familiar with Clarke, Flyers fans, and the Spectrum. He had seen the Flyers' first Stanley Cup title in 1974, and he respected their talent. When the Flyers won the Stanley Cup, Irvin thought there was "no shortage of skilled players on the team; far from it." Irvin saw Clarke as a player who excelled on offense and defense and Parent as a magnificent goaltender who upped his game in the postseason. Barber, Leach, and MacLeish were first-rate players who largely left the brawling to the other members of the "Mad Squad." Still, Irvin was aware of what he called the "handwringing" concerning the high-gloss treatment given to the Flyers' fighting. It was the part of their game, Irvin said, that made the Broad Street Bullies the "terror of their opponents and the darlings of box office managers around the NHL." The records for penalty minutes and the attention paid to Dupont, Schultz, Saleski, and Kelly overshadowed at times the play of the Flyers who, in Irvin's words, "were skillfully putting the puck into the other team's net or keeping it out of theirs."

Like many others, Irvin knew of the Philly Flu. He'd heard of players who suddenly found themselves afflicted with ailments that prevented them from suiting up in the Spectrum. These same players, Irvin said, "would then make a miraculous recovery and suit up for the next game, somewhere else."

Born in 1932 and forty-three years old at the time of Super Series '76, the Calgary, Alberta, native was a future inductee in both the Hockey Hall of Fame and the Canadian Association of Broadcasters Hall of Fame for his lengthy career as a sports broadcaster and author. Irvin served as color commentator on CBC's *Hockey Night in Canada*, often working the broadcasts of Montreal Canadiens games with play-by-play partner Danny Gallivan. Gallivan addressed his broadcast partner as "Richard," even though Irvin's full name is James Dickenson Irvin Jr. In the 1970s and 1980s, Irvin was both color commentator and studio host for Canadiens telecasts, and his movement between the broadcast booth and ice level meant he was often absent from both the start and finish of the three periods. He worked for *Hockey Night in Canada* from 1966 to 1999, making him the longest-serving member of the CBC broadcast. He also changed roles and provided play-by-play radio commentary for Canadiens games not televised on *Hockey Night in Canada*. Irvin's father, Dick Sr., was a hockey coach credited with being the first to change lines while the puck was in play. Dick Jr. wrote that articles about that piece of Irvin strategy noted the "three-minute shifts." What he was witnessing from the Flyers against the Soviets was Shero's strategy of using his players in one-minute shifts, the Bullies skating hard and heading off the ice.

Shero's short shifts kept his players fresh, and the Flyers needed the rest as the Russians returned to the attack. Maltsev, Mikhailov, Kharlamov, and Gusev applied pressure, with Gusev's shot gloved by Stephenson.

Irvin: "Stephenson made a pretty good stop on a very quick shot. The Soviets have been so impressive the way that they can shoot the puck."

As the period approached the eight-minute mark, Dornhoefer was drilled along the boards by Aleksandrov. MacLeish let loose a hard shot that was turned away by Tretiak and cleared by Vikulov. MacLeish bore down on Tretiak but was brought down by defenseman Vladimir Lokotko. Dornhoefer and Schultz banged the Soviets around deep in their own zone, but Aleksandrov retaliated, charging into Dupont along the far boards. The Russians resumed their weaving patterns and got off two shots—the first by Viktor Kutyergin and the next by Glazov—that were handled by Stephenson.

The Red Army was ratcheting up its intensity, and Cole said the Soviets were taking over again. The Bullies were waiting, and their fore-checking continued to frustrate the Red Army. Cole said the Flyers were "forechecking the Red Army back in their own zone. [The Russians] can't seem to figure this out at all."

The Soviets' frustrations could be traced to the Flyers knowing, as Jimmy Watson says, the Red Army's game plan: "They looked to move the puck around, spread you out, get you up ice, and then get odd-man rushes." Popov got loose across the Bullies' blue line before being belted by Mel Bridgman. Kutyergin picked up the loose puck and blasted a bullet from the right point that went over Stephenson's arm at the 10:48 mark. Cole called it a goal "fired with blistering speed that Stephenson didn't see."

Meanwhile, Popov was down on all fours and was helped to the Soviets' bench by Glazov and Kharlamov. Popov was a solid third-liner, experienced in international competition. He had already helped the Red Army roll to Soviet titles in 1971–1973 and 1975. Because the Red Army used the USSR's military draft to enlist the nation's top hockey talent, competition was keen to make the team. Popov withstood challenges to his position on the club, and his play in Super Series '76 was considered by many his best in international competition.

Kutyergin surprised the Bullies with his heat-seeking slap shot, and his score came sans helmet, his headgear having been knocked off when he and Kelly crashed along the glass. The goal came with an assist from Popov and marked the Red Army's sixth shot on Stephenson. The game had tightened, and with so much on the line, Clarke cursed the Soviets' score. CBC cameras showed Clarke bent forward on the ice, nearly convulsed in anger, as the red lamp lit up signifying the goal. Potvin pointed to the Bullies' breakdown on defense. It was a mix-up, he said, the Flyers having four players on one side of the ice.

Kutyergin's goal quieted the crowd, but the Soviets, as was their style, showed little emotion. "They never smiled," McNab observed following Buffalo's game with the Wings, "even when they scored."

Having reduced their deficit to 3–1, the Russians rallied behind Kharlamov, Maltsev, Mikhailov, and Vasiliev, all of whom turned up the pressure on the Flyers' defense. Leach saw the Red Army advancing and thought this was the passing game the Soviets had perfected. Of all the Soviet players, Kharlamov stood out the most to Leach. The Russian winger streaked up and down the ice and was, in Leach's opinion, a magician with the puck.

The Red Army's offensive forced a power play situation as Van Impe was whistled for high-sticking. Volchenkov twice wound up from inside the Flyers' blue line and slapped hard shots at Stephenson, the first of which Wayne blocked and the second stopped before getting on goal. Kharlamov nearly had an empty net goal, but Stephenson leaned into the crease to block the shot.

Irvin told viewers that this was the first time the Soviets had the flow of play going their way. Potvin pointed out that the Russians controlled the puck very well once they got inside the Flyers' zone: "The Flyers had been able to keep them out of the zone, but now the Soviets are piercing."

The Red Army, said Cole, was coming on strong. Irvin noted with 5:48 remaining in the period that the Russians had directed 16 shots at the Flyers' goal, 7 on net. Potvin pointed out that the Soviets "seem to be gaining a little bit of their poise."

The Bullies killed off the penalty, and Dornhoefer directed a shot that ricocheted off the glass. Dornhoefer was again active in his shift, the black-bearded forward keeping the puck in the Russian zone. Writing for the *Hockey News* in its January 9, 1976, issue, Bill

Fleischman said Dornhoefer exemplified the Flyers' consistency as much as Clarke, Lonsberry, or Watson. "Dornhoefer is a vital part of the Rick MacLeish-Lonsberry line," wrote Fleischman, "a fact that is more noticeable even when the veteran right winger's shooting radar isn't functioning."

Dornhoefer would throw his 6-foot-1, 190-pound frame at enemy players, or turn his back on goalies to throw them off their game. The latter aspect of Dornhoefer's game moved Vancouver Canucks coach/general manager Phil Maloney to state, "Gary Dornhoefer has been standing in the crease since he was 10 years old."

It was Dornhoefer's way of contributing when he wasn't scoring. "When I'm not scoring, I feel I have to do other things to help the team," Dornhoefer said at the time. "I've found that by bothering the goaltender you can pick up a lot of points." Hart wrote that Dornhoefer's screening the enemy goalie for a teammate's shot was "a custom which made him the target of every defenseman (and goaltender) in the league, save his own." Nykoluk said Dornhoefer was the best in the league at getting in front of the goalie. "It takes a lot of courage to stand there," Nykoluk told Fleischman. "You know you'll get knocked on your butt and the puck can do strange things when someone is shooting at you."

In 1976, Dornhoefer was in his twelfth season as a Flyer, and he had his share of cuts, bruises, and broken bones. Hart said once that Dornhoefer's objective throughout his eventual fourteen-year career was to play one season without an injury. Hart thought Dornhoefer, more than any player he'd seen, "consistently sacrificed his body for the good of the team." Dornhoefer was once hit in the back of the head by a puck that was headed for MacLeish, but Hawk dodged it at the last second. "I ducked and the puck hit Dorny," MacLeish told Fleischman. Despite his physical pains, the thirty-two-year-old Dornhoefer had a reputation as one of the fiercest competitors in the NHL, which was vividly illustrated against the Soviets.

Fleischman said Dornhoefer's friends suggested that when he retired, his elbows should be sent to the Hockey Hall of Fame, and Hart agreed that Dornhoefer was as much known for his razor-sharp elbows as his acerbic wit. The Bullies joked that Dornhoefer spent time between periods sharpening his elbows. Before the Flyers became the Broad Street Bullies, Dornhoefer was one of the few members of the team who played aggressively in enemy buildings. He was a favorite of Spectrum fans and, in Fleischman's words, "a classy veteran who turns tiger on the ice."

Turning tiger against the Russians, Dornhoefer joined Kindrachuk, Schultz, and Leach in pressuring Tretiak, but the Soviet goalie stood firm. Tretiak's game was based on his ability to play the angles and place himself in the best possible position to block the shot. The Flyers were finding that Tretiak positioned himself deeper in the crease than did his NHL counterparts, who were known for challenging shooters. Phil Esposito thought Tretiak's position in the crease too deep, but Tretiak was playing the position as Russian goalies were taught. "He made some great saves," Dupont remembers. "He played an exceptional game."

With just over two minutes to go in the period, Leach and Aleksandrov got their sticks up high in a brief tussle and were sent to the penalty box for roughing. Gilmour tacked on an extra two minutes to Aleksandrov's penalty, citing unsportsmanlike conduct. NHL players had been saying since the 1972 Summit Series that the Soviets employed questionable tactics. Clarke considered the Soviets the dirtiest players he'd ever seen. Paul Henderson recalled the Russians spearing with their sticks. Esposito said the Russians speared players behind their kneecaps. The Soviets were known to turn on each other as well. Red Army players were heard sniping at one other in their game against the Rangers. Cole thought some of the comments the Soviets made to each other were incredible. "They chew each other out," he noted.

"They were yelling at the referees all the time," remembers Dupont. "They wanted to run the game. They should've concentrated on trying to beat us."

Aleksandrov's hot temper and salty language led to a misconduct penalty for cursing at Pavelich; the Russians didn't realize the linesman understood their language. Aleksandrov was among the more combative Soviet players, once violently spearing Valentin Gureyev in a Soviet League game. As the period wound down, Clarke and Kharlamov faced off in the circle to Tretiak's left; Clarke won the draw. Moments later,

Clarke was called offside by Russian linesman Yury Karandin, and the Flyers' captain shook his head in disagreement with the call. Clarke then headed toward the Russian official to voice his displeasure but was intercepted by a teammate and steered toward the bench.

Kharlamov took the puck into the Flyers' zone but had his pocket picked by Kindrachuk. Carrying the puck into the Soviets' end of the ice, Kindrachuk fed Joe Watson, who once again drove the net. This time, Tretiak blocked Watson's shot. Dornhoefer centered to Joe Watson, whose point-blank shot was blocked by the sprawling Tretiak. Cole exclaimed on air that Tretiak again came up with "a great save!"

Tretiak provided more acrobatics, this time on a blistering blast by Bladon. He followed this by dropping to his knees to deflect a rifle shot from Leach. With some forty seconds remaining in the period, Tretiak blocked Barber's shot, and Leach's attempt at a rebound goal was high. Ross Lonsberry's long drive with three ticks remaining went wide.

Irvin thought the Red Army had regained its poise and produced more scoring chances. The Russians' rally reflected coaching adjustments made by Konstantin Loktev and assistants Anatoli Firsov and Veniamin Aleksandrov. Firsov and Aleksandrov were Hall of Fame talents who had played for the Red Army. Firsov was a forerunner to Kharlamov in that he was a small but quick player with superior skills and speed. Video shows Firsov to be a blur as he defeated double-teams, deked defensemen, and powered the puck past goalies.

Born in Moscow in February 1941, Anatoli was a month old when his father was killed in Russia's war against Nazi Germany. Raised by a single mother in a family with three children, he grew up knowing financial difficulties. Finding refuge in sports, he played bandy in the winter and soccer in the summer. Not until age fifteen did he play ice hockey, and though he struggled initially with the equipment—hockey sticks are larger than their bandy counterparts—Firsov would become one of the great players in Soviet history.

A forward, Firsov first suited up for Spartak Moscow in 1954 and then for CSKA Moscow from 1961 to 1974. He earned prestigious Soviet Union civilian awards—Orders of the Badge of Honor and the Red Banner of Labour—for his deeds and services to the Soviet state.

Firsov's coaching career began in 1972 when he began serving as a player-coach for the Red Army, and four years later he was an assistant on the team battling the Broad Street Bullies.

Aleksandrov's career in Soviet hockey lasted from 1955 to 1969, playing with CSKA Moscow. During his fifteen years as a player, Aleksandrov's teams won ten Soviet titles, including four straight twice (1958–1961, 1963–1966). A four-time USSR All-Star, Aleksandrov set a Soviet championships record in 1963 that still stands, scoring 53 goals in a single season. From 1956 to 1968, Aleksandrov played for Russian national teams that won two gold medals and one bronze in the Winter Olympics; six golds, three silvers, and two bronze medals in the world championships; and nine European championships.

Aleksandrov's play in exhibition matches in North America in 1957 so impressed the Chicago Black Hawks that they added the forward to their negotiation list. On December 14, 1963, Aleksandrov and the Soviet National Team met the Toronto Marlboros in an exhibition game. The Toronto team included junior stars from other clubs, including Bobby Orr, Serge Savard, and Derek Sanderson. Aleksandrov earned induction into the Russian and Soviet Hockey Hall of Fame in 1963 and the IIHF Hall of Fame in 2007. He earned lasting fame in the Soviet Union as a member of the one of the great lines in Russian history, teaming with Loktev and Aleksandr Almetov on a unit that reportedly recorded more than 250 goals in approximately one hundred games. Before joining Loktev's Red Army's staff, Aleksandrov was head coach of SKA Leningrad in 1973–1974.

Aleksandrov teamed with Firsov and former linemate Loktev to design strategies that led to the Red Army averaging five goals per game against NHL opponents in Super Series '76. One period remained in the climactic final game against the Flyers, and the Soviets sought to continue their comeback. The Bullies, meanwhile, looked to reclaim control of the contest.

Twenty more minutes would tell the final story of Super Series '76.

CHAPTER 9

Fort Wayne

As the third period began, there at center ice with referee Lloyd Gilmour stood Bobby Clarke, Reggie Leach, and Bill Barber. Opposing the LCB Line was Soviet center Slava Solodukhin and wingers Vlad Vikulov and Boris Aleksandrov. It was a notable change for Central Red Army, which had started the game with Valeri Kharlamov, Aleksandr Maltsev, and Boris Mikhailov opposite the LCB Line.

Heat from players and spectators caused the temperature inside the Spectrum to rise to approximately 65 degrees. In the Canadian Broadcasting Corporation booth, play-by-play announcer Bob Cole, working with Dick Irvin Jr. and Denis Potvin, spelled out what was at stake in this final period.

> Cole: "Here we go into the final twenty minutes of Super Series '76. I think fans across the country realize this is The Game. Champion against champion."

Not only did fans realize it, players and coaches on both teams knew this was The Game of the Super Series. Like his comrades, Vladimir Lutchenko eagerly anticipated every meeting with an NHL team, the defenseman eager to prove his worth to the professionals. In the 1972 Summit Series, Lutchenko ranked as the Soviets' second highest-scoring defenseman. He was complimented by Russian sportswriter Vladimir Dvortsov, who wrote for the Soviet state-owned news agency TASS, that Lutchenko played very well defensively and showed that even against the

Canadians a defenseman can use clean bodychecks effectively. "He played the real style of Soviet hockey—smart, elegant and clean."

Arthur Chidlovski praised Lutchenko as one of the best defensemen in Russian hockey history. Lutchenko was respected, Chidlovski recalls, for his steady play and consistency.

Owning a powerful left-handed shot, the 6-foot, 202-pound Lutchenko set a record in 1975 by scoring four goals in a game against Sweden in the Izvestia Cup. Yet he was most respected for his abilities on defense and was considered by teammates and opponents to be a consistent and sometimes brilliant player. Playing his entire career with the Red Army, Lutchenko was pivotal in his team's winning Soviet championships and European Champions Cup crowns. On the international stage, Lutchenko helped the Soviet National Team claim world championships titles, European championships, and Olympic gold medals. His haul of hardware included silver medals and a bronze in the world championships and silvers and a bronze in the European championships.

Playing in the 1972 and 1974 Summit Series and Super Series '76, Lutchenko relished the opportunity to test himself against North American players. "We had always beaten them in the Olympics and world championship," he said at the time. "I'd often heard that their best players were in the NHL, and it bothered me that we weren't playing against them." He believed the Summit Series proved finally that the Russians were as good at hockey as the North Americans.

Flyers goalie Wayne Stephenson shared Lutchenko's excitement at the epic confrontation between the two teams. Nicknamed "Fort Wayne," Stephenson was born in Fort William, Ontario. He was in his sixth NHL season and, having built a fort-like wall around the Flyers' goal, was in the process of backstopping the Bullies to one of the greatest triumphs in franchise history. Still, Stephenson felt unusually tight the night before this game.

Stephenson had huge skates to fill in replacing Bernie Parent, whose absence offered an opportunity for Wayne. Fred Shero fully supported Stephenson, dismissing any notion that his Bullies would suffer. "It's really not a gamble," Shero said. "He is not some half-assed backup goalie we are throwing in there."

Stephenson was also the Flyer with the most experience playing against the Soviets, due to his six years of international competition. On this afternoon against the Red Army, Stephenson was eighteen days shy of his thirty-first birthday. His early life had been nomadic. His father, Fred, owned an air conditioning business and moved his family from Ontario to western Canada and then to Winnipeg when Wayne was a teenager. Playing well in his junior career in the Manitoba Hockey League, Stephenson moved on to the Canadian national ice hockey team. For a six-year span from 1966 to 1971, he competed in tournaments in North America and Europe, helping Canada claim bronze medals in the 1966 and 1967 world championships. In the 1968 Winter Olympics in Grenoble, France, Stephenson backstopped Canada's bronze-medal performance, earning one shutout and surrendering a combined three goals in victories over West Germany, East Germany, and Team USA. Stephenson's save percentage in the three games was an excellent 93.9. Team Canada's only losses came to the gold medalist Soviet Union squad and silver medalist Czechoslovakia.

Turning pro in 1971, Stephenson signed with the St. Louis Blues and spent some of the 1971–1972 season in the Central Hockey League with the Kansas City Blues. He made his NHL debut in 1972, backing up Ernie Wakely. Stephenson was busier in the 1971–1972 campaign, playing in forty-five of St. Louis's seventy-eight regular-season games; the following season he started forty games. Stephenson was traded from the Blues to the Stanley Cup champion Flyers on September 16, 1974. The deal was yet another steal engineered by Philadelphia general manager Keith Allen. In return for Wayne, the Flyers gave up their NHL rights to Randy Andreachuk of the World Hockey Association, along with a second-round pick in the 1975 draft.

Stephenson played sparingly behind Parent in 1974–1975 as the Bullies repeated as Stanley Cup champions. Relegated to spectator status, he longed to return to the starter's role he'd had in St. Louis and on Team Canada. "I knew I wasn't going to play much, though I can't say I liked the idea," Stephenson once recalled. "I knew I'd be strictly a backup goaltender."

Stephenson kept to himself in Philadelphia, and the rowdy Bullies recognized his reserved nature and respected it. "Wayne was a real intelligent guy, a family man," Joe Watson remembers. "He was always reading books, and we let him go his own way. It was never really an issue. He delivered for us on the ice, and goalies are a different breed anyway."

Stephenson employed an old-school stand-up style. A student of his sport, he played the angles, relying not on reflexes but on positioning to turn away enemy shots. Teammate Bob Kelly calls Stephenson a good goaltender whose play engendered great confidence among his teammates. "He was a bigger part of our success in those days than people think," says Kelly. Larry Goodenough agrees, stating that "Wayne was a hell of a goalie."

Playing sixty-six regular-season games in goal for Philadelphia in 1975–1976, Stephenson was selected to the NHL All-Star Game. Against the Red Army, he was the Flyers' final line of defense. Through two periods Stephenson surrendered just one score, the goal deflecting in off Joe Watson's skate. Stephenson's performance against the Soviets came in arguably the most memorable game in Flyers' history.

"Wayne played very well," Jimmy Watson remembers. "He had played against the Russians a lot and told us to just play our game."

Stephenson always maintained that his most memorable outing came the year before, on April 29, 1975, in Game 1 of the semifinals against the New York Islanders. On that day, Parent was injured in warm-ups when a shot by Dornhoefer hit Bernie below the right knee. The injury left Parent unable to walk and put Stephenson in a starting role just minutes prior to puck drop. Stephenson did not have time to be nervous, yet he also didn't have time to study the opponent. He had, however, built a reputation as being able to play at an elevated level on short notice, and he would do the same against the Islanders. Having started just ten games in the regular season, Stephenson came off the bench and blanked the talented Isles. Since Parent was still injured for Game 2, Stephenson started again and led the Flyers to an overtime victory and a 2–0 series lead.

Even when he shut out an opponent, Stephenson still found something wrong with his performance. He was his own worst critic, but by

1976 he was learning not to be as hard on himself as before, when he admittedly would take the game home with him.

Stephenson was bringing it home for the Flyers against the Red Army, and fronting Fort Wayne was a lockdown defense that left little room for daylight. Even when the Soviets breached the Bullies' blue line, they found themselves frustrated by Fort Wayne's walled-off interior. Stephenson rebuffed the Russians, then watched as his teammates took the battle to his opposite in goal, Vladislav Tretiak.

After Gilmour dropped the puck to start the third period, Clarke battled Solodukhin at center ice and the puck was controlled by the Flyers. Barber passed to Leach, crossing right to left in front of Tretiak, but the Rifle's attempt at a tip-in failed. Goodenough followed with another shot, this one sailing wide. The Russians cleared the puck, and Vikulov brought it into the Flyers' zone.

Moose Dupont poked the puck off Vikulov's stick, and Leach found Clarke with a cross-ice pass. Clarke dropped the puck back to a trailing Dupont, who then fed the captain with a neat give-and-go. Clarke's backhand shot was blocked by Tretiak, who was knocked backward into his net in a scrum involving Barber, Leach, Valeri Vasiliev, and Alexei Volchenkov. Believing Leach had pushed the puck past a prone Tretiak and into the net, Clarke and Barber raised their arms in exultation. But the red lamp behind the Red Army goal did not light up, and the Flyers did not argue.

Killing off Aleksandrov's penalty, the Russians returned to full strength. Dornhoefer slapped a shot from inside the blue line, the puck flying high and to Tretiak's right, then bouncing off the protective glass behind the net and going into the crowd. Kharlamov, his artistic stick-handling still on display, raced into the Bullies' end of the ice. The Flyers broke up his drop pass for Mikhailov, and Rick MacLeish drilled the puck into the Russians' zone. Aleksandr Gusev took control and fed Mikhailov on a break.

Cole: "Here they come! Mikhailov at center, back to Gusev. Pokes a high one in; Stephenson makes a grab at it."

As the Soviets stormed back, Irvin referenced for the second time the presence of Nikolai Ozerov at ice level. Ozerov was the Soviet Union's leading sports commentator, a veteran broadcaster whose career would span several decades from the 1950s into the 1980s. He was a prominent Soviet athlete and actor from a family of high achievers. His great-grandfather Mikhail Vinogradov earned renown as a nineteenth-century composer; his father, Nikolai Sr., was an opera singer; and his mother, Nadezhda, was a stage actress who gave up her career to raise her sons, Yuri and Nikolai Jr.

Ozerov took up tennis at age nine and three years later won the Moscow boys' championship. When famed French tennis champion Henri Cochet visited Moscow in the late 1930s, he watched the husky Ozerov train and prophesied, "This fatty will go far." Cochet proved prescient; Ozerov eventually won twenty-four Soviet tennis titles in men's singles, men's doubles, and mixed doubles from 1940 to 1963. Ozerov's outstanding play transcended sports and was used by the Stalinist government to inspire the Russian people as Hitler's hordes approached Moscow in 1941. Rather than flee the city, Ozerov and three other tennis players were commissioned by political leaders to play exhibition matches that were broadcast throughout Moscow to raise the morale of fearful citizens.

Ozerov began his career as a radio sports commentator on August 29, 1950, when renowned sports journalist Vadim Sinyavsky invited him to report on a soccer match between CSKA Moscow and Dynamo Moscow. Listeners praised his reporting, prompting Ozerov to focus on a career as a sports commentator. He would cover Soviet ice hockey at thirty world championships and eight Winter Olympics and was featured as a commentator in thirteen movies. He trotted the globe, eventually visiting some fifty countries. While he also broadcast soccer, he became synonymous with ice hockey. Just as Foster Hewitt was an icon in Canadian broadcasting, Ozerov filled the same role in Russia, his voice indelibly linked to Soviet hockey. Ozerov and Hewitt joined Sweden's Lennart Hyland and Czechoslovakia's Josef Laufer as sportscasters whose work on radio and television was instrumental in popularizing ice hockey internationally. Ozerov's broadcasts became legendary. When the Soviet National Team took the lead on Team Canada in Game 1 of the

1972 Summit Series, Ozerov mockingly told his audience, "So these are the vaunted Canadian pros." In the aftermath of the Russians' rout, Ozerov remarked that "the myth of unbeatable self-praised Canadian hockey professionals is over!"

The trained actor could do comedy as well as drama. When the Soviets played the World Hockey Association stars in 1974, Ozerov had fun with aging Gordie Howe and Bobby Hull. "Gordie Howe is a legend of Canadian hockey," Ozerov told his audience. "He is forty-six, has over one thousand scars on his body, his hair is gray, but it's still not enough for him. Life is expensive, and Howe needs money. He plays himself and forces his children to play too." Of Hull, Ozerov stated, "Canadian hockey pros don't wear helmets. They wear nothing. The only one who wears anything is Bobby Hull. He wears a wig."

Ozerov had a serious side, and when he thought North American players were trying to intimidate the Soviets with hard hits, Ozerov would shout into his mic, "No, this is not the hockey we need!" Chidlovksi was among the millions of Russian fans who listened faithfully to Ozerov. "Ozerov's name can't be separated from hockey," he says. "In a way, he was Mr. Hockey, or, keeping up with the terminology of his prime time in broadcasting, Comrade Hockey. During these glorious decades in Soviet hockey, generations of viewers watched his hockey reports from Moscow and Toronto, Voskresensk and Helsinki, Montreal and Stockholm, Prague and Kiev."

Chidlovski recalls Ozerov's reports from the 1972 Summit Series as belonging to the classics of TV broadcasting: "I am not sure if it was the drama of the series, the level of hockey shown in the Summit, or the passion in Ozerov's voice that made these games in September 1972 one of the best sports spectacles ever shown on Soviet TV."

Chidlovski is one of many who revered Ozerov. Visiting a post office in Russia, Ozerov saw an older man who looked familiar. Looking closer, Ozerov realized the man was Vyacheslav Molotov, former Soviet prime minister and foreign minister, and second only to Stalin among Russian diplomats at the international conferences in Teheran, Yalta, and Potsdam during World War II. Ozerov introduced himself and offered

Molotov a ride. "My wife won't believe it," Molotov told him. "Ozerov himself gave me a ride!"

Ozerov's broadcasting style stressed enthusiasm and optimism. Russian theatre and cinema actor Mikhail Ulyanov said that those living in the Soviet Union from the 1950s to the 1980s cannot imagine that time without the voice of Ozerov and "his passion and enchanting love of sports." The heavyset Ozerov, his graying hair brushed straight back and the mic inches from his mouth, was fifty-four at the time of the Red Army's game in Philadelphia and was less than happy with being positioned at ice level in the Spectrum. Though he protested, he did not gain an improved vantage point, leading Irvin to say that the usually persuasive Ozerov was now 56–1 in arguments.

As Ozerov broadcast to his Russian audience during the third period, Dave Schultz sent a rink-wide pass to Saleski. Big Bird blasted a straight-on shot that Tretiak turned away. The Hammer followed with a drive, and moments later, Orest Kindrachuk and Maltsev battled for the puck in the corner. As the Flyers and Soviets took their positions near the right faceoff circle, CBC cameras closed in on the sweaty visage of Gilmour, Cole noting, "He is showing signs of fatigue. It's been a hot contest."

The Red Army roared up ice, and Alexander Volchkov split the Flyers' defense and closed on Stephenson before dropping the puck to Victor Kutyergin. Seeking his second goal, the Soviet forward delivered a direct blast. Stephenson gloved the shot and tossed it to Jimmy Watson. As Shero changed lines on the go, the Flyers continued their fierce forechecking.

Clarke was knocked down by Volchenkov, who waved his right hand dismissively at a penalty call. The two-minute hooking penalty gave the Flyers a man advantage, and Shero sent in his power play unit of Clarke, MacLeish, Leach, Goodenough, and Barber. Against the Soviets, Barber was burnishing his reputation as the best left winger in the NHL. The season before, he had finished fourth in the voting in the league's All-Star voting for top left wing. Buffalo's Rick Martin was the runaway selection for the first team, followed by the Rangers' Steve Vickers and Danny Grant of the Detroit Red Wings. Those inside the Flyers organization took exception, believing writers were emphasizing scoring and not overall play.

By 1976, writers were taking notice of Barber's complete skill set. He led the voting for top left wing, securing 101 votes to far outdistance runner-up Vickers. The media's recognition of Barber as the league's best left wing was particularly fitting, since the upcoming 1976 NHL All-Star Game, scheduled for January 20, would be played in the Spectrum. "Finally, people are finding out he does more things than the other guy [Vickers]," Shero told Bill Fleischman. "He's better than Vickers."

Against the Red Army, Barber was showing himself to be not only the best left wing in the NHL but also on par with two stars acknowledged to be the best—Kharlamov and Aleksandr Yakushev of the Soviet Wings. He followed with a drive aimed at Tretiak that went off Clarke, who had positioned himself in front of the Russians' net. MacLeish sent in an angled shot that Tretiak kicked aside at the last second. Clarke scooped up the rebound behind the net and, curling to his left, tried a wraparound goal that Treitak stopped. Potvin noted that the Flyers were "pretty hungry for that fourth goal." Irvin agreed, saying that the Bullies didn't want the Red Army to "get to within one."

Clarke won the face-off, and Dornhoefer played the puck along the boards before sending it to Clarke in the corner. From behind the red line Clarke found Goodenough, who was storming in from the right point.

Cole: "Goodenough goal!"

Goodenough proved to be just that—good enough. His score was particularly impressive since he fell while releasing the shot. "Fell on my ass!" Goodenough recalls. "The play was behind the net. The puck was passed to Clarkie and he put it right on the tape [of the stick]. Tretiak gave me the top [shelf], and I wanted it so bad I panicked. I was shooting high, but it went right through Tretiak's legs. I wasn't shooting for the five-hole. After the game Clarkie told me, 'If I knew it was you, I wouldn't have passed it to you!' That's why I loved those guys. We were a blue-collar team representing a blue-collar town."

Clarke leaped twice in the air, his hops reminiscent of his celebration following his overtime goal in Boston in Game 2 of the 1974 Stanley Cup Finals. He then turned to Goodenough, who was hugged by Barber as the Spectrum shivered from an explosion of cheers. Dave Leonardi lifted a sign taunting Tretiak: "NEXT GOALIE!"

Potvin: "Clarke saw the open man and fed it to him, and Goodenough put his head down and fired that puck towards the net. An important goal!"

Goodenough, nicknamed "Izzy" (as in "Is he good enough"), was in his second season with the Flyers. A native of Toronto, he was a twenty-two-year-old rookie the spring before when the Bullies repeated as Stanley Cup champions. Taken by Philadelphia as the twentieth pick overall in the 1973 NHL Entry Draft, Goodenough was called up to the Flyers late in the 1974–1975 regular season and played the final twenty games. He also played an additional five games in the Stanley Cup playoffs, including Games 4 and 5 of the finals, assisting on a pair of second-period goals in Game 5 by Leach and Schultz to fuel a 5–1 final that gave Bullies a 3–2 lead in the series.

Shero paired the rookie with veteran Ted Harris, who was approaching his thirtieth birthday and had won four Stanley Cups in the 1960s with Montreal. Harris's toughness fit well with the Bullies. He was Bobby Orr's first opponent in an NHL fight and had several memorable bouts with New York Ranger Orland Kurtenbach. The 1975–1976 campaign would see Goodenough start in seventy regular-season games. By season's end, the 6-foot, 195-pound defenseman produced a plus-45 rating, based in part on his 42 points and 8 goals. None of Goodenough's goals, however, would ever have the impact as his power play score against the Soviets.

Goodenough's goal came at the four-minute mark, Clarke and Dornhoefer credited with assists. Following Goodenough's score, the Red Army sought to retaliate. Solodukhin carried the puck into the Flyers' zone, and the Russians employed all the moves in their repertoire to pressure the Bullies. The Flyers regained control, and their offensive artistry was noted by the CBC crew, Cole stating that the Flyers "pass the puck beautifully."

Lonsberry followed with a drive off the glass. Gusev cleared the puck, but MacLeish reclaimed it and sent a centering pass that was batted away by Tretiak, who then blocked a rebound shot as well. With the tempo remaining high, Ed Van Impe crashed into Mikhailov along the boards. When the Soviet center arose, his red uniform was covered with white ice. On the opposite side of the rink, Vasiliev stopped Barber at the blue line with a high elbow, and Barber collided with Kharlamov when the latter attempted to dance through the Bullies' defense. Leach and Gusev tussled in the corner in the Soviet zone, and Clarke forechecked Vasiliev behind the net. Vasiliev followed by tangling with Barber in the corner and forcing a face-off. Saleski's shot off the draw was smothered by Tretiak. In the booth, Potvin said that if not for Tretiak, "the score would be much higher."

Potvin's stint as color analyst for this historic game would serve him well in his post-playing career. Taken by the Islanders with the number 1 pick in the 1973 NHL Entry Draft, Potvin won the Calder Trophy in 1974 as the league's top rookie and in 1976 won the first of three Norris Trophy awards as top defenseman. He would wear the "C" on his sweater as Isles captain throughout their dynasty years, winning four straight Stanley Cups from 1980 to 1983 and playing for a fifth straight in 1984 before bowing to Wayne Gretzky, Mark Messier, and the Edmonton Oilers.

Three years following his retirement in 1988 as a player, Potvin was inducted into the Hall of Fame. His work in Philadelphia this day proved a precursor to his role as part of the Florida Panthers' first broadcast team in 1993–1994. From 2010 to 2014, Potvin was a color analyst with the Ottawa Senators. He returned to doing color for the Panthers, retiring in 2019 after twenty-one seasons behind the mic in Florida. Irvin remembers Potvin's analysis in Philadelphia as excellent. "Denny saved us," he recalls.

Potvin, Cole, and Irvin watched as Kutyergin carried the fight to the Flyers, stickhandling the puck up ice and issuing a high drive that was caught by Stephenson. With twelve minutes remaining, Saleski's pass was stolen by Aleksandr Lobanov, who was hit and spun around by Joe Watson. Sergei Glazov took the puck and, in Cole's words, did "a bit of a dance" as he retreated to his own blue line with it.

With play again getting chippy, Schultz was bumped on the boards by Kutyergin, and Terry Crisp dueled with Volchenkov behind the Russian net. Popov, Vikulov, and Vladimir Lokotko teamed on a rush, but the Flyers stood firm. Barber knocked down Volchenkov, and MacLeish unleashed a sizzling backhand that thumped off Tretiak's leg pad. A drive by Dupont went high, and Goodenough's attempt from the right slot was covered by a diving Tretiak.

With just over nine minutes remaining, the Red Army continued to try to break through the Bullies' defense. Mikhailov went in on a rush but was sandwiched by Schultz and Saleski. Kharlamov sped toward Stephenson and tried a centering pass, but the Flyers clogged the passing lanes. Vasiliev controlled the loose puck, prompting Cole to remark that the "Soviets are coming on strong again."

Kutyergin tried to break the Bullies' blue line defense, but again the Soviets were thwarted by a thicket of big bodies. Vasiliev slammed into Dornohefer along the boards, and Lobanov and Maltsev orchestrated a rush that resulted in a shot from Glazov. As the attempt went wide to Stephenson's right side, Clarke fell to the ice. CBC cameras showed the captain's face bloodied above the right eye, courtesy of an unintentionally high stick by Kutyergin. The Russian dropped his stick and went to Clarke to apologize. Clarke waved him away.

With seven minutes to play, the Flyers were outshooting the Red Army, 45–11. The Soviets seemed to be in an icy maze of indecision. Everywhere the Russians looked, they saw the Bullies blocking their paths and passing lanes, turning the Soviets' accustomed downhill skating into an uphill struggle. Loktev did not look to make many more adjustments, and since the Soviets were not inclined to dump-and-chase the puck, as NHL teams would have done, they continued to circle and weave.

"The Russians were used to having the puck, not chasing it," Joe Watson recalls. "They didn't have the system to dump and chase." MacLeish later told reporters that the Russians kept looking for the perfect opportunities: "Even in the last five minutes they just kept circling. Either they have a lot of patience, or they just can't adjust." Dupont recalls it being the latter. "They played their system," he says. "They never did adjust."

The Flyers were content to let the Soviets control the puck between the blue line all game, knowing that puck possession alone wouldn't do the Red Army any good if it couldn't score. Clarke believed the Bullies could allow the Russians to have the puck between the blue lines and still beat them.

Chidlovski credits Shero and the Flyers for planning and executing a strategy that worked to near perfection: "The Flyers played a good game, a technical game," he says. "Fred Shero outsmarted the Soviets. [The Russians] were expecting rough play, penalties, and scores on power plays. Blame Loktev for that."

Hockey writer Shirley Fischler said there was no question in anyone's mind that the Flyers had thoroughly intimidated Red Army players and thrown them off their game. "After all that aggressiveness, however, remember that the Flyers' game is basically one of talent and hard work—which is what they did *AFTER* scaring the crap out of the Soviets," Fischler wrote.

As time wound down, Dornhoefer muscled Volchenkov, and Dupont bumped Vikulov off stride. MacLeish pilfered the puck and went in on Tretiak, who blocked the shot. Dornhoefer followed with a drive, and Bridgman bounced an attempt off Tretiak's pads. Saleski drove Tretiak into the crease with the force of his shot, the 48th of the game for the Flyers, which was an all-time high against the Soviets and broke the mark of 46 set by the Sabres against the Wings. The Flyers believed Tretiak prevented the game from becoming a blowout. "If it hadn't been for Tretiak we would've won 10–1," Joe Watson says. "We were all over them."

Kharlamov quickly returned the puck into the Flyers' zone but was stopped by Jimmy Watson. Nicknamed "Chan" due to his cleft chin, the twenty-four-year-old younger brother of fellow defenseman Joe Watson was enjoying an All-Star season, his second of four straight and five overall from 1975 to 1980.

The road to NHL stardom had been a road less traveled for Jimmy, one of six children born in Smithers, British Columbia, to Joe Sr. and Mary Watson. To support his family, Joe Sr. spent summers working as a logger and winters working as a butcher. All six children were boys, and five of them played hockey, mostly makeshift games outdoors on nearby Lake Kathlyn, whose surface froze to a depth of three feet when temperatures plunged in midwinter to as low as minus-20 degrees Fahrenheit. From late October to early April, the Watson boys played ice hockey. The rest of the year they played street hockey, with tin cans serving as pucks. The Watson boys enjoyed other sports as well; they played baseball and were fans of the Detroit Tigers. Jimmy was seven years old when Joe left Smithers at age sixteen to play junior hockey in Estevan, Saskatchewan. Jimmy used the occasional phone call from Joe, along with newspaper and radio accounts of his games, to follow his brother's career. Like Joe, Jimmy's dream was to play in the NHL and win the Stanley Cup. Joining the Calgary Centennials of the Western Canada Hockey League, however, Jimmy was unhappy with his own play and thought of returning to Smithers.

Joe stepped in, inviting Jimmy to visit Philadelphia to see what the NHL was about. "It was," Jimmy recalls, "the best thing that ever happened to me." Returning to the Centennials with a new outlook, Jimmy amped up his play and was named the WCHL's best defenseman for the 1971–1972 season. Though he was expecting to a high pick in the 1972 NHL Entry Draft, Jimmy wasn't selected until the third round, when the Flyers made him the thirty-ninth pick overall. Following a year with the AHL's Richmond Robins, Jimmy was called up to the big club, joining Joe on the Flyers' roster. Teamed with the veteran Van Impe, Jimmy played with poise and intelligence. Among those impressed was Shero, the coach warming to the rookie whose 1973–1974 season produced a plus-33 defensive rating and 20 points in seventy-eight games.

Jimmy was even better in his first NHL postseason. He stepped into the sizeable void created when fellow defenseman Barry Ashbee was sidelined with a career-ending injury to his eye in the semifinal series against the rival Rangers. As the final seconds wound down in Game 6 of the finals against Boston, Jimmy hugged Tom Bladon, another fuzzy-cheeked Flyers defenseman, and repeated the words, "Can you believe it?" to everyone in listening distance. Jimmy and Joe joined their father in the jubilant locker room, Joe Sr. having made the long trip from Smithers to Vancouver to Denver to Philadelphia to watch his sons play for the championship.

Amid his celebratory, champagne-soaked surroundings, Jimmy tried to make sense of the fact that he was a rookie who had just won the Stanley Cup. "What did we just accomplish here?" he thought. "What did I just do?"

What he had done was realize two career goals in a single season. When he returned home to Smithers that summer, Jimmy's friends asked what he would do for an encore. "We're going to do it again," Jimmy replied. The Flyers did, and Jimmy played a vital role with a plus-41 rating, 7 goals, and 25 points. Two of his goals were game winners, and his steady, sometimes spectacular play his second season earned him his first All-Star Game appearance. It also earned him a reputation as a clutch player, someone who could be counted on when the situation demanded it. Forget stats, Bob Kelly says. Jimmy Watson was a guy who made plays when he had to.

Still, the Flyers had fun with the Watson brothers' lack of scoring. Hart created the "Grizzly Cup" to be awarded annually to the player from Smithers who scored the most goals during the season. Jimmy and Joe went along with the good-natured ribbing, Jimmy telling Hart his strategy was that if he got a goal by Christmas, he was virtually a lock. Jimmy claimed the Grizzly Cup the first two years, outscoring Joe 2–1 and 7–6. Joe's victory came in Year 4, when he tallied four goals to Jimmy's three. The other two years the Watson boys tied one another in goals scored.

Hart noted that the Watsons were "*defense*-minded defensemen, to whom goals are something to be prevented at all costs, not something to be scored." Yet Jimmy and Joe displayed a flair for the dramatic by scoring goals at opportune times. Like center fielder Garry Maddox of the 1976 division champion Philadelphia Phillies, Jimmy Watson was the "Secretary of Defense" for the Flyers, improving his on-ice rating from plus-41 in 1974–1975 to plus-65 in 1975–1976.

At the time he took the ice with the Flyers against the Soviets, Jimmy was considered by Ashbee to be one of the two best defensemen in the NHL; Potvin being the other. Ashbee told the *Hockey News* in its January 2, 1976, issue that Jimmy Watson played with poise, be it clearing the puck from the defensive zone or carrying it into the opponent's end of the ice. His physical size also allowed him to move opponents from the goal crease, a fact the Soviets soon became aware of.

As Jimmy's game evolved, so did his role as one of the club's leaders. Like Joe, Jimmy could be vocal when teammates needed to hear it. When Flyers' spirits flagged, Jimmy would announce, "Let's go, boys! We can do it!" Not many knew it then, but Jimmy's encouragement was as much for himself as for others. He played through back problems stemming from an off-ice injury suffered when he was eighteen years old. Working a summer job with a water company near Smithers, Jimmy hurt his back as he hefted a heavy water pipe. His back would never fully heal, later developing into a degenerative disc condition.

Amid a campaign in which he would win the team's Barry Ashbee Trophy as top defenseman, Jimmy Watson rode Kharlamov off the puck in the Bullies' zone. With less than four minutes remaining in the game, the Russians tried to regroup. The Bullies worked to prevent it. Clarke chased down Kharlamov, and he and Barber sent shots toward the Soviet goal. Mikhailov and Kharlamov responded for the Red Army, breaking out in a two-on-one against a back-skating Van Impe. Mikhailov's shot was blocked by Stephenson, who followed by sprawling on the ice to stop a rebound shot by Maltsev.

Cole: "A big hand for two fine saves by Stephenson!"

The crowd roared its appreciation. A year earlier, Dana T. Graf wrote that as well as Stephenson played in relief of Parent, he could sense that extra something, "that geometric savoir faire," was missing. Graf found himself "second-guessing every move Wayne would make, visualizing in each case how Parent would have reacted." There was no second-guessing Stephenson this day. With 2:45 to go, he used his stick to brush aside a backhand attempt by Maltsev.

Cole: "All of Canada is very proud of the Flyers today. It's safe to say that everybody has been behind them from coast to coast."

With a minute to play, the countdown to victory began. Potvin noted on the broadcast that the Flyers were disproving the notion that they could only win by playing rough. "I think they're showing expertise in hockey today."

As the final seconds expired, Flyers fans began a rhythmic chant of "We're number one!" They stood and cheered as Van Impe controlled the puck and then picked it up as the scoreboard clock showed zeroes.

Cole: "A standing ovation for the Philadelphia Flyers! Philadelphia has defeated the Soviet Red Army team quite convincingly today, 4–1!"

Irvin told viewers he didn't think there had been a similar reaction in the Spectrum since the Flyers beat the Bruins for the Stanley Cup in 1974. As the Bullies surrounded Stephenson in a celebratory hug, the scoreboard flashed a sign reading "Kate 44–3–1."

Potvin credited the Flyers for playing "an excellent game . . . a flawless game. They are really the number one hockey team."

With the issue of the world championship settled and the Broad Street Bullies proving they were the best hockey team on earth this January day, Leonardi flashed one final sign: "BRING ON MARS!"

Unable to adjust to Shero's disciplined defensive scheme, the Red Army was outshot 49–13. In the third period, the Flyers tested Tretiak eighteen times; the Soviets, meanwhile, put just three shots on goal against Stephenson. The Bullies had not only seized the day, they had *sieged* the day.

"We are the world champions," a happy Shero told reporters. "If they had won, they would have been the champs. I said back in June that winning the Stanley Cup didn't make us the world champions until we met and beat the Russians. We beat them head-to-head. We beat a hell of a machine. Ninety-nine percent of the National Hockey League didn't think we could do it."

Shero stated that the Red Army didn't want to battle the Bullies physically in the corners. "And that's where games are decided," he said. Shero thought that rather than joust with the Flyers for the puck, the Russians bailed out.

Dave Anderson of the *New York Times* saw Clarke and noted "a rosette of blood" on the captain's forehead. The gash, courtesy of Kutyergin's stick, would require twelve stitches to close. Clarke waved it off as "an accident" and said Kutyergin apologized when it happened. Turning his attention to the outcome, Clarke said that it didn't prove Canadian hockey was superior to Soviet hockey; "it just means the Flyers are better than their best." Clarke thought the Flyers "played our game, the way we usually played." Told of Loktev's comments that the Flyers played like "animals," Clarke issue a wry grin. "I guess he meant we were like Russian bears."

Other Flyers were less diplomatic. Bladon believed the Soviets played scared, and Dupont said the Russians skated like amateurs. "They're not so great," Moose declared. "They looked like fools today." Crisp couldn't understand the Soviet strategy, why they kept trying to make the perfect play at the blue line. Every coach he ever had warned against such tactics. The best thing about the Flyers' victory, Crisp opined, was that the Bullies showed those who thought the Soviet system was the best that "it's not the be-all and end-all."

Too tense to sleep in the days before the game, Jimmy Watson was euphoric. "I've never been so happy. This compares with winning the Stanley Cup." His brother Joe defended the Flyers' physicality. "Sure we play it rough," he said, "but taking the body is part of the game. . . . Let's face it, we won on discipline." Joe said that because this was his only chance to play the famous Red Army, it was the greatest game of his career.

Van Impe remarked that he knew the Russians didn't like the rough stuff, but that's how the game is played in the NHL. "It's our game," he said, "and if they don't start laying on the body themselves, they should stay home." Kelly said the Flyers allowed the Red Army to pass the puck as much as they wanted in their own end, adding that the Soviet style was indeed beautiful to watch: "We had the best seats in the house."

Meanwhile, the Bullies stood at their blue line and waited for them to advance.

Kelly thought the thing about the Red Army was that when the Flyers made a run at them, they wouldn't retaliate with a fight but would instead spear, kick, or jab. Saleski, whom Tim Burke of the *Montreal Gazette* thought played the greatest game of his career, had a large ugly welt on his chest from what he called "the worst spear I ever got in my life." The spear was so hard, said Saleski, that the Soviet player broke his stick on it.

In the Red Army locker room, Loktev downplayed the outcome. "One game against the Flyers doesn't mean anything," he said. "If we played them a seven-game series anything could happen." The Soviet coach paused. "The Flyers are a good team. But they were playing animal hockey." The Bullies, he stated, were intent on physically "destroying" opponents. "We have the Olympic Games coming up and we didn't want to risk injuries to our players. We are not frightened by the Philadelphia players, but nobody likes to have teeth missing or have damage done to other parts of the body."

Loktev thought the Flyers worked well together and that Shero was progressive in his coaching methods. He said his Red Army club knew the Bullies were a strong team that could play any brand of hockey. "They are noted for their vicious acts on the ice, but they do not need to play that way," Loktev said.

Tretiak dismissed the Flyers' victory. "I am disappointed with the Flyers," he told reporters. "I shall always remember how they hunted our leading players, and how they kept striking the cage with their sticks whenever I was covering the puck." The years did not soften his feelings. "Philadelphia beat us," he later wrote in his autobiography, "but could anyone consider it a fair victory?" Tretiak called the Flyers the champions of the world—"in penalties."

The Russians' protests brought a mixed response from players and media. Potvin thought the Flyers had played a hard-hitting but clean game. Bobby Hull was said to be indignant at the Bullies' tactics, as was Anderson who wrote in the *New York Times* that the Bullies "bisected" the Red Army "and upheld the Spectrum's reputation as the cradle of licensed muggings. The triumph of terror over style could not have been more one-sided if Al Capone's mob had ambushed the Bolshoi Ballet Dancers. Naturally, it warmed the hearts of the Flyers followers, who would cheer for Frankenstein if he could skate."

Robert Fachet wrote in the *Washington Post* that the Flyers were probably "a better hockey team and would have won without the softening-up process to which they resorted. Unfortunately, we will never know, and the Soviets always will have the excuse that they were just trying to stay alive."

Milt Dunnell of the *Toronto Star* disagreed. "Loktev knew the conditions before he came," he wrote. "Nobody loves playing in Philadelphia. Once he accepted a game with the Flyers, under NHL rules, with an NHL referee, he was in the same boat as the Toronto Maple Leafs or Vancouver Canucks when they come to town. Loktev wanted to know what it's like to play the Flyers in Philly under NHL conditions. Well . . . that's what it's like."

Dunnell broke down Shero's winning strategy, writing that as a student of the Soviet style of play, Shero had the Red Army beaten before the teams stepped on the ice:

From his analysis of their films, he had noted the reluctance of the Ruskies to give up the puck. Their game is puck control. So Shero flooded the centre ice zone with checkers. Their instructions were that the first man to emerge from the Soviet zone could be ignored as a likely sniper—also the second man to handle the puck. Concentrate on that third man.

Thus, Shero was able to practically destroy the intricate Russian passing game—which was what Canadians admired most. In the physical hockey which the Flyers play, the Soviets were wheelbarrows against tanks.

Frank Orr of the *Toronto Star* cited the Soviets' claims of "animal hockey" as their excuse for the walkout and praised Shero as "Sunday's hero" and the Flyers as "champs of the world." As the Flyers coach held court, Ed Snider burst into the interview room and proclaimed Shero's strategies as "the greatest coaching job ever in the history of hockey."

CBS Radio's Herb Goren, a longtime NHL observer, thought the Soviets "made their biggest mistake when they didn't insist on a Russian referee for the last game."

Writing in the *Montreal Gazette*, Burke said, "The Flyers salvaged Canada's pride in her national sport with a near-perfect hockey master-piece. . . . It came as a glorious finale to Super Series '76."

The Associated Press stated that the Flyers "intimidated" the Soviets and forced the Russians to "cry uncle." Chuck Burghardt of the (Meriden, Connecticut) *Morning Record* wrote that the Russians were "big babies."

United Press International (UPI) toed a middle line:

The Soviets found the Philadelphia Flyers' home ice colder than their hometown of Moscow Sunday as they met the Stanley Cup champions in a game which almost didn't get through the first period. At stake was the reputation of the National Hockey League, pitted against that of Russia, where the Soviet Union is turning out some of the most talented players in the world. The aggressiveness of the Flyers appeared not only in the final score, but it also was reflected in who carried the game to whom.

UPI sports editor Milton Richman wrote that the Flyers' aggressive-ness caused the Russians to take drastic steps. "Soviet coach Konstantin Loktev suddenly pulled his team off the ice, presumably because one of Russia's key players, Valeri Kharlamov, was checked too hard by Flyers defenseman Eddie Van Impe. That was supposed to be the reason, but it wasn't. The whole thing was a big act, the same kind of act the Russians generally try in international diplomacy or international sports to get the upper hand. This time they didn't."

The Canadian newspaper the *Globe and Mail* quoted Alan Eagleson as stating that Loktev "overreacted" to the tense situation in the Spec-trum when he pulled his players from the ice. In the Soviet Union, *Pra-vda* published a cartoon of bulky Bullies players brandishing oversized clubs as they skated on the ice. The perception was endorsed throughout

Russia. Upon the Red Army's return to the Soviet Union, Loktev was summoned to the Kremlin. Expecting to have to answer for his team's loss to the Flyers, Loktev was startled when Soviet premier Leonid Brezhnev asked why he continued the game in Philadelphia, why the Red Army didn't forfeit the contest.

Eagleson found the Russians' protests interesting. The NHL Players' Association executive director said the Soviets were preaching the party line. The Flyers play hard and tough, he said, but their play against the Red Army wasn't dirty: "They're an aggressive team."

Roger Kahn cited Van Impe's body check on Kharlamov and Kutyergin's cutting Clarke and noted that hockey is "a rough, existential game and intimidation is a part of it, as surely as the ice is hard."

NHL players likewise differed in their opinion of what happened that day at the Spectrum. While Potvin thought it a masterful performance by the Flyers, Montreal Canadiens defenseman Serge Savard called what happened in Philadelphia "a disgrace."

Their cold war on ice over, relations between the Flyers and Russians thawed in the postgame. The players exchanged presents. The Flyers received small pins and pennants, the Soviets Lucite plaques containing the Flyers' crest. "We went over to their dressing room, and they were drinking vodka and beer," Joe Watson recalls. "So we drank vodka and beer with them. They were good guys. I was wearing a $5 Flyers cap and one of their guys was wearing a $150 Russian hat. He offered to trade hats with me. So, I left with his $150 hat, and he left with my $5 hat." He laughs. "I still have that hat!"

The Red Army and the Broad Street Bullies left the blood-spotted Spectrum ice and went their separate ways. Two days after losing to the Flyers, the Red Army played the Soviet Wings to a dubious 7–7 tie in Landover, Maryland. Campbell was unimpressed. The Soviets were skillful and fundamentally sound, he said, but their style wouldn't win in the NHL. Nor would it sell tickets. "Do you want to see this every night?" he asked reporters after the unimpressive and perhaps orchestrated tie.

The Russians headed to the Winter Olympics, where they claimed another gold medal when Kharlamov netted the winning goal in the final game to edge Czechoslovakia, 4–3. The Flyers, meanwhile, were feted by freedom lovers around the globe. "We got letters from people all over the world congratulating us on our victory," Joe Watson says. The Bullies then proceeded to put the finishing touches on their record-setting season and barged into a third straight Stanley Cup Final.

Awaiting them in their Triple Crown quest were the Montreal Canadiens.

CHAPTER 10

The Bullies' Final Battle

DAVE SCHULTZ WAS "THE HAMMER," A FEROCIOUS ENFORCER FOR THE enemies at the gates, the Broad Street Bullies. Guy Lafleur, "The Flower," symbolized the grace and style of the NHL's monarchs, the Montreal Canadiens.

That the 1976 Stanley Cup Finals featured the Hammer versus the Flower spoke volumes of the significant crossroads the NHL found itself at in the spring of 1976. Hockey fans viewed this much-anticipated series as white hats versus black hats, good versus bad, a battle for the soul of their sport.

All-Star center Rick MacLeish and future Hall of Fame goalie Bernie Parent helped the Philadelphia Flyers hold aloft the Stanley Cup in 1974 and again in 1975. Poised to make a run at NHL history in 1976 and join the Montreal Canadiens and Toronto Maple Leafs as the only franchises in history to that point to claim at least three consecutive Cups, the Flyers lost Parent and MacLeish to injuries, and hard-hitting All-Star defenseman Ed Van Impe to a trade. Still, Philadelphia versus Montreal represented a classic final that fans clamored for all winter. The series promised a clash of contrasting styles symbolized by the sport's leading protagonists and antagonists—Scotty Bowman's Canadiens and Fred Shero's Flyers. It was billed as force versus finesse, strength versus speed, and in this epic final hockey's future hung in the balance. The Flyers had proved that toughness could pay off in Stanley Cup currency. Seeing other clubs emulate the Bullies' style, the Canadiens realized their sport had reached a critical intersection in the spring of 1976.

The Habs were acutely aware that their task to turn back the Bullies would not be easy. Lafleur thought the Flyers were big, tough, and could fight. Ken Dryden agreed, later writing in his book *The Game* that "the Broad Street Bullies were a hugely intimidating team." There was a time when Dryden saw what he said was the admirable and contemptible, side by side. It was reflected in the "simple, courageous game they played, their discipline and dedication, Bobby Clarke, Bernie Parent, their no-name defense, Fred Shero." They had succeeded in turning the hockey waste-land that had been Philadelphia into something Dryden considered "vibrant and exciting."

The contemptible side of the hard-working Flyers, Dryden thought, was their alter ego, the Bullies. What finally turned him wasn't the Bullies' brawling and intimidation; it was their sense of impunity. They held in contempt opposing players, coaches, referees, league rules, fans, even the sport itself. "They searched out weakness," Dryden wrote, "found it, trampled it, then preened with their cock-of-the-walk swagger—C'mon, ya chicken, I dare ya!'" Gordie Howe, for one, brushed off salty language on the ice. All NHL players, Howe stated, are bilingual. "They speak English and profanity." Following Super Series '76, Bowman encountered Konstantin Loktev and, according to Al Strachan of the *Montreal Gazette*, told the Red Army coach there were many times he wanted to pull his team from the ice when facing the Flyers. The reason he didn't, Bowman told Loktev, was because the NHL would "suspend me for life."

The Flyers were undermanned heading into the finals. A healthy Parent had won back-to-back Vezina Trophies as the NHL's best goalie in 1973–1974 and 1974–1975 as well as consecutive Conn Smythe Trophies as playoff MVP. He pitched shutouts in back-to-back Cup-clinching victories. Putting a padlock on the pipes, Parent's clutch performances stirred memories of Terry Sawchuk and Parent's mentor, Jacques Plante. Backup goalie Wayne Stephenson played solidly in the spring of 1976, owning a postseason goals-against average of 2.67. In Philly's Cup-winning years, Parent's playoff GAA had been 2.02 in 1974 and 1.89 in 1975. "Wayne played well," defenseman Joe Watson recalls. "But he wasn't Bernie."

MacLeish was clutch as well, scoring the Cup-winning goal in Game 6 of the 1974 finals and troubling Vladislav Tretiak in the 1976 Super Series with his speed and accuracy. "He's Mr. Everything," Shero said at the time. The Hawk produced 22 points in seventeen playoff games in 1974 and 20 points in seventeen postseason games in 1975. His presence on the second line in the 1976 finals would have prevented Bowman from double-shifting his top two defensive centers, Doug Jarvis and Doug Risebrough, on Clarke. Since he didn't have MacLeish to worry about, Bowman believed his checking line of Jarvis, Bob Gainey, and Jim Roberts would take a toll on Clarke.

"Montreal tried to wear [Clarke] down," remembers Watson, who cited Gainey as a particularly effective grinder. "Gainey was a great checker. The Soviet coach [Konstantin Loktev] called Gainey the best player in the world, and it was because of his checking."

Van Impe was known for his checking as well. He delivered the hit heard 'round the hockey world when he decked Valeri Kharlamov. Yet the defensive star who provided a steadying influence was dealt to Pittsburgh for goalie Gary Inness. "It was very surprising, we were all kind of shocked," Joe Watson recalls. "Eddie was a key player on our team. He commanded a lot of respect on the ice and in the locker room. Eddie was a big, physical guy. Against a team like Montreal, the way they could skate, I would've liked to have had Eddie back there [on defense]."

Even without MacLeish, Parent, and Van Impe, the Flyers believed they could beat the Canadiens. Flyers team chairman Ed Snider and Shero were among those who felt the 1975–1976 Bullies were better than their Cup-winning predecessors. "To me, I think this is the best team I ever coached in Philadelphia," Shero said in the spring of 1976. The Flyers sent a franchise-record eight members of their squad—Shero, Clarke, MacLeish, Stephenson, Bill Barber, Reggie Leach, Andre Dupont, and Jim Watson—to the All-Star Game that winter in Philadelphia.

Additional honors poured in in 1976. Clarke claimed his third Hart Memorial Trophy as league MVP, and Leach captured the Conn Smythe by setting a blistering pace in the playoffs with a record 19 goals in sixteen games. Leach, Clarke, and Barber—the LCB Line—set an NHL record for goals in a season with 141. Clarke set a club record for points in a season with 119. The Flyers earned a team-record 119 points and tied the 1929–1930 Boston Bruins for most consecutive victories on home ice with 20. Shero, named Coach of the Year in 1974 after his system of disciplined, positional hockey helped lead the Flyers to their first Cup, was arguably the game's leading strategist.

"He came up with a system, and nobody ever had a system until Freddy came up with it," Joe Watson says. "A lot of people tried to emulate Freddy's success." Included among them was the man many consider hockey's greatest coach. "All the emerging teams are using systems," Montreal's Scotty Bowman said at the time. "With this team I know it will be difficult, but we're going to have to resort to a system ourselves."

It was a startling concession. Montreal may not have been the "Flying Frenchmen" of years past—in 1975–1976 they had nine French Canadians on their twenty-man roster, compared to fourteen of nineteen from their great 1957–1958 squad—but Bowman and company still favored the freewheeling style that had led to decades-long dominance. Bowman's admission surprised many, but not Shero. Since losing to the Canadiens in a hard-fought semifinal in 1973, the Flyers had dropped just two decisions to Montreal in ten meetings dating back to January 1974. The Bullies went 2–1–1 against the Habs in 1975–1976, extending Montreal's winless streak at the Spectrum to three years.

"Talent-wise, this team doesn't compare with the Canadiens," Shero said. "Aside from Clarke and Parent, we don't have a man who could make their squad. But when we have to beat them, we do. Why? Because Montreal relies on one individual to have a super game or make a super play. With them, everything is one-on-one."

Shero's system had stifled attack-based teams Boston and Buffalo in the two previous finals. Montreal was attack-based as well. Lafleur, the league's leading scorer, typified the artistry and élan of former Habs Howie Morentz, Maurice "Rocket" Richard, and Jean Beliveau. Like Beliveau, Lafleur would glide on the ice with almost effortless grace until he suddenly disappeared in a blur on a breakaway. "He's like a magician," Bowman said. Like Rocket Richard and Bernie Geoffrion, the Flower owned a flame-belching shot. Lafleur was one of an incredible nine future Hall of Famers on a club that would win four straight Cups from

1976 to 1979 and go 16–3 in the finals. Lafleur, Gainey, Yvan Cournoyer, Ken Dryden, Guy Lapointe, Jacques Lemaire, Larry Robinson, Serge Savard, and Steve Shutt all got the Hall call. Jarvis, Risebrough, and Pete Mahovlich were key contributors as well. The 1976 Canadiens set records at the time for wins (58) and points (127). With a suffocating defense fronted by the Big Three—Robinson, Savard, and Lapointe—and a free-flowing offense, Montreal stormed through the postseason.

Awaiting Bowman and the Canadiens were Shero and the Bullies. Fans and media saw this series as much a morality play as a matchup of styles. League MVP Clarke and his record-setting LCB Line would be taking on Vezina Trophy winner Dryden and a defense that surrendered the fewest points in the league. The Flyers' ferocious forechecking would be matched against Montreal's backchecking; the Habs' celebrated speed and savoir faire against the grit and spit of the Broad Street Bullies. In the eyes of traditionalists, the game's Holy Grail had been seized by heathens the previous two seasons, and the barbarians were back to storm the citadel once again. As the series with the Flyers loomed, the Canadiens felt pressure to restore order to a sport many believed had been given a black eye by the Bullies. A violent sport had turned vicious, as *Sports Illustrated* declared in a 1975 cover story on the NHL during the Flyers' reign. Bowman and his Habs believed that because of the fighting Flyers, hockey itself was fighting for its own survival.

"Unless the NHL puts a stop to this business quick, you're going to find more and more teams resorting to what the Flyers do," Bowman said. "Teams that only a couple of years ago wouldn't have thought about fighting except in spur-of-the-moment situations are actively looking for musclemen now."

It was an interesting comment from Bowman. A master strategist—he would use thirty-four different line combinations in Game 4 of the finals against the Flyers—Bowman was headman of the NHL's most stylish team. Like Shero, however, Bowman understood the importance of physical play. At his previous coaching stop in St. Louis, Bowman's Blues had been nicknamed the "Black and Blues." Ironically, it was Bowman's Blues who had beaten up the undersized Flyers and given birth to the Broad Street Bullies.

Bowman may have despised the Flyers' orchestrated mayhem, but he had immense admiration for Clarke and studied Shero's system. This moral ambivalence coursed through the Canadiens. In his book *Robinson for the Defence*, the legendary Montreal defenseman Larry Robinson wrote that the Flyers had seven or eight highly skilled players. They were skilled down the middle with Clarke and MacLeish, who Robinson thought were excellent players, and Orest Kindrachuk, a hard worker whom Robinson believed to be vastly underrated. The Flyers had excellent wingers in Barber, Leach, and Gary Dornhoefer, and another plus factor in Shero, who Robinson said knew how to squeeze the last drop of effort out of his players. Since Shero knew his Flyers weren't figure skaters, Robinson said, he took the components of his team and devised a system that maximized their strong points and minimized their weak ones. Each player had a role in that system, and once the system was in place, Shero made sure his players stuck to it. Dryden saw the Flyers as a club that needed a system to win. They were a good but limited team, he thought, and to be effective, they needed to play just one way and play that way so well that their system could overcome more talented teams.

Shero shrugged off criticism of his club's rock 'em, sock 'em hockey. "If it's pretty skating they want to see," he said, "let 'em go to the Ice Capades." He believed his Flyers would win when they had to. "Our team never ceases to amaze me," he said. "When we are challenged, we rise to the occasion." Clarke fired back at experts who believed the Habs had the horses to beat the Bullies. "Everyone always says they have the most talent, but they haven't won," he said. "Maybe they really don't have the most talent."

By the time the finals opened in the Montreal Forum, the hockey world was abuzz with anticipation. "This is the one everyone's been waiting for," Flyers announcer Don Earle told his TV audience. "The Flyers and Canadiens in the finals." Philadelphia sportswriter Jay Greenberg called it the "ultimate Stanley Cup Final." The players agreed. "The Flyers were wired," Robinson said. "So were we."

In Toronto, hockey writer Frank Orr implored the Canadiens to "bring the Cup home." In Boston, hockey writer Leo Monahan believed the Cup was staying on Broad Street. He thought that teams who play crash hockey, who muscle it out in the corners are the teams who gain the Cup. "In the past two years, this has meant the Philadelphia Flyers, and I'll put my money on Fred Shero's bellicose crew this time, too," said Monahan.

The Flyers struck first. After referee Ron Wick dropped the puck for the opening face-off, Clarke and rookie defenseman Jack McIlhargey set up Leach, and the Rifle fired what Earle called "a frozen rope" past Dryden for a 1–0 lead just twenty-one seconds in. Later, Ross Lonsberry freed himself from Robinson in front of the net and beat Dryden with a backhander to make it 2–0 after one period. Some twenty minutes into the finals, the favored Canadiens were reeling. Robinson was impressed by the Flyers' "fierce will to win." The Bullies, he said, let the Habs know from the start that they intended to take the game to them. Shero's LCB Line had gotten the jump on Bowman's checking line. Leach's goal was a laser, and Robinson said it should have awakened the Canadiens. Instead, they continued to lurch and stumble. The Habs left the ice thankful the siren sounded to end the period—and even more thankful they weren't in a deeper hole. "Dryden made a save on my brother Jimmy," Joe Watson recalls, "and if we score there we're up [3–0] and that game is over."

Instead, Montreal regrouped. Dryden believed that to beat the Flyers, the Canadiens would have to neutralize the Bullies' intimidation. Doing so would free up the rest of Montreal's game, which the Habs believed was superior. A video review of Game 1 reveals an intriguing meeting of stars and styles. Robinson provided a glimpse of things to come with hard hits on Clarke and Leach along the boards, but the Bullies gave as good as they got. With just over five minutes left in the first period, Schultz took offense at Mario Tremblay's tactics and floored the Canadiens' fiery forward with a three-punch flurry. "He was a physical presence for us, and other teams knew it," Joe Watson says of the Hammer. "They didn't step out of line."

Stephenson was a presence as well, handling the Habs early in Game 1. Fort Wayne turned in a magnificent save on Lemaire's rebound shot. Earle and Gene Hart told viewers the Canadiens looked overanxious, and Robinson thought the Canadiens were nervous playing in their first final since 1973. Broadcast analyst Ted Lindsay noted that the Flyers' forechecking and positional play was pivotal in Montreal's mistakes. With Canadian premier Pierre Trudeau in the Forum crowd, Montreal seized the momentum in the second period. The Canadiens' speed and their offense-minded defensemen—Robinson, Savard, Lapointe, and company had 14 of Montreal's first 22 shots—began catching the Flyers up ice and created numerous rushes. Roberts and Robinson roofed hard shots over Stephenson's right shoulder to tie the game. Larry Goodenough's power play goal in the third put the Flyers back in front, 3–2, their first success on the man advantage.

Lemaire tied it again when he slid a loose puck in the slot past a screened Stephenson. With 1:22 left and the opener seemingly headed for overtime, Shutt fed Lapointe on the left wing and Lapointe drilled a circle drive into the net. The score sent Forum fans into a frenzy—"like Team Canada playing the Russians," Mahovlich said. The goal gave Montreal the lead for the first time, and the Canadiens' 4–3 victory was secured when Dryden made several saves in the final seconds, including a toe stop on a wicked twenty-foot blast by Jimmy Watson with five seconds left. "I was just trying to cover space," Dryden said. Jimmy still thinks about his shot that nearly forced OT. "It was on the corner of the net," he recalls. "I still can't believe it."

Game 1 was in the books, and several trends had been established. Montreal's speed resulted in numerous odd-man rushes; three of the Canadiens' four goals, including Lapointe's game-winner, came on a two-on-one. "When you played Montreal, I swear it seemed like they had eight guys on the ice," Joe Watson remembers. "They beat you with their team speed and their checking. They were always checking."

The Frenchmen were also flying. Clarke told reporters that Montreal's defensemen skated better than Philadelphia's forwards. "Seemed like they were coming at us 100 miles per hour," he said later. "I think we can still beat them, but it is going to require making a few adjustments." Jimmy Watson remarked that while the Flyers had to play to 100 percent of their capabilities to beat the Canadiens, Montreal only had to play at 75 percent to beat the Flyers. "That's what speed can do," he remembers.

Montreal's big, mobile defense, fronted by the 6-foot-4, 225-pound Robinson and 6-foot-3, 210-pound Savard, helped the Habs achieve a two-to-one advantage in shots on goal in Game 1. Montreal's muscle men stood firm in the face of the Flyers' ferocity. After Schultz pounded Tremblay, Yvon Lambert retaliated against Don Saleski. Robinson continued to crash and bash, colliding heavily with Joe Watson and then with Schultz. "The Canadiens are a punishing team," Hart told his viewing audience. "They've belted the Flyers all night." Lindsay agreed, adding, "They're a big club. We'll have to wait and see what that takes out of the Flyers."

In Game 2, Jarvis, Gainey, and Roberts limited the LCB Line to one shot apiece. Jarvis was particularly effective, winning 14 of 18 faceoffs against Clarke. A bloodied Robinson—he had caught a high stick dangerously close to his right eye—sent another message to the Bullies in the third period when he drilled Dornhoefer along the boards. Some onlookers recall Robinson's hit as the hardest body check they've ever seen. It broke the boards and caused the game to be halted while a maintenance man walked onto the ice with a hammer and pounded the damaged slats back into place. A sizable dent remained, and players on both sides skated past the area, sneaking looks and shaking their heads in amazement. Dornhoefer was hurting but not intimidated. While workmen fixed the Forum boards, Flyers' winger Paul Holmgren saw Dornhoefer leaning over the boards, yelling at Robinson, "Is that the hardest you can hit?" Still, it was reported that Dornhoefer spit blood for several days.

Robinson's resounding body check was the signature play in a game that saw spectacular stops by Stephenson on Shutt and Lemaire and by Dryden on Jimmy Watson and Saleski. The Canadiens claimed a 1–0 lead late in the second period when Lemaire pilfered the puck from Goodenough and scored a shorthanded goal. Montreal made it 2–0 early in the third on a blurring shot by Lafleur from just inside the blue line. The Hammer halved the Flyers' deficit when he beat Dryden with just over two minutes remaining. As they did in the opener, the Flyers flurried in the final seconds, but Dryden deflected their desperate attempts, securing a 2–1 win. It was the first time Shero trailed 2–0 in a series, and the first time the Flyers faced such a deficit since their 1971 quarterfinal sweep by the Black Hawks.

"We're in a hole, no doubt about it," said Shero, but the Bullies were heading home, and Bowman knew what that meant. "I think the visitor is partly psyched out at the Spectrum," he said, relating to reporters how an NHL referee recently had to be escorted from the arena due to the angry mob. Kindrachuk spoke to the urgency facing the Flyers. "We have to win our two games in Philly. We just have to be a little sharper."

Game 3 saw the series switch to the Spectrum, where the Flyers had lost just three times in their last fifty-two games and were 23–2 in the playoffs since 1974. The Canadiens geared themselves for the Flyers, their frenzied fans, the Spectrum, Kate Smith, and what Robinson called "The Song"—"God Bless America." When Shero put enforcers Schultz and Kelly on the wings, Bowman countered by shifting a pair of defensemen—6-foot-2, 210-pound Rick Chartraw and 6-foot-2, 205-pound Pierre Bouchard—to forward to give Montreal more muscle.

The Flyers struggled with the Canadiens' size and strategy. Bowman composed a line that saw Lemaire flanked by the 6-foot-5, 210-pound Mahovlich and the 6-foot-2, 200-pound Lambert, prompting Hart to tell viewers it looked like the red-sweatered Habs had "redwood trees" on the ice. Joe Watson thought the Canadiens were so big and tall that when they reached with their sticks it looked as though they could reach across the rink. Considering they hadn't won in Philadelphia in three years, it might have been easy for the Canadiens to catch the Philly Flu in hockey's House of Horrors. Instead, Montreal sent a message early when Chartraw delivered a hard hit on Joe Watson. Robinson thought Chartraw's hit drove home the point that the Canadiens weren't going to be intimidated. It made the Bullies very uncomfortable, Robinson thought, to be on the receiving end.

Later in the period, Shutt scored on a seventy-five-foot floater that danced like a Phil Niekro knuckleball and seemed to pass through Stephenson as if he were made of ectoplasm. "The puck was sitting on its edge so when I shot it, it took off fluttering," Shutt said later. "The shot must have dipped two feet on Stephenson." Stephenson said that this was the case: "All of a sudden it dropped and curved." The Flyers tied it when Clarke fed Leach and the Rifle launched a low rocket to the far corner of the net. Leach's blast was a line drive; Dryden didn't react until the puck was already past him. Leach made it 2–1 in the first when he took advantage of a Bill Nyrop turnover and dribbled the puck past Dryden for his NHL-record eighteenth goal of the playoffs. Shutt tied it a minute into the second when he stuffed in his own rebound. The score stuck at 2–2 as Stephenson performed brilliantly in net, stopping 12 of 13 shots in the second period, including breakaways by Murray Wilson, Gainey, and Cournoyer. It could have been 10–2, Robinson thought, except that Stephenson was phenomenal in goal. Eager to put a stranglehold on the series, Bowman had his forwards flooding the Flyers' zone. On the TV broadcast, Flyers backup goalie Gary Inness, who was not activated for the series since Parent was serving as backup, warned that the reigning champions couldn't continue to allow the Canadiens to crash the net.

Midway through the third period, Montreal's persistent pressure paid off. Chartraw tied up Schultz in front of the net and Pierre Bouchard took a pass from Wilson and fired. Bouchard's forty-five-foot wrist shot slipped through the legs of Chartraw and a screened Stephenson for the winner. The Flyers, a team that had always risen to the occasion, were scrambling for answers. Shero's style—winning small battles along the boards—wasn't working. As Lindsay noted, the Habs had seized control of the boards and were forcing the Flyers into the middle of the ice, where they struggled to contain the Canadiens' creativity on the fly.

Bowman's checking lines frustrated the Flyers, leading an exasperated Dornhoefer to tell reporters that Gainey, Risebrough, Roberts, Jarvis, and company were checking the champions so closely he could tell "what brand of deodorant they're using." The Canadiens were beating the Bullies at their own game. Bowman pulled a page from Shero's playbook with his emphasis on a defensive "system"—a forerunner of the neutral-zone trap that Lemaire and Robinson took to New Jersey as coaches and won the Stanley Cup with in 1995. Montreal was winning not only the mental chess match but the physical war as well. Robinson reasoned that if the Canadiens could eliminate the Flyers' physical edge, their skills would allow them to beat the Bullies. Strip away Shero's system, Robinson thought, and the flaws underneath would be exposed.

The Bullies, meanwhile, believed the Canadiens to be the best team they had seen. "I haven't seen a better team since I've come into the league," Clarke told the media. Barber thought the Flyers were playing their best, "but there's not much we can do." Shero said his team "played very hard but we still got outplayed a little." Dornhoefer believed the Canadiens to be "a lot stronger, physically, than we are." Clarke said Montreal had the bodies, "and they're using them." Leach thought Montreal's lines were outstanding, and on top of that, they had Dryden and huge defensemen. The latter, combined with Bowman's use of the trap, forced the Flyers to shoot from the top of the circle because, as Leach learned, that was as close as they were going to get. Montreal's size and strength also left Philly's defensemen with little room to operate. The Flyers started dumping the puck out, sometimes without looking, and it was a puck Robinson thought had been carelessly cleared that led to Bouchard's winning goal in Game 3. Joe Watson recalls the Canadiens scoring "goals they shouldn't have."

The loss was only the Flyers' fourth following Smith's song, and the Canadiens were responsible for three of those defeats, including two in the 1973 quarterfinals. Asked by a reporter if he thought the Flyers would "come out charging" for Game 4, Dryden frowned. "That implies the Flyers have been holding back in the first three games and I don't think that's true," he said, adding that Montreal's 3–0 series lead was the most deceiving in Cup history. "Remember, each game has been decided by one goal and each has ended with the Flyers storming around our goal, taking point-blank shots. A deflection here, an inch or two there and they could have two wins quite easily. . . . Never forget one thing—the Flyers have won the Stanley Cup championship the last two years. It's an honor they've cherished, and they won't give it up cheaply."

The Flyers had a reputation for roughhouse hockey, but it was the Bullies who were feeling battered. In Game 3, Leach, Kindrachuk, and McIlhargey needed medical assistance, the latter requiring fourteen stitches to close a face wound. "It's just something I can't believe is happening," Clarke said. He credited Bowman's coaching, noting that the Canadiens were dressing twelve forwards and five defensemen while the Flyers were dressing ten forwards. "They have fresh people coming at you all the time."

Schultz said the Flyers needed to reach back to their Broad Street Bullies days and "kick some ass." Shero opened Game 4 with Schultz and Saleski on the wings. The Hammer set an early tone, swapping punches with Savard. "He knocked a couple of Savard's teeth out," Joe Watson remembers. Desperate to turn their fortunes around, the Flyers brought in Kate Smith in person. The raucous Spectrum crowd roared, and for good reason: It was noted on the TV broadcast that the Flyers were 47–4–1 when Smith's song was played and 4–0 when she sang it in person. It looked like Lady Luck was smiling on the Bullies when Leach lifted a drive past Dryden from forty-five feet out just forty-one seconds in. On *Hockey Night in Canada*, Dick Irvin Jr. told Danny Gallivan and their TV audience that Leach had Dryden "mesmerized." Leach heard that Dryden feared the Rifle's shot. Reggie's strategy was to shoot high early in the game to intimidate Dryden. Once the shooter got inside the goalie's head, Leach believed the battle was practically won.

The sold-out Spectrum was "Flyered" up, but the Bullies' physical play worked against them. In a fast and furious first period, the Canadiens sandwiched power play goals by Shutt and Bouchard around a Barber goal to tie the score at 2 each. As accelerated as play was on the ice, it was just as fast-paced behind the benches. Shero put fourteen different line combinations on the ice in the first twenty minutes, and Bowman, seventeen. Seven minutes into the second period, the Flyers reclaimed the lead as Dupont netted a power play goal and celebrated with his customary Moose Shuffle. The play had been set up by Clarke, who dug the puck from the corner and fed Moose. The LCB Line was showing signs of life, having produced two goals and assisted on a third. Bowman stepped up the pressure on Clarke. He had Jarvis and Risebrough on Clarke in the first three games, and then triple-shifted in Game 4, adding Lemaire to the mix. Kindrachuk could hear Dryden yelling, "Lean on them! Tire them out!"

In their signature win over the Soviets four months earlier, Shero's blue line defense rattled the Russians. A review of each of the four games of the 1976 finals reveals that Shero didn't use the trap at all against the Canadiens. "Montreal was so fast, it was hard to set up [defensively],"

Joe Watson explains. "They were big and fast, and they came at you in droves."

With eleven seconds left in the second, the Canadiens tied the game again at 3–3 when Cournoyer backhanded a rebound for a power play goal. With time running out in the third, Lafleur scored on a point-blank blast, and fifty-eight seconds later, Mahovlich made it 5–3 with Montreal's third straight score. The Broad Street Bullies' reign was over, and it had ended with a surprising sweep. The Bullies had gone down, but not without a fight, a fact acknowledged by the new champions. Dryden told reporters in the champagne-soaked clubhouse to take note: Hockey's new kings were celebrating but were doing so sitting down. They were too tired to stand. Robinson told reporters that if he had hit all season like he hit against the Bullies, he'd be ground down. "I'd be 4–8 and weigh 150 pounds," he said.

The former champs felt the ferocious pace as well. Slowed by strained ligaments in his knee and by the tight-checking Canadiens, Clarke was worn thin. By series' end, he was fifteen pounds below his playing weight. Pain and frustration were evident in his pale blue eyes. The Canadiens thought the stretched ligaments in Clarke's right knee showed their effects in Games 3 and 4. "There's only so much a guy can do for a team," Mahovlich said. Kindrachuk played despite a painful back injury, and several other Bullies were battered and bloodied. Leach looked around the locker room and saw a banged-up team. A series sweep, he thought, is not indicative of how close these finals were. In the traditional post-series handshake lines at center ice, Bowman gripped Clarke's hand. "I'd just like to have you on my side once," Bowman told Clarke.

The purists were pleased. Flower Power had conquered the Hammer, and many hailed Montreal's victory as the dawn of a new day in the NHL. "This is not only a victory for the Canadiens, it is a victory for hockey," Savard said afterward. "I hope that this era of intimidation and violence that is hurting our national sport is coming to an end. Young people have seen that a team can play electrifying, fascinating hockey while still behaving like gentlemen."

Robinson said later that the Canadiens "ended the Broad Street Bullies. Never again would they dictate their system or style of game to us." Irvin believes the Canadiens' win was a turnaround for hockey. He thought the sport's white hats had beaten the black hats and that it proved to be a changing of the guard. Amid the funereal feeling in the Flyers' locker room, Dornhoefer called the Canadiens the greatest club he'd ever seen: "They were a step-and-a-half ahead of us all the time." Stephenson said the Flyers "gave everything. . . . If we started this thing all over again next week, I'd give us as good a chance to win as them." Clarke called Montreal the "better team in this series," but told *Argosy* magazine in the off-season that when the Flyers get MacLeish and Parent back, "I think we can beat them." Pete Mahovlich wasn't so sure. "I don't think Parent would've played any better than Stephenson," he said. But Mahovlich acknowledged the absence of MacLeish. "You can't take away a guy who scored 17 and 19 points in the playoffs and expect to fill the hole," he said.

Mahovlich felt Montreal had too much depth for the Flyers. "Their injuries caught up with them," he said. He believed the Bullies played the Canadiens even for the first thirty minutes of each game, but then Montreal would take over. Still, the Habs were impressed by the former champs. "Tell the Flyers they played a hell of a series," Jimmy Roberts remarked to reporters. "They're a great team." Robinson called the finals "the toughest four games I've ever played." Lafleur, speaking softly, described it as "a very tough series. Philadelphia deserves credit. They played hard every game."

The breakup of the Bullies that began with the trading of Bill Clement in 1975 and Van Impe in 1976 continued with Schultz being dealt during the off-season. Philadelphia wouldn't return to the finals until 1980. By then, Montreal's dynastic run was giving way to the Islanders. The 1975–1976 Flyers remain one of the greatest squads in franchise history. Robinson calls the 1976 Stanley Cup Finals his favorite because the Flyers were "at their peak." Injuries and notable absentees hurt the Flyers' run at a historic hat trick of titles and also led to one of the great "what if" questions in Flyers history.

What if the Bullies had been at full strength for the finals? "If we had [Parent, MacLeish, and Van Impe] in the lineup, we could have played pretty even hockey," Kelly says. "I know we were beaten in four straight, but three games were decided by one goal and the last game by two. Any time you're missing stars, it has an impact."

Joe Watson agrees. "That was as good a team as Montreal put together," he says, "but if we had our full team, it might have gone seven. Larry Robinson said the biggest win in his life was beating the Flyers in 1976." Watson pauses, then issues a loud laugh. "Bastards!"

Irvin believes that as good as Montreal was, if the Flyers had Parent and MacLeish for the finals, the series would have been different. "It would not have been a sweep," he states.

In the end, Flyers fans saluted their beloved Bullies. A sign inside the Spectrum at the end of the final game said it all:

"WE LOVE YOU ANYWAY"

They loved them because the Flyers turned the toxic wasteland that was pro sports in Philadelphia into a budding paradise. The Phillies, 76ers, and Eagles ended extensive postseason droughts, and the city was soon celebrating its first ever World Series champion and Super Bowl squad, and its first NBA champion since 1967.

Epilogue

Making the Modern NHL

In the first quarter of the twentieth century, Moscow resident Boris Fomin wrote the melody for a song titled "Dorogoi Dlinnoyu" ("By the Long Road"). Fomin's melody, coupled with the lyrics provided by poet Konstantin Podrevsky, focused on wistful reminiscing about one's younger days. Decades later, Gene Raskin, also of Russian descent, put English lyrics to Fomin's melody for a song titled "Those Were the Days." In 1968, the song served as Mary Hopkin's debut single, and it soared to number 1 in the UK and number 2 in the United States.

For fans, coaches, and players, Super Series '76 stirs similarly strong reminiscences. Those were the days, indeed, and the memories and photographs remain vibrant and vivid: Valeri Kharlamov of the Red Army colliding along the boards in Madison Square Garden with the Rangers' Ron Greschner; Army goalie Vladislav Tretiak blocking a shot by the Bruins' Jean Ratelle in Boston Garden; the Canadiens' Doug Risebrough diving to the ice to control a loose puck in the Montreal Forum; the Bullies' Bob Kelly and the Red Army's Boris Mikhailov tangling in the Spectrum; Konstantin Loktev pulling his players from the ice in a walkout.

These were the times of their lives, and the passage of time has seen the years fall away. The classic arenas have disappeared from cityscapes. The Spectrum no longer sits on Broad Street; the historic building was torn down in 2011. Nor do we see Freddy the Fog behind the bench, Bill Barber on the wing, Moose Dupont dropping an opponent at the blue line, or the Watson brothers shutting down enemy forwards. The days of the Broad Street Bullies are over. Yet what took place on the skate-scarred ice of the Spectrum on January 11, 1976, remains an important part of hockey history.

The Flyers' influence was not lost on the Russians. Their protests about the Bullies' "animal hockey" aside, the Soviets in subsequent years became more physical, more willing to check. Frustrated by the Flyers' defense, the Russians adopted more of a transition game. The Soviet style became one of instant creativity, an all-ice commitment in which there were fewer patterns to disrupt and thus fewer opportunities for the opposing defense to get set. North American players likewise learned from their European counterparts. NHL teams improved their passing skills and shot selection and enhanced their training and conditioning. It led to a more wide-open brand of hockey popularized by the Edmonton Oilers dynasty in the 1980s.

As Super Series '76 closed, the Russians and North Americans both claimed victory in the NHL-Soviet "World Series." Including victories by the Wings, the Soviets won the series, 5–2–1. Yet the Russians failed to beat the NHL's elite teams, losing to 1975 Stanley Cup finalists Philadelphia and Buffalo and tying with eventual 1976 champion Montreal, a fact seized upon by Clarence Campbell.

"Who the hell did they beat?" the NHL president asked at the time. "Montreal was first in our league. They didn't win but anybody who saw that game—and that includes the Soviets—agreed that the Canadiens gave them a hell of a beating. Philadelphia is second in our league. They beat the Russians. Buffalo is third in our league. They beat the Russians." Campbell said the NHL expected the Soviets to win some games, but the important result was that the Russians did not defeat the NHL's top three teams. Regardless, the Russians still claimed victory. "Despite the loss in Philadelphia," Tretiak later wrote, "we won the Super Series." Like Tretiak, Soviet Wings coach Boris Kulagin was unimpressed by the Flyers' victory. "I feel confident that if the Soviet Central Red Army team played eight games against the Philadelphia Flyers," Kulagin said, "the Flyers would lose the series."

Red Fisher of the *Montreal Star* disagreed. The Soviets, he wrote, were "grand and talented visitors," but their eight-game tour did not represent an NHL season. "The Soviets won this series, 5–2–1, but all of the dialogue in the wake of Philadelphia's awesome wipeout of the Central Army team focused on the Soviets' failure to beat the National Hockey League's best three teams. Their best was unable to beat our best, which makes the over-all results considerably less than important."

The Flyers and the Red Army played a singular game for the ages. In combining their skills, styles, and strategies and in bringing together European and North American players on the same ice, they gave a glimpse into hockey's future and a preview of the modern NHL. "The Russians had never seen anything like the Philadelphia Flyers," Bill Clement says. "They learned that they had to toughen up."

The Soviets' strong showing in Super Series '76 raised the question of whether the Russians should be allowed to compete for the Stanley Cup, the trophy emblematic of hockey supremacy. Writing for *Hockey Illustrated* in 1976, Leo Monahan thought it "sacrilege" to suggest the Russians be included in the NHL playoffs. "To allow Russia to play for the Cup would dishonor the memory of North America's oldest athletic trophy."

Providing a counterpoint, Frank Orr felt it might be better to have a World Cup involving the champions of the NHL, WHA, Russia, Finland, Czechoslovakia, Sweden, Finland, and other countries. Orr also suggested "an interlocking" schedule between the NHL, WHA, USSR, and European clubs: "Each NHL and WHA team would be guaranteed four visits from top foreign sides as part of their schedule, and the WHA and NHL clubs would make at least one overseas trip each."

Amid talk of whether the NHL or Soviet hockey was superior, the WHA was almost an afterthought. Yet while Super Series '76 spurred debate as to which team was hockey's greatest—the Flyers, Canadiens, or Red Army—one more club deserving consideration was WHA champion Winnipeg. Paced by the prolific Hot Line of Bobby Hull and Swedish wingers Anders Hedberg and Ulf Nilsson, the Jets won fifty-two games in the regular season and stormed to their second AVCO Cup crown by going 12–1 in the playoffs, including a four-game sweep of Gordie Howe and the Houston Aeros. The Hot Line combined for 141 goals and 342 points, then added 32 goals and 65 points in the postseason. Yet the Jets were more than just the Hot Line. Joe Daley was the best goalie in the

WHA, and forwards Peter Sullivan and Veli-Pekka Ketola each scored 32 goals. Lars-Erik Sjoberg was one of the WHA's top defensemen, and former Bruins' defenseman Ted Green added experience and toughness.

Hockey historian Roy MacGregor calls the Hot Line the best scoring trio in the sport from 1974–78. MacGregor told Geoff Kirbyson in a 2016 article in the *Winnipeg Free Press*. "You had the guy with the best shot in hockey (Hull) and combined him with the best playmaker (Nilsson) and the fastest skater (Hedberg)." Kirbyson wrote that the Hot Line "married the north-south North American game with the east-west European game to create magic on ice." Kirbyson noted in his 2016 article that *Winnipeg Tribune* writer Vic Grant called the Jets one of the best hockey teams in the world. On January 5, 1978, the Jets became the first club team to defeat the Soviet national squad, winning 5–3. Kirbyson believed the Soviet team that played WHA clubs in 1977–1978 was a "half step" ahead of the Red Army team that played in Super Series '76.

The Soviets had defeated the Jets three times on spacious international ice in Japan one week earlier, and Tretiak was held out of the game in Winnipeg until 13:03 of the second period, when the Hot Line had already fueled a 4–0 lead. The Soviets cut their deficit to 4–3 before Hull beat Tretiak in the final seconds for the hat trick score that sealed the deal. Like the Flyers, the Jets played a physical game against the Soviets, forechecking fiercely. CKY-TV's Peter Young told Kirbyson that Winnipeg's forechecking foiled the Soviets' breakouts and that the Kharlamov line "looked like confused little peewees." Bob Irving, part of a radio broadcast team doing the game, told Kirbyson, "These were the powerhouse Russians and Hedberg, Nilsson, and Hull had their way with them."

The Russians would have their say in subsequent meetings with North American clubs. One year after the Red Army returned to North America and went 6–2 against WHA teams in Super Series '76–77, including a 3–2 victory over Avco Cup finalist Winnipeg and a 6–1 loss to league champion Quebec, Spartak Moscow went 3–2 against NHL clubs, including a 5–2 defeat against Stanley Cup champion Montreal. The Russians won Super Series '79, the Soviet Wings going 2–1–1 against the NHL, the tie being a 4–4 final against the Flyers. Super

Series 1980 saw Dynamo Moscow and the Red Army win their respective series against NHL teams, the Red Army falling to the Canadiens, 4–2, but defeating the league champion New York Islanders, 3–2.

Super Series 1983 witnessed the official birth of the "Red Machine" moniker with a Minneapolis newspaper's coverage of the North Stars' 6–3 loss to the Soviet national team headlined, "The Red Machine rolled down on us." Indeed, the Soviets rolled over the NHL, 4–2, losing to the Oilers, 4–3, but finally beating the Flyers, 5–1. Soviet dominance continued in Super Series 1986, the Red Army going 5–1, with a 6–3 win over the dynastic Oilers, and Dynamo Moscow going 2–1–1. The NHL didn't win a series against the Soviets until 1989, defeating Dynamo Riga, 4–2–1; the Red Army, meanwhile, continued its dominance by beating NHL clubs, 4–2–1, with one of their losses coming to Mario Lemieux's Pittsburgh Penguins. In Super Series 1990, the Isles, Canadiens, and Hartford Whalers fronted a 3–1–1 win over the Wings. In that same Super Series, NHL teams tied Khimik Voskresensk, 3–3, but fell to the Red Army, 4–1. Included in the latter was the Flyers' 5–4 loss to their old rivals. Dynamo Moscow likewise won its series over the NHL, 3–2.

Super Series 1991 marked the end of Soviet-NHL Super Series. While Khimik Voskresensk tied, 3–3–1, the Red Army handled the NHL once again, going 6–1, and Dynamo Moscow also won, 3–2–2, in the process defeating the Stanley Cup champion Penguins and the Flyers, the latter a 4–1 final that mirrored their 1976 score.

Along with the Super Series, there were other meetings between Soviet and NHL stars. Challenge Cup '79 was a three-game "Series of the Century" played at Madison Square Garden in place of that year's annual NHL All-Star Game between the Wales Conference and Campbell Conference. Fueled by Lafleur and Mike Bossy and accompanied by the theme from the blockbuster movie *Star Wars*, NHL stars stormed Tretiak to take the opener, 4–2. The Russians retaliated in Game 2, overcoming a 3–1 deficit to defeat Ken Dryden, 5–4. The Soviets romped in the decisive Game 3, with Mikhailov igniting a 6–0 victory over Gerry Cheevers and Vladimir Myshkin replacing Tretiak and playing flawlessly in goal. Rendez-vous '87 resulted in a split of the two-game series, the NHL winning Game 1, 4–3, and the USSR taking Game 2, 5–3.

North American pros also played the Soviets in round robin Canada Cup tournaments in 1976, 1981, and 1984. The 1976 Team Canada squad ranks as one of the greatest teams in the history of sport, hockey's version of the NBA's original Dream Team of Michael Jordan, Magic Johnson, Larry Bird, Patrick Ewing, and company. Team Canada's roster read like a Who's Who of Hall of Famers: Clarke, Hull, Lafleur, Bobby Orr (finally able to play against the Soviets following years of injuries), Bill Barber, Phil Esposito, Gil Perreault, Larry Robinson, Denis Potvin, and head coach Scotty Bowman. Kharlamov, Mikhailov, Petrov, and Aleksandr Yakushev remained in Russia as the team transitioned to a lineup that listed young stars Slava Fetisov, Igor Larionov, Vladimir Krutov, Sergei Makarov, Vasily Pervukhin, and Alexei Kasatonov teamed with standard bearers Tretiak, Aleksandr Maltsev, and Valeri Vasiliev. Krutov, Larionov, and Makarov formed the KLM Line and joined with defensemen Fetisov and Kasatonov on the "Green Unit," so named by the Canadiens because they practiced in green jerseys. Orr, Hull, and Perreault starred for Team Canada in its 3–1 win, while Maltsev was a standout for the Soviets.

Canada downed Czechoslovakia in the finals, and after the 1980 Canada Cup was postponed due to international political tensions arising from the Soviet Union's invasion of Afghanistan, the USSR and Team Canada prepared to meet in 1981. The Soviets were coming off their historic upset loss to the United States in the 1980 Olympics, and they appeared to be still reeling when they were dazzled by the Dream Line of Gretzky, Lafleur, and Perreault in a 7–3 defeat in the Montreal Forum. The tournament's final game rematched the Russians and Team Canada. The Soviets studied film of Gretzky's on-ice wizardry and built a game plan to contain him. With Tretiak having his last hurrah in international play, the Soviets celebrated an 8–1 rout and Cup championship. "Just can't compete," Gretzky lamented. It was reported that when the Russians returned to Moscow, a woman kissed Tretiak on the cheek and thanked him for beating "those Canadian bastards!"

Canada Cup 1984 had Team Canada coached by Glen Sather of the Oilers. The lineup was comprised largely of players from the NHL's two most recent great teams—the Oilers and Islanders. The Soviets dominated Team Canada, 6–3, in their first tournament game. It marked the second straight defeat dealt to NHL stars by the Red Machine. Messier responded with a stiff body check and high elbow that bloodied the face of Vladimir Kolvin and sent the Russian to the bench for treatment. Video review shows Messier standing in the penalty box and shouting at the Soviets. Reflecting the Flyers' attitude from 1976, Messier said it was "win at all costs, Us against Them, two ideologies colliding."

The collisions continued in the semifinals, Team Canada winning an emotional 3–2 overtime thriller. "We're a great hockey country, they're a great hockey country," Gretzky told reporters. "It's about time everybody realizes that." Team Canada stopped Sweden in the finals, and three years later, head coach Mike Keenan put together arguably the greatest line in hockey history—forwards Gretzky, Messier, and Lemieux, with defensemen Paul Coffey and Ray Bourque. The Soviets countered with their renowned Green Unit. The 1987 Canada Cup had Team Canada and the Soviets advancing to the best-of-three finals. Alexander Semak's OT goal in Game 1 gave the Russians a 6–5 victory. Game 2 was another 6–5 final in OT, Team Canada evening the series as Gretzky and Lemieux teamed to provide the winning score. The third and decisive game was again 5–5 in the third period when Gretzky and Lemieux worked their magic one more time, the Great One on his way to being tournament MVP feeding Super Mario, who wristed the winning score over goalie Sergei Mylnikov's shoulder.

It's fitting that three of the greatest games in the history of North America versus Soviet hockey signaled the end of an era. Soviet players began emigrating to the NHL in 1989, and the collapse of the USSR two years later contributed to the influx of Russian players into North America. It marked the greatest migration of talent from one league to another since the late 1940s when Negro Leaguers joined the major leagues.

Pavel Bure, aka the "Russian Rocket," and the "Wizards of Ov"—Sergei Fedorov, Slava Fetisov, Vladimir Konstantinov, and Slava Kozlov—began lighting up NHL arenas with electric play and leading their respective clubs into Stanley Cup Finals. The Wizards of Ov helped Detroit into the 1995 Stanley Cup Final. Awaiting the modern-day "Soviet" Wings were the New Jersey Devils, and there was irony in former Canadiens player and Devils coach Jacques Lemaire's using a neutral-zone trap in the fashion of Fred Shero to produce a four-game sweep. "It was the same damn trap," Joe Watson says.

The next season, Detroit dealt for Igor Larionov, and the famed "Russian Five"—Fedorov, Fetisov, Konstantinov, Kozlov, and Larionov—set an NHL record with sixty-two wins, their 131 points one shy of tying the 1976–1977 Canadiens' mark. In 1997, Bowman and the Russian Five helped Detroit end its title drought by sweeping Eric Lindros and the "Legion of Doom" Flyers in the finals.

The impact of Russian players on the NHL has been significant. Through Colorado's 2022 Stanley Cup victory over two-time defending champion Tampa Bay, more than 140 Russians have taken the ice in the Stanley Cup playoffs. Including Avalanche winger Valeri Nichushkin, thirty-six Russian players have been on Stanley Cup championship teams. Goalie Andrei Vasilevskiy backstopped the Lightning to consecutive Cup titles in 2020 and 2021 and three straight trips to the finals. Winger Nikita Kucherov and defenseman Mikhail Sergachev were key contributors to the Lightning's success as well, which saw Tampa Bay reach four conference finals in five seasons.

Unfortunately for Nichushkin, the NHL announced during the 2022 finals that due to Russia's invasion of Ukraine the previous February, Russian players would not be allowed to take the Stanley Cup home to their native land. NHL associate commissioner Bill Daly said before Game 1 of the finals that the league would consider a "make-up Cup trip in the future," like they did during the pandemic. The NHL's hard stance regarding the Stanley Cup did not extend to Russian players' eligibility for the draft in July 2022. Daly said ahead of draft day that it wouldn't surprise him if one or more Russian players slipped in the draft proceedings "based on the inability to access them."

During the 2022 season, there were fifty-seven Russian players on NHL rosters. Their country's unpopular war with Ukraine caused the league to experience an uncomfortable overlapping of sports and politics. It was the largest European military conflict since World War II, and NHL commissioner Gary Bettman said that everyone connected with the league was doing their best under "incredibly trying circumstances."

The Russian players, he added, were in "an impossible situation." The NHL stopped business relations in Russia, declined to discuss holding future games there, ended its posting to social media sites connected to Russia, and issued a statement condemning the invasion. Russian players largely kept a low profile during the war. Alex Ovechkin issued a statement, "Please, no more war," and Calgary defenseman Nikita Zadorov posted "NO WAR" on Instagram.

Hall of Fame goalie Dominik Hasek, a Czech, said in February 2022 that the NHL did not go far enough in its measures. Taking to Twitter, Hasek called Ovechkin, who campaigned for Vladimir Putin in 2017 "a liar." Wrote Hasek, "Every adult in Europe knows well that Putin is a mad killer and that Russia is waging an offensive war against the free country and its people. The NHL must immediately suspend contracts for all Russian players! Every athlete represents not only himself and his club, but also his country and its values and actions."

Unlike Wimbledon, which banned tennis players from Russia and its ally Belarus, the NHL did not consider banning players. Had the league done so, stars such as Vasilevskiy, fellow goalie Igor Shesterkin of the New York Rangers, and forwards Alex Ovechkin of the Washington Capitals, Evgeni Malkin of the Pittsburgh Penguins, and Kirill Kaprizov of the Minnesota Wild, among others, would have been unavailable to their Stanley Cup–contending clubs.

Sports agents representing Russian players told the Associated Press in March 2022 that because their government was considering declaring what it called fake news about Putin's "special military operations" to be a crime, players were concerned about family and friends living in Russia. Malkin's parents were in Russia, as were Ovechkin's wife, children, and parents. As Putin places a greater emphasis on ice hockey than on other sports, some felt that allowing Russians to continue playing in the NHL during the war was promoting Putin's government. The league released a statement in spring 2022 that players from Russia "play in the NHL on behalf of their NHL clubs, and not on behalf of Russia."

North American and Russian players have come a long way since Super Series '76. Dick Irvin Jr. believes both sides benefited from decades of intense competition against one another. "Each learned from the other," he says. Writing an opinion piece for the *Washington Post* in March 2022, Dryden recalled NHL vs. Soviet hockey in the 1970s as "the most passionate and hard-fought in both countries' hockey histories." The reason was nationalism and Cold War politics. "It was *Us* vs. *Them*," he wrote. Those passions were eventually cooled by mutual respect, and Us versus Them, said Dryden, became "*US.*"

The proof is the modern NHL, which has melded the styles of Europe and North America. Old rivalries die hard, however, and Russians and North Americans have not forgotten what took place in Philadelphia in January 1976. Tretiak once recalled Shero traveling to Moscow and presenting the Flyers' victory over the Red Army as "well-deserved." The Flyers, Shero said, were not a group of gangsters; "we simply have more guts than any other team." Tretiak thought Shero's reasoning lacked objectivity, as did his claim that the Russians were confused by the Bullies' disciplined and patient play. The Red Army was confused, Tretiak said, but for other reasons. They didn't know barbarians could put on skates and get away with hunting hockey players. He said the Russians had witnessed the "dirty play" of North American professionals in 1972 and 1974, "but what happened in Philadelphia was an apotheosis of professional hockey thuggery." Years later, Tretiak said he couldn't think about that game with the Flyers without shuddering.

Jimmy Watson takes an opposing view. He is not being overdramatic, Jimmy says, when he speaks of the importance of the Flyers' victory over the Red Army. He believes the dramatic win did a lot for the Flyers, for the NHL, and for North America's pride. There is some humor attached to the Soviets-Flyers game. When Gene Hart visited Russia, he asked a guard why a certain group of men were chained. "Those men were on the ice," the Russian responded, "when Joe Watson scored his goal!"

Joe Watson was in Moscow when young Muscovites asked about the Bullies' victory over the Red Army. "You're not old enough to have seen that game," he told them. Didn't matter, the Muscovites answered: "It is ingrained in our history what the Broad Street Bullies did to our Red Army!" Back home, Watson was in a South Jersey parade when he was greeted with chants of "Beat the Russians!"

Larry Goodenough recalls meeting Tretiak and hearing him say he was the best goalie in the world. "You can't be the best," Goodenough told Tretiak.

"Why not?"

"Because I scored on you!"

Shero considered the Flyers' win against the Red Army as arguably the greatest in franchise history. He also thought it perhaps the costliest. "It probably cost us the Stanley Cup," he said once. "I noticed something missing from our team after that game. We had defeated the best in the world."

The Flyers versus the Red Army remains the most controversial game in hockey history. It's the game that saved the NHL, and it's talked about still. "We were the Stanley Cup champions," Jimmy Watson says. "If we had not beaten the Russians, that would've tainted the Stanley Cup, and how could we say the NHL is the best hockey in the world? We knew all of this going into that game. We had read about the Russians and heard what tremendous players they were, but we had the right coach and the right team. We were not going to lose that game."

The Broad Street Bullies staked their claim to being the best hockey team in the world. The Soviets claimed victory in the Super Series. Decades later, it's clear that hockey itself was the ultimate winner from those eight games in the winter of 1976.

"Super Series '76 was spectacular," says Jimmy Watson. "It totally blended the two styles together. We learned from the Russians, they learned from us, and that's been good for our sport. It's elevated the NHL to a worldwide game."

ACKNOWLEDGMENTS

As with any work of this size, there are many people who contributed to the final product. To my wife, Michelle, thank you for your love and support and for reading early drafts and offering input. To my daughters, Patty and Katie, and their families, thank you for your enthusiasm and encouragement.

To Niels Aaboe of Lyons Press, who believed in this project from its inception, and to Rick Rinehart, Chris Fischer, and Meghann French, thank you for your hard work and expertise.

It was my privilege and honor to get to know members of the famed Broad Street Bullies, including brothers Joe and Jimmy Watson, Andre "Moose" Dupont, Bob "Hound" Kelly, Bill Barber, Larry Goodenough, and Bill Clement. Each of you shared memories and insider information on one of the most iconic teams in sports history. Your recollections, always candid and often humorous, provided a rare behind-the-scenes look at a team that transcended the NHL and one that joined the 1972–1974 Oakland A's "Mustache Gang," the 1975–1977 Oakland Raiders, and the 1987–1091 Detroit Pistons "Bad Boys" as winning clubs whose controversial style brought substantive change to their respective sports.

To Ray Shero, son of Bullies head coach Fred Shero and a longtime NHL executive, you provided valuable insight into the pioneering coaching ways of your father and into the skill and talent of the Flyers Stanley Cup championship teams of the mid-1970s. Fred's induction into the Hockey Hall of Fame was long overdue, but fortunately, the omission has been corrected and the legendary coach, who was ahead of his time in so many ways and instituted many innovations adopted by his coaching contemporaries, is finally and rightfully enshrined with the game's greats.

Hall of Fame sportscaster Dick Irvin Jr. of *Hockey Night in Canada* fame recalled broadcasting this classic contest between the two-time reigning Stanley Cup champion Flyers and the Soviet and Olympic champion Central Red Army. To Mr. Irvin, thank you for being exceedingly gracious with your time and providing great memories of the NHL as it was in the 1970s. You also took time to emphasize that the champion Flyers were more than the Broad Street Bullies. They were, as you stated, a well-coached club that featured Hall of Fame and all-star talent and was one of the hardest-working outfits in NHL history.

Arthur Chidlovski, arguably the foremost historian of Russian hockey, recalled watching this epic confrontation on television as a youth growing up in Moscow and remembered how the prospect of Russia's hockey heroes sharing the same ice with the internationally renowned Broad Street Bullies stirred tremendous interest in the Soviet Union. Thank you, Arthur, for your thoughts on Russian hockey greats like Vladislav Tretiak, Valeri Kharlamov, and Boris Mikhailov, which helped put personality into the printed stats. You also detailed the impact of Super Series '76 and the role it played in bringing about the blending of the European and North American styles of hockey that led to the creation of the modern NHL.

Bill Lyon, whose elegant prose graced the *Philadelphia Inquirer* sports section for decades, was a treat to speak with. Sadly, Bill has since passed, and his wonderful writing is greatly missed. Bill began covering sports for the *Inquirer* in 1973, and his memories of the highs and lows of reporting on the Broad Street Bullies remain a treasure.

It was a great honor to speak with these and others, and to be the first to write the full story of this magical era and memorable game: the game that saved the NHL.

APPENDIX

Super Series 1975–1976: Soviets versus NHL

(STATISTICS COURTESY OF ARTHUR CHIDLOVSKI)
Sunday, December 28, 1975
Soviet Red Army 7, New York Rangers 3
Madison Square Garden
Attendance: 17,500
Soviet Red Army: Tretiak, Vasiliev-Gusev, Lutchenko-Tsygankov, Kuzkin-Volchenkov, Mikhailov-Petrov-Kharlamov, Vikulov-Zhluktov-Alexandrov, Popov-Solodukhin-Maltsev, Glazov, Volchkov, Kutyergin
New York Rangers: Davidson, Vadnais-Bednarski, Greschner-Jarrett, Beverley-Sacharuk, Gilbert-P. Esposito-Vickers, Middleton-Stemkowski-Tkaczuk, Fairbairn-Holland-Johnstone, Dillon, Polis

FIRST PERIOD
1. New York–Vickers (Esposito, Gilbert) 0:21
2. Red Army–Alexandrov (Petrov, Gusev) 4:04 PPG
3. Red Army–Vikulov (Zhluktov, Alexandrov) 5:19
4. Red Army–Kharlamov (Vasiliev, Petrov) 19:42 PPG
Penalties: Jarrett 2:46; Greschner 7:20, 10:13, 18:16

SECOND PERIOD
5. Red Army–Petrov (Kharlamov, Mikhailov) 1:26
6. Red Army–Vikulov (Zhlutkov, Alexandrov) 14:21

7. Red Army–Mikhailov (Kharlamov, Gusev) 16:54
Penalties: Popov 7:34, Gusev 8:46, Johnstone 19:11

THIRD PERIOD

8. Red Army–Petrov (Mikhailov, Kharlamov) 3:16 PPG
9. New York–Gilbert (Esposito) 15:31
10. New York–Esposito (Vickers, Sacharuk) 17:47 PPG
Penalties: Vasiliev 0:38, Esposito 1:40, Fairbairn 8:04, 12:42, Volchkov
    16:04, Polis 19:38, Vadnais (major) 19:38
Shots:
Tretiak (Red Army) 10 14 17–41
Davidson (New York) 12 9 8–29

Monday, December 29, 1975
Soviet Wings 7, Pittsburgh Penguins 4
Pittsburgh Civic Arena
Attendance: 13,218
Soviet Wings: Sidelnikov, Liapkin Tyurin, Krikunov Glukhov, Babinov
Kuznetsov, Shalimov, Shadrin, Yakushev, Lebedev, Anisin, Bodunov,
Kotov, Repnyev, Kapustin, Lapin, Klimov
Pittsburgh Penguins: Plasse, Burrows, Owchar, Durbano, Stackhouse,
Wilkins, Campbell, Pronovost, Apps, Gilbertson, Hadfield, Schock,
Arnason, Kelly, Larouche, Kehoe, Morrison, Faubert

FIRST PERIOD

1. Wings–Anisin (Bodunov) 1:45
2. Wings–Shadrin (Shalimov) 4:33
3. Wings–Shalimov (Liapkin) 12:10
4. Wings–Yakushev (Shadrin, Tyurin) 15:25
Penalty: Campbell 7:12

SECOND PERIOD

5. Wings–Shadrin (Liapkin, Shalimov) 1:39
6. Pittsburgh–Larouche (Kehoe, Faubert) 5:35
7. Wings–Repnyev (Kapustin) 6:02

8. Pittsburgh–Schock (Hadfield, Arnason) 6:53
9. Pittsburgh–Wilkins (Pronovost, Gilbertson) 14:52
Penalties: Soviet Wings (bench) 3:31, Larouche (misconduct) 12:26

THIRD PERIOD
10. Wings–Liapkin (Schalimov, Shadrin) 0; 30
11. Pittsburgh–Morrison (Hadfield) 3:02
Penalties: Stackhouse 9:41, Yakushev 4:18, Kapustin 17:23, Schock
    17:32
Shots:
Plasse (Pittsburgh) 15 8 12–35
Sidelnikov (Wings) 5 7 18–30

Wednesday, December 31, 1975
Soviet Red Army 3, Montreal Canadiens 3
Montreal Forum
Attendance: 18,975
Soviet Red Army: Tretiak, Vasiliev-Gusev, Lutchenko-Tsygankov, Kuzkin-Volchenkov, Mikhailov-Petrov-Kharlamov, Vikulov-Zhluktov-Alexandrov, Popov-Solodukhin-Maltsev
Montreal Canadiens: Dryden, Van Boxmeer-Lapointe, Savard-Robinson, Awrey-Bouchard, Roberts-Risebrough-Lafleur, Lambert-Tremblay-Lemaire, Cournoyer-Wilson-Mahovlich, Shutt-Gainey-Jarvis

FIRST PERIOD
1. Montreal–Shutt (Mahovlich) 3:16
2. Montreal–Lambert (Risebrough, Savard) 7:25
Penalties: Wilson 0:38, Vasiliev 4:43, Cournoyer 16:33, Zhluktov 19:45

SECOND PERIOD
3. Red Army–Mikhailov, (Vasiliev) 3:54
4. Montreal–Cournoyer (Lafleur, Lemaire) 9:39 PPG
5. Red Army–Kharlamov (Petrov, Mikhailov) 16:21
Penalties: Solodukhin 7:38, Gusev 8:23, Savard 9:52

THIRD PERIOD
6. Red Army–Alexandrov (Zhluktov, Tsygankov) 4:04
Penalty: Vasiliev 0:27
Shots:
Dryden (Montreal) 4 3 6–13
Tretiak (Red Army) 11 11 16–38

Sunday, January 4, 1976
Buffalo Sabres 12, Soviet Wings 6
Buffalo Memorial Auditorium
Attendance: 16,433
Soviet Wings: Sidelnikov (Kulikov, 24:32–28:26); lineup N/A
Buffalo Sabres: Desjardins, McIntosh-Korab, Fogolin-Hajt, McAdam-Guevremont, Lorentz-Richard-Ramsay, McNab-Stanfield-Spencer, T. Martin-Luce-Gare, R. Martin-Robert-Perreault

FIRST PERIOD
1. Buffalo–Guevremont (Spencer, Hajt) 6:10
2. Buffalo–Perreault (Korab) 7:10
3. Buffalo–Martin (Stanfield) 11:32
4. Wings–Repnyev (Shalimov, Yakushev) 13:45 PPG
5. Buffalo–Martin 14:23
6. Wings–Kapustin (Kotov) 19:16
Penalties: Shadrin, Ramsay 0:36, Repnyev, Fogolin 11:21, Korab 11:45

SECOND PERIOD
7. Buffalo–Lorentz (Gare, Guevremont) 4:32 PPG
8. Buffalo–Robert (McNab) 5:32
9. Wings–Repnyev (Kapustin, Kuznetsov) 5:59
10. Buffalo–Korab (Martin, Perreault) 8:26 PPG
11. Wings–Shalimov 8:40
12. Buffalo–Gare (Stanfield, Korab) 11:44
13. Buffalo–McNab (Martin, Spencer) 13:17
Penalties: Kapustin 2:49, Terekhin 7:55, Korab 14:41, 19:45

THIRD PERIOD

14. Wings–Kapustin (Kuznetsov) 3:28
15. Buffalo–Stanfield (Martin, Perreault) 9:41
16. Wings–Lebedev, (Babinov, Krikunov) 11:32
17. Buffalo–Gare (Stanfield, Ramsay) 14:04
18. Buffalo–Spencer (McNab, Robert) 18:04 PPG
Penalties: Shadrin 6:08, Sidelnikov (served by Shalimov),
Spencer 6:30, Guevremont 6:52, Kuznetsov 7:20, Tyurin 17:14
Shots:
Sidelnikov–Kulikov (Wings) 17 17 12–46
Desjardins (Buffalo) 9 7 6–25

Wednesday, January 7, 1976
Soviet Wings 4, Chicago Black Hawks 2
Chicago Stadium
Attendance 18,500
Soviet Wings: Sidelnikov, Liapkin-Tyurin, Krikunov-Terekhin, Babinov-Kuznetsov, Shalimov-Shadrin-Yakushev, Lebedev-Anisin-Gostyuzhev, Kotov-Repnyev-Kapustin, Rasko
Chicago Black Hawks: T. Esposito, Russell-Tallon, White-Redmond, Koroll-Mikita-Marks, Mulvey-P. Martin-D.Hull, Bordeleau-Sheehan-Rota

FIRST PERIOD

1. Wings–Terekhin (Yakushev, Krikunov) 8:46 PPG
2. Chicago–Redmond (Mulvey) 9:11
Penalties: White 3:21, Rota 7:41, Redmond, Rasko 20:00

SECOND PERIOD

3. Wings–Kapustin (Rasko, Kuznetsov) 4:03
4. Wings–Shalimov (Terehin, Liapkin) 8:41 PPG
5. Wings–Liapkin (Turin, Yakushev) 17:13 PPG
Penalties: Russell 3:15, Repnyev 3:15, Tallon 7:33, Russell 7:57,
Kapustin 9:25, Redmond 9:31, Shalimov 10:49, Mulvey 16:22, Terekhin
17:38

THIRD PERIOD

6. Chicago–Hull (Mikita, Mulvey) 7:44
Penalties: Rota 5:25, Redmond, Shadrin 7:53, Redmond 13:28, Mulvey 18:18
Shots:
Esposito (Chicago) 9 12 9–30
Sidelnikov (Wings) 8 6 4–18

Thursday, January 8, 1976
Soviet Red Army 5, Boston Bruins 2
Boston Garden
Attendance: 15,003
Soviet Red Army: Tretiak, Vasiliev-Gusev, Lutchenko-Tsygankov, Kuzkin-Volchenkov, Mikhailov-Maltsev-Kharlamov, Vikulov-Zhluktov-Alexandrov, Popov-Kutyergin-Lobanov, Solodukhin, Volchkov
Boston Bruins: Gilbert, Park-D.Smith, Doak-Edestrand, Sims, Schmautz-Ratelle-Marcotte, Bucyk-Sheppard-Cashman, O'Reilly-A. Savard-Forbes, Gibson-Hodge-Nowak

FIRST PERIOD

No Scoring
Penalties: Smith 16:03, Alexandrov 17:20

SECOND PERIOD

1. Boston–Forbes 2:54
2. Red Army–Kharlamov (Maltsev) 4:41 PPG
3. Red Army–Kharlamov (Maltsev) 11:00
4. Red Army–Maltsev (Vasiliev) 13:19
5. Boston–Ratelle (Hodge) 17:31 PPG
Penalties: Schmautz 3:31, Cashman 11:00, Zhluktov 17:26

THIRD PERIOD

6. Red Army–Tsygankov (Alexandrov, Vikulov) 0:43
7. Red Army–Alexandrov (Zhluktov) 8:58
Penalties: Tsygankov, Hodge 4:30, Schmautz 9:22

Shots:
Gilbert (Boston) 8 5 6–19
Tretiak (Red Army) 19 8 13–40

Saturday, January 10, 1976
Soviet Wings 2, New York Islanders 1
Nassau Veterans Memorial Coliseum
Attendance: 14,865
Soviet Wings: Sidelnikov, Liapkin-Tyurin, Krikunov-Terekhin, Babinov-Kuznetsov, Shalimov-Shadrin-Yakushev, Lebedev-Anisin-Gostyuzhev, Kotov-Repnyev-Kapustin, Rasko
New York Islanders: Resch, D. Potvin-J. Potvin, Marshall-Hart, Lewis-Fortier, Westfall-Drouin-Parise, Harris-Trottier-Gillies, Nystrom-St. Laurent-Howatt, Stewart, MacMillan

FIRST PERIOD
No Scoring
Penalties: Drouin 2:24, Anisin 5:25, Repnyev, Marshall 7:48, Lebedev, St. Laurent 8:46, St. Laurent 10:56, Hart 16:35

SECOND PERIOD
1. Wings–Shalimov 6:31 SHG
2. New York–Trottier (D. Potvin, Gillies) 14:59 PPG
3. Wings–Anisin 19:46
Penalties; Gostyuzhev 2:27, Krikunov 5:30, Babinov 10:00, 14:54, Harris 10:17

THIRD PERIOD
No Scoring
Penalties: Kuznetsov 1:58, Kuznetsov 11:41, Bobinov, Parise 15:10, Terekhin 18:30
Shots:
Resch (New York) 7 9 4–20
Sidelnikov (Wings) 11 6 8–25

Sunday, January 11, 1976
Philadelphia Flyers 4, Soviet Red Army 1
The Spectrum
Attendance: 17,077
Soviet Red Army: Tretiak, Vasiliev-Gusev, Lutchenko-Lokotko, Glazov-Volchenkov, Mikhailov-Maltsev-Kharlamov, Vikulov-Solodukhin-Alexandrov, Lobanov-Kutyergin-Popov, Volchkov
Philadelphia Flyers: Stephenson, Jim Watson-Van Impe, Dupont-Goodenough, Bladon-Joe Watson, Leach-Clarke-Barber, Dornhoefer-MacLeish -Lonsberry, Saleski-Kindrachuk-Schultz, Kelly, Bridgman

FIRST PERIOD
1. Philadelphia–Leach (Barber) 11:38
2. Philadelphia–MacLeish (Lonsberry) 17:37
Penalties: Alexandrov 2:24, Dornhoefer, Glazov, 3:34, Dupont 7:00, Van Impe 9:10, Red Army (bench–delay of game) 11:21, Dornhoefer 17:56

SECOND PERIOD
3. Philadelphia–Joe Watson (Saleski, Kindrachuk) 2:44 SHG
4. Red Army–Kutyergin (Popov) 10:48
Penalties: Dupont 1:08, Van Impe 11:31, Alexandrov (double minor), Leach 17:08

THIRD PERIOD
5. Philadelphia–Goodenough (Clarke, Dornhoefer) 4:07 PPG
Penalty: Volchenkov 3:14
Shots:
Stephenson (Philadelphia) 2 8 3–13
Tretiak (Red Army) 17 14 18–49

Sources

Altman, Stephen. "Bernie Parent—C'est Magnifique!" *Sports Special Hockey*, November 1974.

Anders, Doug. "The NHL Outlook—Underrated Flyers Set to Make Believers out of League." *Super Sports*, April 1975.

Anderson, Dave. "A Hockey Lesson for Dr. Kissinger. *New York Times*, January 12, 1976.

Barber, Bill. Interview with the author, March 2011.

Barniak, Jim. "Barry Ashbee's Saga: Involuntary Retirement." *Hockey Digest*, November 1974.

———. "Ed Van Impe: A Lion in Winter." *Sunday Bulletin* (Philadelphia), October 5, 1975.

Beliveau, Jean. "Beliveau Wants a Shot at The Russians." *Sports Canada*, October 1969.

Bernstein, Ross. *The Code: The Unwritten Rules of Fighting and Retaliation in the NHL.* Chicago: Triumph Books, 2006.

Bertucci, Frank. "Are the Classy [or Klutzy] Flyers Worthy of Another Stanley Cup?" *Action Sports Hockey*, May 1976.

Blumberg, Joel, and Barry Wilner. "A Guide to the Six Best Hockey Rinks in North America." *Action Sports Hockey*, February 1976.

Bock, Hal. "Bobby Clarke Insists: "We Can Beat the Canadiens This Time." *Argosy Hockey*, April 1977.

———. "Bobby Clarke Reveals: 'The Team I Hate the Most.'" *Popular Hockey*, April 1977.

———. "The Flyers' Biggest Mistake." *Hockey Today*, October 1977.

Bort, Ryan. "5 Fascinating Insights from *Red Army*, the New Documentary about the Soviet Hockey Team." *Esquire*, January 23, 2015.

Bortstein, Larry. "The Russians Are Coming." *Hockey*, December 1975.

Boulton, Rick. "Reg Leach: An Indian with a Deadly Aim." *Hockey Pictorial World*, November 1976.

Bridgland, Ralph. "Sabres, Canadiens Explode Superman Myth of Touring Russian Teams." *Hockey News*, January 16, 1976.

Brown, Dick. "Dave Schultz Is Really Mr. Nice Guy." *Hockey Pictorial*, December 1974.

Burghardt, Chuck. "Big Babies." *Morning Record* (Meriden, Connecticut), January 15, 1976.

Burke, Tim. "Flyers Paint Hockey Masterpiece, Destroy Myth of Soviet Superiority." *Montreal Gazette*, January 12, 1976.

———"Flyers Salvage Canada's Pride. *Montreal Gazette,* January 12, 1976.

———. "Wrapping Up the Leftovers from Super Series Classic." *Montreal Gazette,* January 14, 1976.

Canadian Broadcasting Company. Soviet Red Army vs. Philadelphia Flyers, January 11, 1976. Televised broadcast.

Carchidi, Sam. "Flyers Playoff Flashback: Dave Schultz's Famous Fight." *Philadelphia Inquirer,* June 13, 2020.

Cart, Julie. "Soviet Master: Tretiak May Have Been Greatest Goaltender in History of Hockey." *Los Angeles Times,* February 13, 1987.

Chidlovski, Arthur. "The Summit in 1972." http://chidlovski.com/personal/1972/content.htm.

———. "Super Series 1975–76: CSKA and Krylya Sovetov in North America." http://www.chidlovski.com/personal/1974/world/ss75cska.htm.

———. Interviews with the author, February 2011 and October 2022.

Chevalier, Jack. *The Broad Street Bullies: The Incredible Story of the Philadelphia Flyers.* New York: Rutledge, 1974.

———. "Dave Schultz—NHL's Busiest Brawler." *Sporting News,* March 16, 1974.

Clarke, Bobby. "The Game I'll Never Forget." *Hockey Digest,* May 1978.

Clement, Bill. Interview with the author, November 2022.

Coleman, Jim. "Bobby Clarke Will Get Even Better!" *Hockey Digest,* April 1976.

Conflict On Ice: The Defending Stanley Cup Champion Philadelphia Flyers vs. the Soviet Red Army Team for World Hockey Supremacy. Video. Philadelphia Flyers, March 1, 2010.

"Dave Schultz." Hockey Fights. https://www.hockeyfights.com/players/1054.

Denault, Todd. *The Greatest Game: The Montreal Canadiens, The Red Army, and the Night That Saved Hockey.* Toronto: McClelland & Stewart, 2010.

Dolson, Frank. "Beneath Clarke's Baby Face Lies a Mean Hockey Player." *Action Sports Hockey,* December 1974.

Dorr, Vic. "Has Mayhem Over-run the Game?" *Hockey Digest,* April 1976.

Dryden, Ken. *Face-Off at the Summit.* Boston: Little, Brown, 1973.

———. *The Game.* Toronto: Macmillan Canada, 1999.

———. "What Putin the Hockey Player Doesn't Understand." *Washington Post,* March 30, 2022.

Dunnell, Milt. "Russians Flunk Aptitude Tests." *Toronto Star,* January 12, 1976.

Dupont, Andre. Interview with the author, October 2022.

Eskenazi, Gerald. *A Thinking Man's Guide to Pro Hockey.* New York: Dutton, 1976.

Fachet, Robert. "Flyers Intimidate Soviet Army. 4-1," *Washington Post,* January 12, 1976.

Fischler, Shirley. "Hey! Hey! The American Way Is Passe." *Action Sports Hockey,* May 1976.

Fischler, Stan. *Bobby Clarke and the Ferocious Flyers.* New York: Warner Paperback Library, 1975.

———. *Hockey Stars of 1975.* New York: Pyramid Books, 1975.

———. *Hockey Stars of 1976.* New York: Pyramid Books, 1976.

———. "Hockey's Biggest Brawls." *Sport,* January 1968.

———. "How the Flyers Won the Cup." *Action Sports Hockey,* December 1974.

Fisher, Red. "Flyers vs. Central Army." *Action Sports Hockey,* May 1976.

———. "The NHL Versus the USSR: Winning Is the Only Thing." *Hockey Pictorial*, February 1979.

———. "Only One Cup for Two Stars: Stanley Spotlight on Lafleur, Clarke." *Sporting News*, April 5, 1980.

Fleischman, Bill. "Ashbee Ranks Flyers' Jim Watson with Denis Potvin as NHL's Best." *Hockey News*, January 2, 1976.

———. "Can The Flyers Make It Three Cups in a Row?" *Hockey Pictorial*, May 1976.

———. "Dave Schultz Won't Stop Now." *Hockey Digest*, November 1974.

———. "The Making of the Mad Squad." *Hockey Pictorial*, February 1974.

———. "NHL All Star Voting Confirms Theory, Flyers' Barber Best of Left Wingers." *Hockey News*, January 30, 1976.

———. "Reckless Dornhoefer Exemplifies Flyers' Consistency." *Hockey News*, January 9, 1976.

"Flyers vs. Central Red Army." *Action Sports Hockey*, May 1976.

The Flyers Do It Again! Philadelphia: Philadelphia Flyers Hockey Club, 1975.

Foss, Steve. "Why the Flyers Won't Win Again." *Sports Extra Hockey*, March 1975.

Gibbons, Dennis. "Fred Shero vs. the Russians!" *Action Sports Hockey*, December 1974.

Goodenough, Larry. Interview with the author, November 2022.

Graf, Dana T. *Hockey Mad*. Philadelphia: Dorrance, 1976.

Greenberg, Jay. "Canadiens-Flyers Match: Ultimate Stanley Cup Final." *Sunday Bulletin* (Philadelphia), April 11, 1976.

———. *Full Spectrum*. Chicago: Triumph Books, 1997.

———. "Mel Bridgman, New Flyer: Top Draft Choice Is 'All Hockey.'" *Sunday Bulletin* (Philadelphia), October 5, 1975.

Hadfield, Vic. *Vic Hadfield's Diary: from Moscow to the Play-offs*. Garden City, NY: Doubleday, 1974.

Hart, Gene. *Score! My Twenty-Five Years with The Broad Street Bullies*. Chicago: Bonus Books, 1990.

Herman, Robin. "NHL Teams Not Taking Soviets Lightly." *New York Times*, December 28, 1975.

———. "Russian Wings Beat Penguins, 7–4." *New York Times*, December 30, 1975.

———. "The Russians Tour: Wings Team Glum." *New York Times*, January 6, 1976.

———. "Sabres Trounce Soviet Wings, 12–6." *New York Times*, January 5, 1976.

———. "Soviet Wings Win By 4–2, But Hawks Make It Rough." *New York Times*, January 8, 1976.

Hickey, Pat. "Interview with Jean Beliveau." *Sports Canada*. 1969.

"The Hockey Official: "A Man with Iron in His Soul." *New York Times*, December 27, 1964.

Hunter, Douglas. *Scotty Bowman: A Life in Hockey*. Toronto: Penguin, 1998.

Irvin, Dick, Jr. Interview with the author, December 2022.

———. *Now Back to You Dick: Two Lifetimes in Hockey*. Toronto: McClelland & Stewart, 1989.

Jackson, Jim. *Walking Together Forever: The Broad Street Bullies, Then and Now*. Champaign, IL: Sports Publishing, 2004.

Joyce, Gare. *The Devil and Bobby Hull: How Hockey's Original Million-Dollar Man Became the Game's Lost Legend.* Mississauga, ON: John Wiley & Sons Canada, 2011.

Kahn, Roger. "Flyers and Soviets 1976: When Al Capone's Mob Ambushed the Bolshoi Ballet Dancers." *Puckstruck* (blog), January 12, 2016. https://puckstruck.com/2016/01/12/flyers-and-soviets-1976-when-al-capones-mob-ambushed-the-bolshoi-ballet-dancers/.

Kearney, Jim. "The Flyers' Special Formula for Success." *Hockey Digest*, April 1976.

Kelly, Bob. Interview with the author, March 2011.

Kennedy, Ray. "Dr. Jekyll and Mr. Clarke," *Sports Illustrated*, February 23, 1976.

———. "Wanted: An End to Mayhem." *Sports Illustrated*, November 17, 1975.

Kimelman, Adam. *The Good, the Bad, and the Ugly: Heart-Pounding, Jaw-Dropping, and Gut-Wrenching Moments from Philadelphia Flyers History.* Chicago: Triumph Books, 2008.

Kirbyson, Geoff. "A Starry Night." *Winnipeg Free Press.* October 15, 2016.

Klein, Jeff Z. "Bits of Dance and Chess Found in a Vanished Style of Play." *New York Times*, November 12, 2014.

Knight, Hans. "Ted Lindsay Askes: 'What Violence?' All-Time Great Says Flyers Win by Work." *Sunday Bulletin* (Philadelphia), October 5, 1975.

Kreiser, John. "1972 Summit Series Shaped Modern Hockey." NHL.com, September 1, 2012. https://www.nhl.com/news/1972-summit-series-shaped-modern-hockey/c-640724.

Lacher, Ira. "The Flyers Are the Dullest Team in Hockey!" *Action Sports Hockey*, February 1976.

Leach, Reggie. *The Riverton Rifle: Straight Shooting on Hockey and on Life.* Vancouver, BC: Greystone Books, 2015.

Libby, Bill. "Flyers' Bobby Clake Insists: 'We're Not Dirty Players!'" *Hockey Sports Stars of 1975*, Winter 1975.

Love! The Story of The Flyers' Skate to Stanley Cup II. Philadelphia: Philadelphia Flyers Hockey Club, 1975.

Lowitt, Bruce. "Emile Francis Says: 'The Flyers Are Harmful to Hockey.'" *Argosy Hockey Yearbook 1975–76.* New York: Popular Publications, 1975.

Ludwig, Jack. *The Great Hockey Thaw: or The Russians Are Here!* Toronto: McClelland and Stewart, 1974.

Lyon, Bill. "How Bobby Clarke Inspires the Flyers." *Hockey Digest*, November 1975.

———. Interviews with the author, April 2012.

MacInnis, Craig. *Remembering Guy Lafleur: A Celebration.* Vancouver, BC: Raincoast Books, 2004.

MacLean, Norm. "Fred Shero: Coach of the Seventies." *Hockey Pictorial*, December 1974.

———. "Fred Shero on the Russian Series." *Hockey Illustrated*, April 1976.

———. "Flyers No. 1: Shero Claims World Championship by Routing Russians." *Hockey News*, January 23, 1976.

———. "How to Beat Fred Shero at His Own System." *Hockey Pictorial*, November 1977.

———. "NHL Optimistic They'll Top Russians." *Hockey News*, January 2, 1976.

————. "Super Series '76: The Debate Goes On: Who's No. 1?" *Hockey Pictorial*, February 1976.

————. "With Fred Shero, It's All a Matter of Interest." *Hockey Pictorial*, November 1975.

"The Mad Squad." *Newsweek*, January 7, 1974.

Malamud, Slava. "Bobby Clarke: I Was No Fighter." *Hockey Observer*, September 23, 2009.

Mandel, Charles. "Aggie Kukulowicz: The 'Henry Kissinger of Hockey' Smoothed the Way for Summit Series." *Globe and Mail*, October 7, 2008.

Martin, Lawrence. *The Red Machine: The Soviet Quest to Dominate Canada's Game*. Toronto: Doubleday Canada, 1990.

McCarthy, Jack. "Russians Make Believer of Cherry As Bruins Bow to Impressive Guests." *Hockey News*, January 30, 1976.

McKee, Don. "There's Much More to Dave Schultz Than His Fists." *Super Sports*, April 1975.

McNeil, Shane. "Red Army: The Most Dangerous Team of a Generation." TSN, January 30, 2015. https://www.tsn.ca/red-army-the-most-dangerous-team-of-a-generation-1.195201.

Meltzer, Bill. "Great Moments: Flyers Conquer the Red Army." NHL.com, January 10, 2008. https://www.nhl.com/flyers/news/great-moments-flyers-conquer-the-red-army/c-435985.

Monahan, Leo. "Has the Shero System Ruined the Game? Point/Counterpoint: Right Wing: Scoring Makes the World Go 'Round." *Hockey Illustrated*, January 1976.

————. "Should the Russians Compete for the Stanley Cup? Point/Counterpoint: Right Wing: Private Property." *Hockey Illustrated*, February 1976.

————. "To the Shero System Add a Skateful of Bobby Clarke." *Hockey Illustrated* Special 1975–76, October 1975.

Mulvoy, Mark. "Boris and His Boys." *Sports Illustrated*, January 5, 1976.

————. "Détente, Philly Style." *Sports Illustrated*, January 19, 1976.

————. "Hockey's Eclectic Wizard." *Sports Illustrated*, May 20, 1975.

————. "It's Sockey, the Way They Play It Here." *Sports Illustrated*, May 6, 1974.

Myslenski, Skip. "Fred Shero Says the Darndest Things." *Hockey Digest*, December 1974.

Olan, Ben. "Dave Schultz: Challenging the Tough Guys of the Past." *Hockey Illustrated*, January 1976.

————. "Philadelphia Flyers: The Flip Side." *Hockey Illustrated*, February 1976.

Olsen, Jack. "Oh, Brother! A Pair to Watch." *Sports Illustrated*, March 29, 1971.

Orr, Bobby. *Orr: My Story*. New York: Putnam, 2013.

Orr, Frank. "'Animal Hockey' Soviets' Excuse for the Walkout." *Toronto Star*, January 12, 1976.

————. "Flyers' Shero Is Sunday's Hero as Philly Champs of the World." *Toronto Star*, January 12, 1976.

————. "Has the Shero System Ruined the Game? Point/Counterpoint: Left Wing: Every Player Is Important." *Hockey Illustrated*, January 1976.

————. "Should the Russians Compete for the Stanley Cup? Point/Counterpoint: Left Wing: Bring on the Global League." *Hockey Illustrated*, February 1976.

Page, Jim. "Guy Lafleur: The Noblest of Them All." *Hockey Illustrated*, February 1976.

Page, Sam. "Red Army Hockey Documentary a Fascinating Look at Team Chemistry." *Sports Illustrated*, November 11, 2014. https://www.si.com/nhl/2014/11/11/red -army-hockey-documentary-review.

Parent, Bernie. *Bernie! Bernie! Bernie!* Englewood Cliffs, NJ: Prentice-Hall, 1975.

Pozner, Vladimir. "Red Army: The Most Dangerous Team of a Generation." TSN, January 30, 2015.

Puckstruck.com "Coach Overreacted to Tense Situation Pulling Plyers Off, Eagleson Claims." *Globe and Mail*, January 12, 1976.

Rappeport, Rhoda. *Fred Shero: A Kaleidoscopic View of the Coach of the Philadelphia Flyers*. New York: St. Martin's Press, 1977.

Reed, J. D. "But God Blessed Montreal." *Sports Illustrated*, May 24, 1976.

Richmond, Milton. "Flyers vs. Central Army." Action Sports Hockey, May 12, 1976.

"The Russians Are Coming—Again!" *Hockey Pictorial*, November 1975.

Robinson, Larry, and Chrys Goyens. *Robinson for the Defence*. Toronto: McGraw-Hill Ryerson, 1988.

Ryndak, Chris. "Sabres Classics: Buffalo Downs Soviet Wings in 1976 Exhibition Game." Sabres.com, May 21, 2020. https://www.nhl.com/sabres/news/buffalo -sabres-classics-1976-soviet-wings-super-series/c-316968434.

Scappinello, Ray, and Roy Simpson. *Between the Lines: Not-So-Tall Tales from Ray "Scampy" Scappinello's Four Decades in the NHL*. New York: HarperCollins, 2014.

Schoeninger, Bill. "Valeri Kharlamov: The Most Overrated Player in History." *The Hockey Writers* (blog), July 14, 2014. https://thehockeywriters.com/valeri-kharlamov-the -most-overrated-player-in-history/.

Schultz, Dave. *The Hammer: Confessions of a Hockey Enforcer*. Toronto: Totem Books, 1982.

Seitz, Nick. "How Can Hockey Determine a World Champion?" *Hockey*, March 1976.

Seravalli, Frank. "35 Years Ago Today, Broad Street Bullies Ran Soviet Red Army out of the Spectrum." *Philadelphia Inquirer*, January 11, 2011. https://www.inquirer.com/ philly/sports/flyers/20110111_THEGOOD_OL__DAZE.html.

Shero, Fred. *Shero: The Man Behind the System*. Radnor, PA: Chilton, 1975.

Shero, Ray. Email interview with the author, March 2011.

"Soviet Superseries." *Time*, January 26, 1976.

St. James, Emily. "How Soviet Hockey Ruled the World—and Then Fell Apart." *Vox*, February 22. 2019. https://www.vox.com/2015/2/25/8108397/soviet-hockey-red -army.

Stephenson, Wayne. "The Game I'll Never Forget." *Hockey Digest*, February 1981.

Strachan, Al. "For a Short Road Trip, It Was a Long Haul." *Montreal Gazette*, January 14, 1976.

———. "Soviet-Style Game Wouldn't Sell Here." *Montreal Gazette*, January 13, 1976.

Swift, Edward. "Big City Hockey: Philadelphia Is a Winner's Town." *Hockey*, November 1975.

Tretiak, Vladislav. *Tretiak: The Legend*. Edmonton, AB: Plains Publishing, 1987.

Trontz, Jon. "The Hottest Thing in Hockey: The Flyer Fighters." *Hockey Illustrated*, March 1974.

"Vanquished Ranger Players Unanimous: Touring Russians Too Slick For Them." *Hockey News*, January 9, 1976.

Vasiley, Andrei. "Valeri Kharlamov: Little Genius of the Big Game." *Russia Beyond*, December 13, 2014. https://www.rbth.com/sport/2014/12/13/valeri_kharlamov _little_genius_of_the_big_game_42227.html.

Verdi, Bob. "Fred Shero: Hockey Coaches Need a Union." *Hockey Digest*, April 1976.

Watson, Jimmy. Interview with the author, October 2022.

Watson, Joe. Interviews with the author, January 2011 and September 2022.

We're No. 1! The Story of the Flyers' Skate to the Stanley Cup. Philadelphia: Philadelphia Flyers Hockey Club, 1974.

White, Peter. "Confrontation: Flyer Defence Monkey Wrench in Army Attack as Stanley Cup Champs Score rare NHL Win." *Globe and Mail*, January 12, 1976.

Wilner, Barry. "Bill Barber: A Cut above the Rest." *Hockey World*, January 1976.

———. "Can Fred Bring Cup Number Three to the City of Brotherly Love?" *Action Sports Hockey*, May 1976.

———. "The Russians Are Coming . . . Again." *Hockey World*, January 1976.

———. Wayne Stephenson—After Parent." *Hockey Illustrated*, April 1976.

Whyno, Stephen. "Russian NHL Players Mostly Staying Silent about Ukraine War." *Associated Press*, March 2, 2022.

———. "Russians Star in NHL Playoffs as Nation Wages War in Ukraine." *Associated Press*, May 30, 2022.

Index

Philadelphia Flyers and, 39, 79; in Super Series 1976, 32, 110–12

Chidlovski, Arthur: on Clarke, B., 73; coaching to, 185; on competition, xxi, 135; CSKA to, 160; on Kharlamov, 18–19, 26, 59, 64–66; on Lutchenko, 174; Philadelphia Flyers to, 141, 158; on Summit Series, 179; talent to, 30, 70, 80; on Tretiak, 69; Vanyat and, 29; on violence, 150

Chkalov, Valery, 61

Clarke, Bobby: Barber and, 91, 158–59; Bowman and, 73, 210; for Canada, xvi; career of, 74–79, 202–5, 207–11, 218; Chidlovski on, 73; Clement on, 19, 74; Cole on, 137; on communism, xix; on competition, 115, 118, 120–21, 169; CSKA to, 17; diabetes and, 15; Dryden on, 14; Dupont and, 48, 74; enforcers and, xviii, 2, 49–50; in faceoffs, 129–30, 157, 163, 169–70, 181; to fans, 39–40, 164; on Ferguson, 63; in fights, 46; Goodenough and, 181–82; Hart on, 73, 75, 153–54; Hart Trophy for, 7; Howe and, 64; Kharlamov and, 24, 133–34, 138, 141; Kutyergin and, 184, 190, 194; Leach and, 5, 76, 92,

177; leadership of, 3; MacLeish and, 74, 153–54, *p2*; Maltsev and, xxiii, 124–25; in media, 47; Mulvoy on, 48–49, 78, 116–17; Orr, B., and, 52–53; psychology of, 119, 167; reputation of, xxi–xxii, 18–19, 116–17, 199–201; Schultz, D., and, 4, 73, 83–84, 86, 88; statue of, *p1*; strategy of, 5–6; with teammates, 13, 150–51; in traps, 132–33; Watson, Jimmy, and, 147; *See also* LCB line

Clarke, Cliff, 75

Clement, Bill: on Clarke, B., 19, 74; on competition, 115, 144, 215; on enforcers, 14, 81; as fan, 143; in postseason, 93; on Shero, F., 47, 56; style of, 3; on talent, 45; with teammates, 143; in trade, 211

Cleveland Barons, 36

Cochet, Henri, 178

The Code (Bernstein), 2–3

Cold War, xix–xxi, 20, 97, 121, 222

Cole, Bob: career of, 147–48; Irvin, Jr., and, xx, 101, 124–25, 137, 173; in Super Series 1976, 136–39, 141–42, 152, 159–60, 164, 166–67, 169–70, 177, 180–84, 188–89

communism, xvii, xix, 20, 124–25

Condon, John, 100–101

Conn Smythe Trophy, xix, 3,
198–99
Cooper, Bruce, 118
Cosell, Howard, 70
Cournoyer, Yvan, 28, 103, 107,
201, 207, 210
Crisp, Terry, xxii, 42, 89, 130, 135,
184, 190
Crozier, Roger, 13, 92–93
CSKA: *See* Soviet Red
Army Club
Czechoslovakia, 111, 175, 178,
194, 214, 218

Daley, Joe, 215–16
Daly, Bill, 220
D'Amico, John, 85, 132
Davidson, Bob, 69
Davidson, John, 101–2
Day, Clarence, 9
Day, Hap, 116
Deadmarsh, Butch, 46–47
democracy, xvii–xviii, 124
Desjardins, Gerry, 92, 108
Detroit Red Wings, 6, 36–37, 47,
67, 96, 219–20
Dionne, Marcel, 97, 154
Ditmars, Fred, 42
Dornhoefer, Gary: Aleksandrov,
B., and, 135–36, 166; career of,
6–7, 176–77, 181–82, 202, 205,
207–8, 211; on competition,
140; with goalies, 49;
Kindrachuk and, 51; Lonsberry
and, 7, 51; in postseason, 91;

reputation of, 10–11, 44, 166–
70; with teammates, 92, 153,
159; work ethic of, 10, 41, 49
"Dorogoi Dlinnoyu" (song), 213
Dryden, Ken: career of, 63–64,
91, 106–7, 126, 217, 222; on
Philadelphia Flyers, 10–11, 14,
124, 198, 201–5, 207–10
Dunnell, Milt, 192
Dupont, André ("Moose"): career
of, 190, 199, 209, 213; Clarke,
B., and, 48, 74; on competition,
2, 13–14, 52, 93, 139, 143,
190; as enforcer, 40, 140–41;
on global politics, xiv; in
postseason, 55, 90; psychology
of, 54, 146–47, 151; reputation
of, 213–14; on Shero, F., 45; in
Super Series 1976, 159, 161,
165–66, 169, 177, 184–85; in
trade, 139–40; Vasiliev and, 137
Dvortsov, Vladimir, 173–74
Dynasty Line, 5

Eagleson, Alan, 148–49, 194
Earle, Don, 13, 43–45, 44, 202–3
Edmonton Oilers, 214
enforcers: Clarke, B., and, xviii,
2, 49–50; Clement on, 14,
81; on CSKA, xvii; Dupont
as, 40, 140–41; global politics
and, 149–50; Graf on, 2, 164;
Gusev as, 27, 107, 133–34,
159; history of, 8–9, 39–40; in
hockey, 9–10; Lonsberry as, 54;

in media, 8, 47; penalty minutes for, 10–11; Philadelphia Flyers as, 2–8, 11–16, *p2*; psychology of, xix; Shero, R., on, 7; in Stanley Cup, 11; in Super Series 1976, 141–42
Entry Drafts, 6
Erfilov, Vitaly, 68–69
Eskenazi, Gerald, xx
Esposito, Phil: in faceoffs, 78; Gilbert and, 102–3; legacy of, xviii, 4, 59; Orr, B., and, 12, 91; on politics, 97; on referees, 131; with Smith, K., 55; in trade, 15, 96; traps against, 53; Tretiak and, 101
Esposito, Tony, 45, 59, 63, 91, 110
Europe: culture of, 220–21; European championships, 63, 126, 171, 174–75; European Cup, xvi; hockey in, xiv, xx, 19, 21, 66–67, 124, 137, 214–16, 222; Super Series 1976 to, 96
Ezinicki, Bill ("Wild"), 9
Ezkenazi, Gerald, 11–12

Fachet, Robert, 192
Fairbairn, Bill, 51
fans: Clarke, B., to, 39–40, 164; Clement as, 143; of CSKA, 71–72; fights and, 87–88; global politics and, 126–27; Goodenough on, 124; Graf on, xiv–xv, 140–41; hockey, 105, 112, 117–18; Irvin, Jr., on, 93,

109–10; Leonardi as, 146, 160–63, 182; Lyon on, xxi, 2; media and, 31; Moscow Dynamo, 21; Philadelphia Flyers, 42–43, 56, 86–87, 89, 120, 133–34, 189; psychology of, xx, 15–16; Snider and, 42, 55; Super Series 1976 for, 123–30, 161–63; violence by, 50; Watson, Joe, on, xiii, xv, 15; Wilner on, xiv
Fedorov, Sergei, 219–20
Ferguson, John, 18, 63, 83
Fetisov, Slava, 28, 138, 219–20
fights, 46–49, 80–81, 84–85, 87–88
Finley, Charles O., 38, 111
Firsov, Anatoli, 60, 106, 170–71
Fischler, Shirley, 96, 185
Fisher, Red, 214–15
Fleischman, Bill, 123, 167–68, 167–69, 181
Flett, Bill, 6, 41, 77, 88
Fomin, Boris, 213
Forbes, Dave, 114
Francis, Emile, 14, 32, 37, 47–48
Frazier, Joe, 83
French Connection Line, 4–5, 91–92, 91–93, 109–10, 158; *See also* Krylya Sovetov

Gainey, Bob, 199, 201, 205, 207
Gallivan, Danny, 165
The Game (Dryden), 11
Gare, Danny, 109–10
Geoffrion, Bernie, 19

Giacomin, Ed, 47, 53, 82
Gilbert, Gilles, 53, 55, 77, 114–15
Gilbert, Rod, 22, 47, 50, 101–3
Gillies, Clark, xx, 83, 85
Gilmour, Lloyd: professionalism
    of, 130, 132, 137, 145–46; in
    Super Series 1976, xxiii, 124,
    157, 169, 173, 177
Ginnell, Pat, 75–76
Giroux, Claude, 6
Glukhov, Sergei, xvii, 97
Goal a Game Line, 22, 47, 51–52
goalies: backup, 90, 128, 134–35,
    159; for CSKA, 25, 66–70,
    68–69, *p4*; Dornhoefer
    with, 49; in international
    competition, 215–16; Irvin,
    Jr., on, 136; psychology of, xv;
    Shero, F., on, 174; in Super
    Series 1976, 69–70; in USSR,
    67; *See also specific goalies*
God Bless the Flyers, 86
Goldsworthy, Bill, 41
The Good, the Bad, and the Ugly
    (Kimelman), 40
Goodenough, Larry: career of,
    xxi–xxii, 204–5, 223; Clarke,
    B., and, 181–82; on fans, 124;
    on Russia, 133; Saleski and,
    xxii; on Stanley Cup, 1–2; on
    strategy, 157–58; on teammates,
    81, 164, 176; Tretiak and, 223;
    Watson, Joe, and, 151
Goren, Herb, 193

Graf, Dana T., xiv–xv, 2, 13–14,
    35, 140–41, 164, 188
Green, Ted, 12
Greenberg, Jay, 15, 141, 202
Greschner, Ron, 213
Gresko, Alexander, 119
Gretzky, Wayne, 62, 65, 69, 97,
    183, 218–19
Guevremont, Jocelyn, 108
Gusev, Aleksandr: as enforcer,
    27, 107, 133–34, 159; in Super
    Series 1976, 133–34, 138–40,
    159, 165, 177, 183; Vasiliev and,
    28, 128

Hadfield, Vic, 47, 51–52, 105
"Hair of the Dog" (song), 129
Hajt, Bill, 108
Hall, Glenn, xv, 67
The Hammer (Schultz, D.), 11
Harris, Ron, 48, 50
Harris, Ted, 88, 182
Hart, Gene: Albert and, xx,
    151; analysis of, 203–4; on
    Clarke, B., 73, 75, 153–54;
    on competition, 117, 128,
    143; on Dornhoefer, 168–69;
    on Dupont, 140; Earle and,
    13, 43–45; on Leach, 152;
    leadership of, 187; legacy
    of, 55–56; in Russia, 222;
    on Shero, F., 38–39; on
    sportsmanship, 51; style of, 44,
    120; on talent, 79–80; on Van

96; for fans, 123–30, 161–63; Gilmour in, xxiii, 124, 157, 169, 173, 177; global politics and, 97–98, 102–3, 118–20, 146–47; goalies in, 69–70; Gusev in, 133–34, 138–40, 159, 165, 177, 183; LCB line in, 128–29; MacLeish in, 164–66, 168, 177, 180–81, 183–85; media and, xix–xx, 100–101, 164–66; Montreal Canadiens in, 99–100; New York Islanders in, 114–15; New York Rangers in, 100–101; Philadelphia Flyers in, ix–xi, 115–17, 120–21, 133–37, 151–55, 167–69, *p7*; photos from, *p1–p7*; Potvin in, 134–37, 142, 146, 148, 152–53; psychology of, 139–45, 166–71, 190–95; referees in, xxiii, 130–33, 192; Saleski in, 136, 145, 159–60, 165, 180, 183–85, 191, *p5*; Soviet Wings in, 103–5, 108–15, 117–18; sportsmanship in, 146–49; Stephenson in, 159, 162–67, 180, 183–84, 188–89; Summit Series and, 21–22, 130–31; talent in, 24, 95–96, 103–6; Tretiak in, 157–61, 163, 166, 169–70, 180–85, 189–91, 199; to USSR, 98–100; Vasiliev in, 137–38; Watson, Joe, in, 160–61, 164, 170
Super Series 1979–1991, 216–17
Swift, Edward, 87–88

Tannahill, Don, 144
Tarasov, Anatoly: coaching by, 25, 104, 115, 118–19, 146; King on, 20–21; Kulagin and, 62; legacy of, 19–20; referees to, 131; on Russia, 7; Tikhonov and, 25
A Thinking Man's Guide to Pro Hockey (Ezkenazi), 11–12
Tikhonov, Viktor, 25
Time (magazine), 11
Tkaczuk, Walt, 48–49
Tolstoy, Leo, 17
Toronto Maple Leafs, xv, 9, 39, 89–90, 96, 116, 147–48
Tremblay, Mario, 203
Tretiak, Vladislav: Barber and, 135–36; Canada to, 99; career of, 25, 66–70, 213, 216, 218, *p4*; Chidlovski on, 69; on competition, 95–96, 99–100, 107–8, 112–13, 118, 144–45, 149–50; Esposito, P., and, 101; Goodenough and, 223; Kharlamov and, 59–62, 70–72, 70–73, 101; legacy of, ix; MacLeish and, 7, 67, 153; Mikhailov and, 23; in Olympics, 69–70, 144–45; passion of, 105; psychology of, 151–52, 157; reputation of, 25, 95, 126, 128, 177; saves by, 18; Shero, F., and, 222; Stephenson and, 137; in Super Series 1976, 157–61, 163, 166,

About the Author

Ed Gruver, a native of Kearny, New Jersey, is the author of ten books on sports and a contributing writer to twenty-nine sports books. An award-winning writer, his previous books include *Joe Louis Versus Billy Conn: Boxing in the Unforgettable Summer of 1941* (2022), *Bringing the Monster to Its Knees: Ben Hogan, Oakland Hills, and the 1951 U.S. Open* (2021), *Hell with the Lid Off: Inside the Fierce Rivalry Between the 1970s Oakland Raiders and Pittsburgh Steelers* (2018), *Hairs vs. Squares: The Mustache Gang, the Big Red Machine and the Tumultuous Summer of '72* (2016), *From Baltimore to Broadway: Joe, the Jets and the Super Bowl III Guarantee* (2009), *Nitschke* (2002), *Koufax* (2000), *The Ice Bowl: The Cold Truth about Football's Most Unforgettable Game* (1997), and *The American Football League: A Year-by-Year History, 1960–69* (1997). His work also appears in national magazines.